ENDURING IMAGES

ENDURING IMAGES

A FUTURE HISTORY OF
NEW LEFT CINEMA

Morgan Adamson

UNIVERSITY OF MINNESOTA PRESS
Minneapolis · London

A portion of chapter 2 was published as "Toward a New Mode of Study: The New Student Left and the Occupation of Cinema in *Columbia Revolt* (US, 1968) and *Nihon kaiho sensen—Sanrizuka no natsu* (*The Battlefront for the Liberation of Japan—Summer in Sanrizuka,* Japan, 1968)," in *1968 and Global Cinema,* ed. Sara Saljoughi and Christina Gerhardt, 145–64 (Detroit, Mich.: Wayne State University Press, 2018); copyright 2018 Wayne State University Press, with permission of Wayne State University Press. Portions of chapter 3 were published in a different form in "Labor, Finance, and Counterrevolution: *Finally Got the News* at the End of the Short American Century," *South Atlantic Quarterly* 111, no. 4 (2012): 803–23.

Published by the University of Minnesota Press
111 Third Avenue South, Suite 290
Minneapolis, MN 55401-2520
http://www.upress.umn.edu

Library of Congress Cataloging-in-Publication Data
Names: Adamson, Morgan, author.
Title: Enduring images : a future history of new left cinema / Morgan Adamson.
Description: Minneapolis : University of Minnesota Press, 2018. | Includes bibliographical references and index.
Identifiers: LCCN 2018008952 (print) | ISBN 978-1-5179-0308-4 (hc) | ISBN 978-1-5179-0309-1 (pb)
Subjects: LCSH: Motion pictures—Social aspects. | Motion pictures—History—20th century. | New Left.
Classification: LCC PN1995.9.S6 A33 2018 (print) | DDC 302.23/43—dc23
LC record available at https://lccn.loc.gov/2018008952

Contents

Introduction

In December 1967, Guy Debord published *Society of the Spectacle* on the eve of the events of May 1968. Whether or not Debord's analysis of life under the regime of the spectacle actually bore some responsibility for the disruption that followed its publication, what is clear is that the text has come to stand for the emergence of new forms of power and resistance in the transition from industrial modernity to our present. In the book, Debord identified a regime of capitalist production in which authentic social life had been replaced by its representation, a world where the fetishized image created separation and diminished lived experience.[1]

Debord, however, complicated this theory of the image when he recast *Society of the Spectacle* as a film in 1973. Announcing its release, he wrote,

> Until now it has generally been assumed that film is a completely unsuitable medium for presenting revolutionary theory. This view is mistaken. . . . The cinema itself is an integral part of the world, serving as one of the instruments of the separate *representation* that opposes and dominates the actual proletarianized society. As revolutionary critique engages in battle on the very terrain of the cinematic spectacle, it must thus *turn the language of that medium against itself* and give itself a form that is itself revolutionary.[2]

As cinema, Debord's critique of spectacular society entered into the spectacle and became a form of cinematic thinking, an essay film. Though the spectacle is conceived in Debord's writing as "a social relation between people that is mediated by the image," in its filmic form, this alienated image must become the terrain of revolutionary critique and battle.[3] Cinema, which Debord saw as intrinsic to the spectacle, was thus reimagined as a front line in the assault against it.

In this turn from the critique of the image to the deployment of the image as critique, we find the basic kernel of a thesis on cinematic resistance that I trace in this book. By presenting *Society of the Spectacle* as an image—an image that at the same time apprehends, assaults, and reshapes the spectacle—Debord captures the underlying impulse behind what I call *New Left cinema*. Beyond critique, New Left cinema aimed to do more than undermine modes of social existence endemic to spectacular society. If as spectacle, the cinema created separation and alienation, then as resistance, it became an occasion for inventing new social relationships and ways of being and thinking in common. In what follows, I examine how such forms of cinematic resistance played out within global New Left social movements and how their untimely images endure today.

NEW LEFT CINEMA

In the wake of the Arab Spring of 2011 and the subsequent uprisings that year from Occupy Wall Street to Chilean student movements, scholars and pundits devoted increasing attention to the significance of "social media" in circulating revolutionary sentiments and producing affinities between disparate struggles. In particular, the capacity for participants to generate and disseminate documentary images across great geographical and political distances seemed to present new potentials and problems for political struggle on a global scale.[4] Indeed, with each passing year, the amateur production and circulation of digital video has become ever more important in shaping political imaginaries and galvanizing social movements. *Enduring Images* considers what we might think of as the prehistory of this moment: the 1960s and 1970s. This period witnessed the first cycle of international uprisings where relatively lightweight and portable cinematic technologies—16mm film and analog video—were widely available and, as I will argue, became powerful conduits for organizing revolutionary activities. It takes up a diverse set of figures who, like Debord, considered the cinematic image to be a terrain of struggle and who produced essay films that sought to test—in the original sense of *essai* as a trial or attempt—cinema's revolutionary potential.

In tracing the contours of this phenomenon, I am less interested in defining the history and formal characteristics of a cinematic genre than in understanding how, for the New Left, cinema became a vehicle to imagine new political possibilities, modes of social organization, and affective forms of communication, what I will call an *essayistic politics of the common.* As emergent cultural forms, in Raymond Williams's sense of the term, the New Left's cinematic practices and artifacts compose a vast archive through which to reexamine these social movements from the perspective of our present, opening up conversations that have been foreclosed during the last half-century of policing the cultural memory of the New Left.[5] I take the films and movements in question to be opportunities to reconsider the historical narratives about how we arrived at our present. At its core, this book argues that the cinemas of the New Left are sites to examine, through the lens of struggle, the reshaping of global capitalism during the pivotal moment in which they were made.

Before arguing for the potential of its cinema, let me explain what I mean by the New Left. In this book, the New Left refers to, in shorthand, the protagonists of the global revolt that erupted in 1968 against not only the alienation of the commodity that Debord decries but also imperialism, patriarchy and heteronormativity, racism, authoritarianism, and capitalist expropriation. However, to limit the New Left to the movements of 1968 is misleading, as its history—sometimes referred to as the long 1960s—was set into motion in the 1950s and extends well into the 1970s. A general consensus among scholars is that the New Left's ascendance commenced with events like the Montgomery bus boycotts and the rise of civil rights in the United States, the Cuban revolution, the Battle of Algiers, and countless global events that disrupted the postwar global order and laid the groundwork for the following decade.[6]

While these movements are often contained within national histories, it is essential to emphasize their internationalist tendencies, evident in both the New Left's radical and mainstream expressions. For example, figures like Martin Luther King Jr. drew connections between struggles in the U.S. South and struggles against imperialism worldwide, citing pan-African leader Kwame Nkrumah, among others, to articulate a politics of liberation that far exceeded the boundaries of the U.S. nation-state.[7] Expressed most often through what Michael Denning calls an "imaginative geography," the diverse struggles for liberation within the New Left were consistently situated within an international horizon, emboldened through real and imagined solidarities between here and elsewhere.[8] Take, for example, Santiago Álvarez's *Now!* (Cuba, 1965), a film that might be considered a forerunner to the New Left films discussed in this book. It sets images of police brutality against U.S. civil rights protesters to Lena Horne's censored song "Now" (1964) to call for anti-imperialist action in Latin America and elsewhere by exposing the racial violence that exists at the heart of empire. *Enduring Images* outlines the ways that cinema created within and alongside New Left social movements helped elaborate and intensify these international attachments, wresting various cinematic traditions from the national cinemas to which they have been confined and underlining international aspirations and conversations among disparate geopolitical contexts. The New Left in this account is in no way a singular or unified entity; it is constituted by internal differentiation. Nevertheless, it is the international affinities among New Left social movements that this study seeks to emphasize, resisting the impulse to delimit New Left histories to national or regional contexts.

The New Left also describes social movements that worked to distance themselves from the "Old Left"—the Soviet Union, centralized organizations like the Communist Party, and traditional labor unions—while also fighting against capitalist Keynesian management in industrial centers and imperialism in the Global South. As George Katsiaficas notes in his analysis of the New Left's global dimensions, "the New Left sought to overthrow the economic exploitation which the Old Left had opposed, but the anti-authoritarianism of the new radicals also opposed cultural and bureaucratic domination."[9] Thus the New Left expanded politics into a critique of everyday life, while also dramatically extending ideas of revolutionary subjectivity beyond the figure of the industrial worker to include student, peasant, anti-imperialist, Black Power, gay liberation, and women's movements, among others. These movements composed what Katsiaficas calls an "enlarged base of revolution" and are the central sites of investigation in this book.[10]

Distinctions between old and new notwithstanding, Van Gosse has argued that the U.S. New Left's relationship to the Old Left can be construed as one of continuity rather than rupture, especially when locating its origins in elements of the Communist Party, popular fronts, and other radical traditions, such as the black protest movement of the first decades of the twentieth century.[11] Similarly, Andrew Cornell constructs a compelling case to demonstrate that in the United States, the New Left was shaped by the undercurrents of countercultural anarchism that had persisted throughout the postwar era.[12] Untangling the complicated web of red threads that tie the New Left to the Old is beyond the scope of this project, but in examining the New Left, I affirm the plurality of ways that movements overlap, intersect, and diverge across both space and time.

All of this brings me to what is perhaps a more pressing question: why return to the New Left and its cinema in the first place? How many times have we been told that the New Left social movements are finished, that they failed abysmally, that their only legacy is an ineffectual and divisive identity politics? If this is true, why do they continue to exert such a strong pull on the popular imagination, as each subsequent generation of young leftists rediscovers the Black Panthers, Stonewall, Che Guevara, and the Situationists and right-wing pundits continually flag New Left movements as emblems of the demise of "family values" and Western civilization itself? As Kristen Ross argues in *May '68 and Its Afterlives,* myriad techniques have been deployed to convince us that "nothing happened" during the uprisings of 1968 and that containing their cultural memory is essential for the maintenance of the neoliberal consensus that has ensued from the 1980s.[13] In *Photopoetics at Tlatelolco: Afterimages of Mexico, 1968,* Samuel Steinberg similarly explores the ways that the massacre of Mexican students at Tlatelolco Plaza has been simultaneously reified and obscured, its "afterimages" framing narratives of the contemporary Mexican state.[14] In contrast to these important studies, my concern is not primarily how the movements of the New Left persist in cultural memory or the uses and abuses of their history. Rather than looking at the ways that memory forecloses politics, I am interested in revisiting the movements of the New Left, by way of their cinema, to examine how they endure, if only obliquely, in the present.

Far from being finished or resolved, the New Left's meaning is a point of contestation, and the vast archive that the New Left presents to us is a crucial starting place for constructing a history of the present that might point to alternative futures. When speaking about *Hora de los hornos* (*Hour of the Furnaces,* Argentina, 1968), Fernando Solanas argues that, as a film about liberation, "it cannot be anything but an unfinished film, a film open to the present and the future of this act of liberation."[15] The unfinished quality of New Left cinema and of the movements for liberation through which it was conceived is of primary importance to this project. These films are unfinished not in the sense that they will be redeemed or completed by some messianic event to come but in the sense that they are open texts that avail themselves to ongoing struggles, their meaning transformed by each viewing. Against attempts to minimize the legacy of the New Left, I start with the presupposition that the effects of these movements continue to ripple through countless aspects of cultural, political, and economic life and that the counterrevolution launched against them is one of the most vast and complicated in the history of capitalism. This book, then, joins a growing body of scholarly work that critically engages movements of the long 1960s from the perspective of contemporary politics, reexamining our fundamental assumptions about both the past and the present.

Reevaluating New Left social movements by way of their cinema, I am interested in the ways these movements brought the diverse perspectives of an "expanded base of revolution" to bear on cinematic form. Without collapsing the very real differences among these movements, New Left cinema names the cinema that elaborated and intensified existing New Left political projects. Terms that have been used to describe the films I address in the book include *militant cinema, political cinema,* and *counter-cinema.* While these terms are not inaccurate, and are used at times by New Left practitioners themselves, I find each insufficient because they lack historical definition and have been used to describe a wide range of films, from the interwar avant-garde to contemporary documentary. They do not identify any particular politics or militancy, nor do they elucidate what is being countered through the cinema and how. Even the term *third cinema,* which originated with the New Left, has lost its explicative power within the U.S. academy, where it has been used to describe films that are quite different from Fernando Solanas and Octavio Getino's original definition of the term (as I discuss in chapter 1). New Left cinema, on the other hand, designates a set of cinematic practices embedded within the historical context described earlier, those that sought to advance the New Left's political aspirations while sharing its organizational tendencies. If the cinema of the New Left is to be classified as "political," then it is political in Jacques Rancière's sense of the term, an unsettling of the order of things that "invents new forms of collective enunciation."[16]

Like the broader New Left, New Left cinema did not simply vacate the Old Left but drew inspiration from, and even named its collectives after, prominent figures, such as Dziga Vertov and Aleksandr Medvedkin. A number of filmmakers, like Joris Ivens, spanned both old and new leftist cinemas, and a multiplicity of cinematic traditions—including interwar avant-garde, *cinéma vérité,* pop art, and national and regional cinemas—shaped the formal inclinations of New Left cinema. New Left cinema connotes not a uniform style but a set of political and practical commitments that revolve around decentralization, participation, internationalism, deprofessionalization, and antiauthoritarianism, among others—principles that guided many political and aesthetic practices of that era.[17] By taking into account the multifaceted form of the New Left, I do not produce a totalizing account of its cinema, nor do I seek to catalog the diverse and divergent film cultures that came into being in and around New Left political movements globally. Instead, I present a series of case studies intended to underscore salient tendencies within New Left cinema, such as alternative modes of authorship, production, distribution, and exhibition; use of new technologies; and the development of the essay film. These case studies are located within a concrete set of historical situations and phenomena that typify the transition between the industrial era and our present, centering on the ways that new political subjectivities and positions are articulated in and through the cinema.

Given my discussion of the New Left and its cinema up to this point, it is important to clarify what this study does and does not cover. To summarize, New Left cinema as I define it in this book is typified by the New Left's version of the essay film, a confluence of documentary and avant-garde traditions that breaks from both. I focus primarily on films and videos produced by collectives that actively rejected the conventions of cinematic authorship and sought to forge new networks of production and distribution outside of existing channels. These collectives used their cinematic experiments as tools for political mobilization, developing arguments to engage viewers through what Jane Gaines calls "political mimesis," corporeal sensation transmitted through the documentary image.[18] In its attention to the circulation of these experiments within political networks, this book joins recent works, such as Chris Robé's *Breaking the Spell,* that trace the emergence of "alternative media" to the radical film and video traditions of the 1960s and 1970s.[19] For this reason, this study does not address the topic of narrative cinemas that were aligned with New Left social movements like the various "new waves" and postcolonial film traditions in Latin America, Africa, and Asia and underground narrative cinema in the United States, such as the films coming out of the LA Rebellion. This is not to say that narrative cinema at the time did not participate in New Left politics or that there was no overlap between documentary and narrative expressions, but these questions have been considered elsewhere.[20] Focusing on alternate channels of production and distribution, I also leave aside questions about how New Left social movements were represented by popular media and how movements associated with the New Left managed to get their voices heard through mainstream media outlets like broadcast television or Hollywood.[21]

In defining the scope of this project, I want to emphasize that academic research does not stand outside of the New Left's influence. As has been well documented, a host of academic disciplines were brought into being through the New Left's critique of what constituted valid academic knowledge, prying open institutions of higher learning, making them more inclusive, and transfiguring epistemological paradigms.[22] The two primary disciplines within which I situate this book—cultural studies and film studies—are no exception. In his definitive genealogy of the discipline of cultural studies, *Culture in the Age of Three Worlds,* Michael Denning argues that "Cultural Studies was the product of the New Left's critical reflection on the cultural industries and the state's ideological apparatuses."[23] Similarly, the story of film studies (particularly its controversial and influential subgenre "film theory") and its institutionalization within the U.S. academy would be unimaginable without the explosion of political and theoretical discussions of film and its relationship to power and subjectivity in the 1960s and 1970s. With direct connections to the struggles of 1968 that extended into the 1970s, the theoretical conversations (apparatus theory, psychoanalysis, etc.) that moved between the United States and France, but also elsewhere, helped shape the fledgling discipline.[24] Concern for the politics of cultural objects, particularly moving images, was a preoccupation of the New Left, and it remains a preoccupation of interdisciplinary cultural studies today. Thus, in returning to the New Left's cinema, I do not claim a position wholly exterior to it but rather endeavor to think along with it, acknowledging the ways that the horizon of my own disciplinary and interdisciplinary frameworks are shaped by my object of study. Rather than encountering the films and movements in question solely through a critical lens aimed at tracking defeats and uncovering inconsistencies, I use them as sites to reconsider contemporary political economic problems and a potential politics. In her discussion of reparative readings, Eve Kosofsky Sedgwick writes that "the desire of a reparative impulse . . . is additive and accretive. . . . It wants to assemble and confer plenitude on an object that will then have resources to offer an inchoate self."[25] While maintaining a critical perspective, I follow Sedgwick's lead, presenting readings that are "additive and accretive," which, for me, indicates an affirmative materialism that takes seriously the attempts coming from the New Left to generate new political forms.

Toward a Politics of the Everyday

With the object and approach of this study now sketched, let me turn to the theme of the everyday as an entry point into New Left cinema. The New Left's cultural critique was centered on a politics of the quotidian, as captured by Situationist Raoul Vaneigem, who muses in his 1967 book *The Revolution of Everyday Life* that "there are more truths in twenty-four hours of a man's life than in all the philosophies."[26] In exploring the ways culture and politics were fused in such critiques, I am interested in how New Left cinema magnified domains of life that had been excluded from political discourse. This renewed attention to the everyday, which we can trace back to thinkers like Henri Lefebvre and the Frankfurt School, must be located within transformations taking place within post–World

War II global capitalism—the vast expansion of consumerism in industrial centers and the global dissemination of technologies of mass media and the culture industries. Division among the "three worlds"—capitalist, communist, and developing—notwithstanding, Denning argues that the reaction to changes in global capitalism prompted a "cultural turn" in politics that cut across New Left formations, marking political thought and resistance globally as movements drew connections between culture and imperialism, domination and everyday life.[27] The New Left's internationalist disposition resisted the separation of the world into three distinct spheres, as political economic theories such as dependency and world-systems theory "vigorously tried to think the world as one."[28] Despite these efforts, Denning argues, New Left critique never cohered into a transnational critique of culture.

Contra Denning, I propose that an international critique of culture, particularly the phenomenon of mass media, surfaced in the New Left through its cinema, as movements attempted to subvert the operation of cultural industries through the development of counternetworks for the production, distribution, and exhibition of moving images. As I discuss in chapter 1, New Left cinema expanded critiques of international political economy, such as dependency theory, by insisting that the cultural and affective dimensions of everyday life were inextricable from broader systems of domination. Moreover, these cultural and affective aspects of the political could be reconstituted, through cinema, as a basis for resistance. The cinematic artifacts of the New Left were not simply appendages to social movements but generative experiments through which some of the New Left's most radical insights were developed.

New Left cinema and its critique of the everyday was thus situated within a broader assault against the organization of daily life within industrial capitalism. In a series of screeds published in the late 1960s and early 1970s, Ayn Rand dubbed the New Left the "anti-industrial revolution," Dionysian in spirit and impervious to Reason.[29] Though the insults she hurls against the movements of the New Left are facile at best, there is some truth to her assessment of the New Left as a force that called into question the fundamental features of industrial capitalism. The New Left erupted against the backdrop of an enormous expansion of the U.S.

economy during the postwar "American Century," alongside so-called economic miracles like France, Italy, West Germany, and Japan, countries that experienced unprecedented economic growth in the decades following World War II. Concentrating primarily on movements in these industrial centers, the proverbial "First World," this book examines how sites of both the production and reproduction of capitalism—the factory, the university, and the home—became foci of revolutionary activity. However, these "First World" sites only become intelligible by drawing out the international connections that informed the imaginative geographies within New Left movements that I trace in the book. It is within these sites that a new politics of the quotidian and an enlarged base of revolution were hashed out in a way that challenged the underlying global dynamics of power that had produced the postwar economic boom. At the same time, these movements contended, directly and indirectly, with changes in global capitalism that were already afoot, grappling with a new world coming into view while contesting the old.

A question baffled some observers at the time, like Rand: how was it, amid such outward markers of prosperity, that a generation felt compelled to rebel? A default answer to this question, especially in industrial centers, could be summed up in one word: alienation. In addition to immense wealth, capitalism had produced a deep sense of separation: alienation at work, alienation at school, alienation from culture and lived experience. Though I work to complicate this narrative throughout the book, the theme of alienation seems an expedient place to begin a discussion of the New Left's critique of the everyday and a potential politics for its cinema. The fixation on alienation was inspired, for many, by a return to the early Marx, placing issues of consciousness and experience at the center of leftist critiques of mass culture.[30] For example, Vaneigem's *Revolution of Everyday Life* starts with "Power's Perspective," the alienation of the individual within mass culture and traditional politics, and ends with a "Reversal of Perspective" that holds up "self-realization, communication, and participation" as antidotes to capitalist alienation, the keys to a new politics of the quotidian.[31] This "reversal of perspective," which understands the cinematic image not as the vehicle of domination but as the basis for communicative and participatory politics, is an underlying insight of New Left cinema. It is precisely this reversal of perspective that I explore next through the work of Guy Debord, a thinker of alienation par excellence.

ENDURING IMAGES

I began with Debord not to enshrine him as a leader of New Left cinema but because he is often depicted as a kind of prophet, an untimely thinker whose theorization of the commodified image foresaw the increasing role of the spectacle in defining our postmodern, post-Fordist, biopolitical world.[32] His theory of the spectacle is, in many ways, exemplary of the New Left's engagement with culture industries that extended a Marxist humanist critique of alienation to the image. Though the spectacle is not reducible to cinema, for Debord, the cinematic image is an "integral part" of "modern capitalism and its general system of illusions."[33] The cinematic image, in other words, is essential to the spectacle; it participates in and furthers a culture of separation and alienation. Through and against Debord, this section is a first cut into the political, ontological, and historical thesis on cinematic resistance that informs the readings of cinematic movements in this book. Complicating Debord's theory of the spectacle with a divergent theory of the image being developed by his contemporary Gilles Deleuze, I draw out the political consequences of Debord's thesis on the alienated image while arriving at an alternative to it through the cinematic version of *Society of the Spectacle*.

Since its publication, critics, activists, and artists alike have returned to Debord's book to think about what we might describe as contemporary capitalism's "spectacular mode of production" and to generate tactics for resistance against it. In Debord's assessment of the spectacle, the commodity form reigns supreme over social life. Drawing on Marx's critique of the commodity form in *Capital, Volume One* and read through Georg Lukács's theory of reification (with an unstated affinity to critiques of the culture industry by Adorno and Horkheimer), Debord produces a concept of the spectacle as the fullest expression of the commodity's domination. When he writes that "commodities are now all there is to see," he is arguing that we have entered a historical moment in which "*capital* [is] accumulated to the point where it becomes an image."[34] The image and the commodity, for Debord, are one and the same thing. Moreover, in expanding its reach into every facet of social life, the commodity is the only form of reality that the spectacle offers; it constitutes this reality and thus turns reality itself into an image. At the same time, this image is separated from its producers and fetishized; therefore it also stands outside of reality and controls it from a distance. Consequently, the spectacle is a false image, a "nonlife" that turns against its producers.[35] Contained within Debord's conflation of the spectacle and the commodity—a conflation that is pervasive in Marxist critiques of the image—we find a particular metaphysics of the image, which carries with it a number of implicit philosophical assumptions that adhere to what Steven Shaviro calls a "fear of images," a form of neo-Platonism that reproduces a mistrust of the cinematic image.[36] The image, for Debord, is dangerous precisely because it is a bad or false copy that has come to replace the original. Consequently, the image is always false because it is fetishized; it lords over social life and mediates all relations through itself.

Debord's theory of the spectacle has had significant consequences for defining our assumptions about the relationship between aesthetic practice and resistance in the last half-century, as the Situationist theory of *détournement,* or hijacking an image in order to turn it against itself, has been established as a tool for "jamming" capitalist culture. In addition, as Claire Bishop argues, the belief that the spectacle has rent asunder social bonds has tacitly informed social practice art, which has been, in large part, concerned with repairing these broken relationships.[37] Tied to a dialectical critique of alienation, Debord's theory of the image-as-spectacle has played a significant role in defining both artistic and academic approaches to the politics of representation.

But as influential as they may be, Debord's writings on the image take us only so far when trying to articulate a theory of cinematic resistance adequate to the task at hand. Starting from a neo-Platonist position put forward by Debord, the image, cinematic or otherwise, cannot be the basis of resistance. Instead, it can only be reappropriated and exposed as false. These ontological presuppositions about the image as an inherently bad or false copy are challenged when we look to Debord's contemporary

Gilles Deleuze. Although Debord's name never arises in Deleuze's prolific writings from the late 1960s, Deleuze was surely aware of Debord's theory of the spectacle, particularly after its popularization during the events of May 1968. It formed an integral part of the philosophical milieu against which Deleuze's interventions were made. In particular, the Nietzschean project to "reverse Platonism," as he calls it in the appendix to the *Logic of Sense* (1969), might be understood as a counterproposition to Debord's theory of the spectacle, one that not only offers an alternative to Debord's take on the ontological status of the image but also elaborates the political consequences that follow from such a reversal. Beginning with *Difference and Repetition* (1968), and drawing on Nietzsche's concept of the eternal return, Deleuze locates an "anti-Platonism at the heart of Platonism," reading passages from Plato that suggest "simulacra provide the means of challenging *both* the notion of the copy *and* that of the model."[38] Simulacra—bad, degraded, or false copies or images—which Debord finds to be so threatening, for Deleuze affirm "the different, the dissimilar, the unequal"; simulacra are more than representations but take on material force of their own, what Deleuze calls the "power of the false."[39] Deleuze returns to this later concept, the power of the false, at length in *Cinema 2: The Time-Image,* and it is through his philosophy of cinema that Deleuze is able to develop a theory of the simulacra that goes against the thesis that the cinematic image is a fixed representation, a bad copy that is instrumental in "a general system of illusions."

What is important to emphasize here is that the powers of the false that Deleuze first seeks to affirm in 1968 are more than a subversion of Debord's dialectical presumptions about the dangerous image, the "nonlife" that constitutes the spectacle. Rather than simply asserting the power of the negative, Deleuze unravels the binaries between true and false, life and nonlife, that undergird Debord's theory. Furthermore, Deleuze's theory ultimately understands the image not as something static but as that which is infused with a nonlinear time, a virtual force that disrupts the present by signaling other possible worlds. With regard to the time-image, Deleuze writes that "the power of the false ... replaces and supersedes the truth because it poses the simultaneity of incompossible presents, or the coexistence of not-necessarily true pasts."[40] Suggesting that one's reality is one among many coextensive worlds, and that many pasts comingle with the present, the power of the false subverts Platonic binaries by destabilizing any one truth of a given moment in time. According to David Rodowick, the powers of the false refer to those forces that "release the image from the form of identity and restore it to the potential for becoming or eternal recurrence."[41] In Deleuze's time-image, we find not the dead, nonlife alienated from us but the potential for difference and, ultimately, for change.[42]

In *Logic of Sense,* Deleuze underscores the political significance of his subversion of Platonic binaries, which ultimately brings him to an understanding of creative potential of the simulacrum as a force geared toward the production of new political imaginaries:

> Modernity is defined by the power [*puissance*] of the simulacrum. It behooves philosophy not to be modern at any cost, no more than to be nontemporal, but to extract from modernity something that Nietzsche designated as the untimely, which pertains to modernity, but which must be turned against it—"in favor, I hope, of a time to come." It is not in the great forests and woodpaths that philosophy is elaborated, but rather in the towns and in the streets—even the most artificial [*factice*] of them. The untimely is attained in relation to the most distant past, by the reversal of Platonism; in relation to the present, by the simulacrum conceived as the edge of critical modernity; in relation to the future, it is attained by the phantasm of the eternal return as belief in the future.[43]

What does it mean that "modernity is defined by the power of the simulacrum"? Deleuze insinuates that modernity bears within it a creative force, a potential, at once its defining character but also that which "must be turned against it." The simulacrum is the "critical edge of modernity" that opens the untimely potential of the present, but, moreover, it is "a time to come." The "belief in the future" is the belief in possibility for a different future, that is, one that does not come into being through the stagnant repetition of reactive forces. The untimely, the unhinging of linear time, opens up this creative potential of transformation in which the past, present, and future conspire. We no longer need to worry ourselves with the quest for authenticity in our philosophy or our politics: "the time to come" will be amplified on the streets and not in the purity of an ideal nature. In short, in his undoing of Platonic binaries, Deleuze replaces the obsession with alienation with an affirmation of becoming.

In locating the powers of the false within the cinematic image, we arrive at a potential politics that might also contain within it "belief in the future." A belief in the future is an affirmation of a different future in which the creative potential of modernity, the simulacrum, is turned against it. But how might we arrive at a materialist theory of cinematic resistance from this point? Deleuze's writings on cinema gain political weight when we traverse his writing to engage his thinking on power and resistance developed in his monograph on Foucault (published one year after *Cinema 2*). In his discussion of the diagram of power, Deleuze asserts that "the final word on power is that *resistance comes first.*"[44] In this statement, resistance occupies a similar ontological position as the simulacrum in the passage from *Logic of Sense* discussed earlier: it is that which generates the potential for change, an untimely force that opens onto the future. Resistance, like the simulacrum, is creative and affirmative. Cesare Casarino draws out the temporal dimensions of resistance, arguing that the key to understanding Deleuze's enigmatic statement on the primacy of resistance lies in his tacit reading of Spinoza's philosophy.[45] Read through Spinoza, Casarino argues that, "when truly resisting, there was no beginning and there shall be no end, there is no before and no after, there is endurance without duration, and the first and the last are the future anterior of each other."[46] In the concept of "endurance without duration," we find a theory of resistance as that which endures outside of linear time. The ontological primacy of resistance that Deleuze finds in Foucault is thus intrinsically tied to a nonlinear temporality that allows for a belief in the future by potentiating a different future.

How might one assert that, in the case of the image, resistance also comes first? Though Debord's writings seem to fixate on a neo-Platonism that stifles resistance, the cinematic version of *Society of the Spectacle,* I argue, gives us access to a different theory of the cinematic image, one that affirms the primacy of resistance and its nonlinear temporalities discussed earlier. As Jason Smith has argued, we should understand Debord to be first and foremost a filmmaker, and it is through his films that we arrive at his most significant theoretical and aesthetic contributions.[47] If we accept this proposition, then the film version of *Society of the Spectacle* cannot simply be seen as a derivative adaptation of the book. Instead, it offers a substantial reordering and revision of its arguments, in which Debord grapples with the tumultuous birth of a new era that is coming into view in the period between 1967 and 1973. This revision and reordering of chapters from the book emphasize not the alienated image-as-commodity but rather the image as terrain of resistance.[48] While the critique of the commodity remains in the film, a fixation on its totalizing force seems to be replaced by a practice of creating revolutionary assaults against it. Crucial passages such as "commodities are now all there is to see; the world we see is the world of the commodity" are not to be found in the film. The world we see in the film is not simply the world of the commodity but a world of creativity in which the affective power of the image generates a politics of resistance and, ultimately, of transformation.

The film's insights on the image and resistance become clear in the short section on the commodity, which occurs much later in the film than in the book. In this section, the commodity's all-consuming force seems to be undermined, as the passages on the commodity-spectacle from the 1967 text are paired not only with apposite images of cars and girls but also with footage of the Watts riots. By forcing this association, Debord implicitly returns to the Situationists' 1965 pamphlet on Watts titled "The Decline and Fall of the Spectacle-Commodity," in which they argued that the riots indicated the emergence of a "new proletarian consciousness taking shape in America."[49] The pamphlet emphasizes not the hegemony of the commodity-spectacle but, as the title suggests, its inherent fragility exposed by attacks launched against it, attacks possible even from within the centers of industrial capitalism where large sections of the population had been excluded from the prosperity of the postwar era. This footage of the Watts riots is juxtaposed with voice-over on the dominance of exchange-value over use-value in society, as exchange-value becomes its own "autonomous power," subjecting us to a "counterfeit life." The interstice between sound and image, however, disrupts the voice-over and inserts a tension into the film's argument — the life we see in the image is not one of counterfeit or deceit but one of resistance.

With inclusion of the Watts footage, *Society of the Spectacle*'s cinematic

Figure 1. Film still, Watts riots, *La société du spectacle* (1973).

version tracks the reemergence of forms of resistance against capitalism, namely, the riot.[50] The sequence foreshadows the film's conclusion, which prominently features footage of May 1968, events that served as a confirmation of Debord's 1967 prediction of "a second proletariat assault against class society," a point the film underscores. Despite the failures, defeats, and numerous cooptations of May 1968 and the preceding revolutions that the film addresses, *Society of the Spectacle* leaves us with detourned footage of a classic Hollywood film on the U.S. Civil War; the script reads, "After yet another setback, the officer appears in front of the ranks of the First Michigan — the last regiment that remains — and orders yet another charge." The struggle continues. If the book is held up as evidence for the futility of resistance, the film suggests the opposite; a "reversal of perspective" has been achieved.

Thus the film version of *Society of the Spectacle* does not ultimately prosecute an argument that reinforces the total dominance of the spectacle over society. Instead, it complicates the book's arguments by affirming resistance against it. The footage of the Watts riots, taken in 1965, repurposed by Debord in 1973, and viewed by us again today, becomes a kind of eternal return of the simulacrum—the time of resistance, an "endurance without duration." Accumulated within these images of resistance is a density of time, which opens up the image to political, spatial, and temporal dimensions that unhinge it from linear temporality. To say that the image endures does not simply suggest that it persists; the enduring image, like Deleuze's time-image, is a direct image of time—it opens time and exposes multiple temporalities.[51] These images are untimely, in that they potentiate a different kind of time that goes against the grain of the present. But they are also enduring, in the sense that they carry with them a density of time across historical eras, a problem to which I return through the work of Ian Baucom, from whom the title of this book was taken, in chapter 3. How do images of resistance endure, and how do enduring images resist? In this book, I argue that the cinematic image has a unique capacity to carry the affective qualities of resistance across historical eras, disrupting a perpetual present and opening onto possible futures. The meaning of these images does not remain unchanged but is marked by an internal difference and is transformed with each new expression. Instead of writing a history of New Left cinema, I aspire to write a "future history," in the words of Paolo Virno, unfixed from narratives of defeat or determination, "in favor, I hope, of a time to come."[52]

THE SPECTACLE, TRANSFORMED

In addition to revising its position on the ontological status of the image and the possibility for resistance contained within it, the film version of *Society of the Spectacle* measures the theses of the book against the events that transpired in the years immediately following its publication. The film's translation of the text suggests that by 1973, a new era was coming into view and that the spectacle itself did not remain unchanged. For example, during the presentation of the third thesis of the book, which argues that what "the unification [the spectacle] achieves is nothing but an official language of universal separation," the detourned footage that appears on the screen is a speech by Valéry Giscard d'Estaing and another by Jean-Jacques Servan-Schreiber. At first glance, this footage could simply be taken as stock footage of the political spectacle and its separation from lived experience, but the selection of these two figures typifies two poles of France's post-1968 political reconfiguration. Giscard, who spearheaded the Independent Republicans in 1967 (the same year as the publication of *Society of the Spectacle*), would be elected France's president in 1974, and his political ascendance in the period between 1967 and 1973 is consubstantial with the rise of the New Right in France in the post-1968 period, as I discuss in the final chapter of the book. Servan-Schreiber, on the other hand, was cofounder of *L'Express,* a journal of lifestyle and liberal political commentary, and he epitomized a new, cosmopolitan face of the Left that sought to capitalize on the desire for change expressed by the events of 1968 with pseudo-reforms like the project for a "new society." Servan-Schreiber, an early advocate of intra-European economic cooperation, ended up taking a cabinet position in Giscard's government after the latter's election in 1974, epitomizing the collusion of the New Right and elements of the New Left in channeling the revolutionary desire to transform postwar French society demonstrated by May 1968 into a new, neoliberal political formation.

While the 1967 version of *Society of the Spectacle* was an attack launched against industrial capitalism and a Keynesian system that advocated stimulating the economy through effective demand and the expansion of consumer society, the 1973 version opens by immediately registering an impending shift in the political economic organization of society whose new formation is one of cooptation and counterrevolution. The reformulation of *Society of the Spectacle*'s critique of separation in and through what we might call the spectacle of counterrevolution comes in the next sequence, where a figure Debord describes as a "bureaucrat" in the script speaks to Renault workers toward the end of May 1968, announcing that the "Grenelle Accords" had been signed, ostensibly bringing the events of May to a close by forcing major concessions on the part of the workers.[53] Over an answering shot of the Renault workers "showing their discontent and contempt," as the script reads, Debord's voice-over presents the book's fourth thesis: "The spectacle is not a collection of images; rather it is a social relationship, between people, that is mediated by images." The point of this thesis in the original text is clear enough: the spectacle is a social relationship that produces separation. But juxtaposed with this footage of the Renault workers at the conclusion of May 1968, this thesis takes on new meaning. The social relationship between the Renault work-ers is one of being united, but united in a relationship of defeat, shown at the moment of a thwarted revolution. By pairing this footage with the fourth thesis of the original text, the film seems to argue that the conclu-sion of May 1968 marked the inception of a new diagram of power that the film takes as its starting point.

In other words, the aftermath of 1968 opens *Society of the Spectacle* to historical revision. The revisions to the original text occur in and through the film's ability to contrast its theses with new historical developments and insights, which at moments confirm the arguments of the book, while at other times moving beyond them. For example, the section on the commodity includes footage of widespread environmental pollution, signaling concerns beyond the alienation that capitalism had produced by demonstrating a growing catastrophe that poisons not only the minds of the proletarian class but also the air they breathe and the water they drink.[54] Thesis 23, on the specialization of power, is juxtaposed with footage of the Paris Stock Exchange—portending a new era of financialization that comes to eclipse the system of industrial production examined in the book.

In *The Long Twentieth Century,* Giovanni Arrighi argues that the cycles of capitalist accumulation can be mapped according to phases that correspond to Marx's general theory of capital (MCM′), a histori-cal framework to which I return in chapter 3. For Arrighi, there are two distinct phases of capitalist accumulation: the (MC) phases of material investment and the (CM′) phases of financial expansion:

> Thus, (MC) phases of material expansion will be shown to consist of phases of continuous change, during which the capitalist world economy grows along a single developmental path. And (CM′) phases of financial expansion will be shown to consist of phases of discontinuous change during which growth among the established path has attained or is attain-ing its limits, and the capitalist world economy "shifts" through radical restructurings and reorganizations onto another path.[55]

The period that transpires between Debord's publication of the book and film versions of *Society of the Spectacle,* 1967–74, corresponds to the historical moment in which the hundred-year phase of a (MC) cycle of capitalist accumulation comes to an end, the "signal" crisis that marks both an "underling systemic crisis" and a switch to a period of high financialization, according to Arrighi.[56] We might say, then, that Debord's total critique of the commodity in 1967 appears at a historical moment that stood both at the height of the (MC) cycle but also on the precipice of a new phase of capitalist accumulation in which the "radical restructurings and reorganizations" of capitalist forms are beginning to unfold. In this sense, Debord's 1967 theory of the spectacle captures the fullest expression of an era of capitalist production dominated by the logic of the commodity, one written from the perspective of a thinker living in a center of a Keynesian, industrial moment. That moment, as Debord writes it, is on the threshold of crisis and dissolution. The cinematic version of *Society of the Spectacle,* then, provides emendations to the original text that indicate both the birth of a new era of capitalist organization and the capacity to understand the image beyond the domination of the commodity form.[57]

The films and videos discussed in this book share with *Society of the Spectacle* the capacity to think through, in an essayistic manner, the uneven and tumultuous passage from one era of global capitalist organization to another. Through close readings of New Left cinema and the historical context from which it emerges, the conceptual framework of the book reflects upon central and interrelated aspects of this transitional moment in global capitalism: financialization, industrial crisis, the "feminization of labor," the expansion of network technologies and cybernetic management, inflation, and the ascendance of neoliberalism. It argues that New Left cinema presents an opportunity to reexamine these coterminous phenomena, as I explore the ways that each of the films and videos captures both a unique perspective on its own historical moment and an oblique perspective on a world to come—culturally, economically, and politically. Beyond a mode of analysis that understands documentary images as representations of reality and measures their fidelity to that reality, *Enduring Images* examines how New Left cinema intervenes in and transforms culture, politics, and history. In the words of Steven Shaviro, I am interested in the ways that the films and videos in question are "expressive" of social reality, in that they are "both *symptomatic* and *productive*" of it.[58]

Enduring Images pursues an argument that unfolds in the relay between resistance and reaction, revolution and counterrevolution, situating the New Left's cinematic artifacts within broader contexts of the histories and discursive practices to which they both responded and contributed. Among the many films and movements of New Left cinema, I have chosen those that allow me to at once map the salient features of the New Left's international solidarities, participatory aspirations, internal battles, and formal innovations, and develop an argument about the enduring repercussions of the New Left that places struggle at the center of social transformation. Though these themes run throughout the book, each chapter develops an independent argument, which is reflected in the different style and content that frame these individual engagements.

I open the book in chapter 1 with what I call the "New Left's essay film," described not only as a genre but as a political practice that both followed and advanced the New Left's internationalist, participatory, and antiauthoritarian tendencies. My engagement with the "essay film" departs from recent discussions of the genre that define it as a "personal" mode of expression. I argue that this understanding of the essay film closely identifies it with European art cinema and the auteur tradition, particularly in France, and that the development of the essay film in the context of New Left social movements represents a radical break from this tradition. To begin, I focus on collective and anonymous filmmaking projects taking place within and around the events of May 1968 in France, particularly *Cinétracts* (France, 1968), as part of a larger project to dismantle the hierarchies of national cinema and to put forward a new vision of the role that cinema could play within society. I depart from the Eurocentrism of recent histories of the essay film by focusing on the international conversations regarding militant cinema evolving in this era. Turning to Fernando Solanas and Octavio Getino's manifesto, "Towards a Third Cinema," and their film, *Hora de los hornos*—texts I regard as benchmarks in the evolution of the essay film genre—I insist that we decenter our understanding of the genre from its presumed European context and consider the manner in which it was articulated within the international alliances and imaginaries that shaped New Left social movements. Furthermore, I examine how the deployment of the essay form in *Hora de los hornos* enables the filmmakers to present a theory of cultural imperialism and the "colonization of everyday life" that expands postcolonial theories of dependency. This chapter presents the key features of New Left cinema that are developed in these two very different contexts, namely, the demand for participation, the attempted democratization of cinematic technologies and modes of production and distribution, militant political engagement, and the collective production of the essay form. Expanding the theory of the essay film, I argue that in New Left cinema, we see the production of what I call an "essayistic politics of the common," attempts to generate collective cinematic enunciations that express a prefigurative politics.

Chapters 2–4 extend the conversation around the New Left's "enlarged base of revolution," investigating cinematic movements that grew out of student, worker, and women's struggles. Within each of these chapters, questions of internal difference within social movements, particularly race and gender, come to the fore as new political subjectivities and collectivities are articulated through cinema. At the same time, I track how the cinema of these movements traces the shifting political economic landscape that comes into view as new revolutionary epistemologies, temporalities, and subjectivities emerge. Chapter 2, "Toward a New Mode of Study: The Student New Left and the Occupation of Cinema," is particularly interested in new cinematic epistemologies that are generated by the New Left, examining how cinema became a form of militant study geared toward the dissemination of situated knowledge. It draws on questions of cinematic insurgency, collective production, and the essay film developed in the first chapter to explore the connections between New Left cinema and the student movements of the late 1960s through a discussion of the Newsreel collective's *Columbia Revolt* (United States, 1968) and the Ogawa Pro collective's *Nihon kaiho sensen—Sanrizuka no natsu* (The battlefront for the liberation of Japan—Summer in Sanrizuka, Japan, 1968). While coming from diverse geopolitical contexts, both of these films deal with political occupations and are emblematic of the interventionist and horizontal nature of New Left cinema coalescing globally at that moment and of the centrality of the figure of the student within it. I explore how each of these films demonstrates the ways that the student New Left articulated local political struggles with international ones, highlighting the ways that solidarity and new collectivities are formed in the constitution of life behind the barricades, arriving at a form of what

Kristen Ross calls "communal luxury."[59] Drawing on Fred Moten and Stefano Harney's conception of study, I argue that the student New Left employed cinema as a new mode of study capable of generating affects and amplifying antagonisms, while considering the relationship between resistance in 1968 and enclosures around student debt today.

Chapter 3, "*Finally Got the News* at the End of the Short American Century," amplifies the theme of temporality that runs through my reading of New Left cinema, returning to the problem of the enduring image. It highlights the politics of difference within New Left cinema and foregrounds the role of race in the crisis of industrial modernity, via a reading of the essay film *Finally Got the News* (United States, 1970) by the Detroit Newsreel collective and the League of Revolutionary Black Workers. Focusing on forms of autonomous labor organizing, I argue that *Finally Got the News* captures the transition between industrial and financial capitalism in terms of the crisis of the Fordist mode of production as it crystallized in the automotive industry and the city of Detroit. I use the discussion of the film to foreground the struggles against racial oppression that were central to these crises and argue that the film offers a prescient glimpse of the financial counterrevolution that followed. The chapter explores the internal conflicts within the cinema of the New Left around race and class and the ways that production of *Finally Got the News* exemplified these conflicts in the context of the U.S. Newsreel movement. Through an engagement with Ian Baucom's *Specters of the Atlantic,* this chapter further develops the book's historiographical framework and theory of historical transition by way of the concept of the enduring image.

Chapter 4, "Italian Feminist Collectives and the 'Unexpected Subject,'" centers around the formation of new subjective positions that arise through New Left cinematic experimentation by examining the ways that second-wave feminism advanced and complicated the political project of New Left cinema. Across Europe, the United States, and Latin America, the 1970s saw an explosion of political documentaries made by women dealing with various aspects of women's labor, sexuality, and status in society. Situated within this broader context, this chapter focuses on feminist film collectives in Italy whose films explored themes central to the feminist movement in that country, opening the potential for radical subjectivities through what Italian feminist Carla Lonzi called the "unexpected subject." I examine the manner in which the feminist movement conducted a transvaluation of norms and values though films produced by the Collettivo di Cinema Femminista-Roma (Roman Feminist Cinema Collective), *L'aggettivo donna* (The adjective woman, Italy, 1971) and *La lotta non è finita* (The struggle is not over, Italy, 1973), and the ways that the feminist movements challenged the division between productive and reproductive labor through cinematic experiments of the Gruppo Femminista Milanese per il Salario al Lavoro Domestico (Milanese Feminist Group for Wages for Domestic Labor). Thus this chapter evaluates the strategies of collective filmmaking that took hold in women's movements by way of the Italian example and explores the ways that political and tactical innovations of second-wave feminism were translated into radical filmmaking practices, particularly antiauthoritarian and transindividual forms of cinematic inquiry. It does so by tying these themes to larger discussions of the "feminization of labor" in this period and the centrality of the struggles around women's reproductive labor in shaping the character of work in post-Fordism, but also the legacies of resistance that endure from critiques of gender and reproductive labor from this period.

Chapter 5, "Cybernetic Guerrilla Warfare: Early Video and the Ambivalence of Information," shifts focus to interrogate how New Left cinema's tactics and political ethos intersected with new moving image technologies and theories of communication systems. Drawing on themes of collective production and distribution developed throughout the book, this chapter examines utopian imaginations emerging from the New Left about the role new technologies, namely, video, might play in the future of democratic media production. It explores the New Left's imagination of a radical, networked information economy through a close reading of writings and videos produced by the Raindance Corporation, an early U.S. video collective. Specifically, the chapter examines the book *Guerrilla Television* (1971), the journal *Radical Software* (1970–74) and related groups such as People's Video Theater, Videofreex, and Top Value Television. Though these movements have long been framed as part of the tradition of video art, I argue that the guerrilla television movement of the early 1970s should be understood within the broader context of New

Left cinema. Thematically, the chapter explores how the popularization of cybernetic theory in the 1960s intersected with New Left cinema and influenced the early Guerrilla television movement. Deriving its name from the Greek word for "to steer," cybernetics was developed during World War II as an interdisciplinary science concerned with organization and communication of information within systems, particularly the ways that systems use feedback to correct errors and attain goals. In examining the translation of these ideas into the context of the New Left, I look at the theme of "cybernetic guerrilla warfare" proposed by Paul Ryan, an early video practitioner and Raindance member, and how the New Left's early adaptation of video, read through cybernetic concepts, ultimately produced an ambivalent account of the power of revolutionary images to transform social life.

Finally, chapter 6, "Inflation of the Image; or, The Image of Revolution in the 1970s," reflects on the aims and aspirations of New Left cinema explored in the previous chapters and develops a conceptual framework to analyze the fate of the cinema of the New Left and the image of revolution during the emergent counterrevolution of the 1970s, thus serving as a conclusion to the book. It does so by examining two films that use raw footage of revolutionary movements to produce cinematic reflections that critically evaluate the project of New Left cinema: Jean-Luc Godard, Jean-Pierre Gorin, and Anne-Marie Miéville's *Ici et ailleurs* (*Here and Elsewhere*, France, 1974) and Chris Marker's *Le fond de l'air est rouge* (*Grin without a Cat*, France, 1977). *Ici et ailleurs* is a film composed partially of footage of Palestinian militants taken in Jordan from an abandoned project of the Dziga Vertov Group, *Jusqu'à la victoire* (1970), and it contemplates the unfinished and unfinishable nature of *Jusqu'à la victoire*'s revolutionary aspirations. Though an interrogation of the paradox captured in *Ici et ailleur*'s statement "poor revolutionary fool, millionaire in revolutionary images," I analyze the aftermath of the 1960s through the process of inflation, examining the larger implications of inflation's ability to simultaneously multiply and cancel out through the proliferation of images of revolution. In doing so, this chapter examines the unintended consequences of strategies of New Left cinema that functioned to proliferate counterimages and alternative infrastructures for circulating them. I then turn to *Le fond de l'air est rouge*. Similar to *Ici et ailleurs*, the majority of *Le fond de l'air est rouge* was filmed in the late 1960s, and the film's formal construction acts as a historical meditation on the events of the 1960s in light of its present. Arguing against readings of the film that claim it as a work of mourning for the New Left, I assert that the film is a meditation on the themes of visibility and invisibility, acting as an encounter with the vast archive that New Left cinematic movements (many of which Marker was involved with himself) left behind. I argue that Marker's engagement with this archival material contends with the incipient formation of the counterrevolutionary logic of the New Right—neoliberalism as such—a counterpoint that emerges alongside, and in reaction to, New Left social movements. However, I argue that Marker's film develops a materialist understanding of the documentary image, one that allows us to revisit the audiovisual archive of the New Left and see it anew. Outside of the narratives of determinism and defeat, this reading suggests that the enduring meaning of New Left cinema is not fixed but open and ever changing. Furthermore, my wager is that it is only by affirming these enduring meanings that we can open a space for politics within the New Left's cinematic archive.

The epilogue to the book, "A Future History?," looks at the scenes of counterrevolution—spectacles of counterrevolution, as I will call them—that cohered as the 1970s drew to a close and asks, how do we hold images of the New Left at the same time as the world seems to confirm only their inversion, distortion, and cancellation? By way of Chris Marker's reading of "The Zone" in *Sans Soleil* (*Sunless*, France, 1983), I propose a nonlinear historiographical approach to New Left cinema that allows these tensions to remain in balance, affirming the multiple temporalities and possible interpretations of the New Left's audiovisual archive. Against the genre of "capitalist realism," or the discourse that there is no alternative to the neoliberal agenda, I argue that the New Left's enduing images are one site to sketch a path, through the past, toward an alternate future. Drawing on Paolo Virno, I conclude the book by contemplating what it means to understand the cinema of the New Left as a potential "future history" from the perspective of our contemporary historical juncture. In doing so, these images might serve some purpose in helping *us* to endure.

1
The New Left's Essay Film

FROM SUBJECTIVE EXPRESSION TO COLLECTIVE INSURGENCY

Guy Debord's translation of *Society of the Spectacle* from book to cinematic essay gives us insight into how we might apprehend the theoretical and political contributions of *Society of the Spectacle* anew, transforming our understanding of the text from a declaration of the omnipotence of the commodity spectacle to an affirmation of struggle. Among the filmmakers working within and alongside New Left movements, Debord was not alone in his exploration of the essay form. As I examine throughout the book, the essay film became a principal strategy for a new mode of political filmmaking in many different social movements and geopolitical contexts. In and around 1968, essay films coming out of the New Left reflect diverse attempts to articulate new forms of political expression and intervention. The forays into the essay film by New Left filmmakers break open and transform the limits and capacities of the documentary and avant-garde cinematic traditions to contend with the unfolding upheavals taking place at that moment. This chapter explores how the essay film became central to the New Left's cinematic lexicon, providing a both theoretical and historical framework for understanding its significance. Examining the contemporaneous evolution of New Left cinema in France and Argentina, it interrogates the role of the essay film in the break with auteur cinema during the disruption of May 1968 in France and the simultaneous formation of third cinema in Latin America. It does so by conducting what Kodo Eshun and Ros Grey have called a "ciné-geography" in their proposal for the reevaluation of militant cinema of the 1960s and 1970s. Drawing on the concept of relational geography, Eshun and Grey develop ciné-geography "as an interdisciplinary practice of mapping the affinities, proximities and affiliations of ciné-cultures that emerged from and participated in the conflictual and connective militant politics of anti-colonial struggle and revolutionary decolonization in the late twentieth century."[1]

A central question of this chapter is why, given their innovation and intensity, the essay films of the New Left are consistently excluded from critical accounts of the genre. Examples include Debord's *La Société du spectacle,* Fernando Solanas and Octavio Getino's *Hora de los hornos (Hour of the Furnaces,* Argentina, 1968), the Le group Medvedkine's *Classe de lutte (Class of Struggle,* France, 1969), and many others that populate the pages of this book. Examining these as productive omissions that reveal certain commitments in the way that the genre has been defined, I argue that the essay films of the New Left break from an understanding of the essay form that limits it by circumscribing it within the domain of the "personal." Moving beyond a discussion of the genre that confines it to the realm of subjective expression, this chapter works to articulate the essay film with collective insurgency in and through New Left social movements. In doing so, I produce a minor history of the essay film that locates its contributions outside of the auteur tradition. Moreover, the chapter explores the essay film as a mode of encounter that enabled new forms of political enunciation by way of the cinema, what I will call an *essayistic politics of the common.* The essay films of the New Left served as conduits for political encounters across various social and geographic divisions that expressed new alliances forming within an expanding international politics of resistance. Part of the effort to reimagine the role of cinema in society, and in social movements in particular, the 1968 essay films of the New Left in France and Argentina discussed here serve as exemplary experiments in collective production and audience engagement that would come to define New Left cinema. Reading the essay films of the New Left outside the domain of personal expression allows us to expand not only our understanding of the formal innovation of these cinematic movements but also the theoretical and political correspondence between social movements enabled by the cinematic essay.

In conducting a ciné-geography of the New Left's essay film through an examination of the affinities between France and Argentina, my aim is to decenter the essay film from its association with European auteur cinema, situating it within the Tricontinental political alliances taking shape in the Third Worldism of the late 1960s. Through an analysis of seminal essay films of the New Left in France leading up to and during the events of May 1968 (namely, *Loin du Vietnam* [1967] and *Cinétracts,* ciné-pamphlets produced in the midst of May 1968), I argue that the New Left's essay film is developed in France not simply as an autochthonous outgrowth of a national cinematic culture but as a rupture induced by a series of militant political struggles deeply tied to France's own colonial history. Similarly, this chapter engages the theorization of the essay film by Fernando Solanas and Octavio Getino in conjunction with the development of their original conception of third cinema, an anticolonial cinema of liberation that rejects both Hollywood and European auteur traditions. Through an analysis of *Hora de los hornos,* I amplify the way that detaching the essay film from the domain of the personal in the context of New Left cinema allows for a mode of cinematic thinking capable of advancing nuanced theoretical arguments regarding the dynamic interplay of culture and global systems of dependency, on one hand, and financial debt at the dawn of the neoliberal era, on the other.

Of primary importance in my presentation of the New Left's essay film is a critical reevaluation of the collective and participatory practices of production, the alternative networks of distribution, and the new approaches to exhibition and audience engagement that were deeply entrenched within the social movements from which they were born. This attention to the material practices of New Left cinema brings to light collective forms of thought and social relations produced in and through the cinematic image that exceed the purview of auteur cinema. It also points to the crucial role of the cinema as a form of expression integral to social movement activity in the New Left. Examining these practices within the broader context of what Claire Bishop has deemed the "social turn" in contemporary art, the chapter concludes with an evaluation of the liberatory aspirations of New Left cinema beyond critiques of participation presented by theorists like Jacques Rancière. I argue that the ambitions of New Left cinema were not necessarily foolhardy but arose out of an overarching rejection of forms of spectatorship and cinematic production in the industrial era, creating a new cinematic culture that actively took part in dismantling those cinematic conventions. Moreover, the New Left's essay film registered the breakdown of modern distinctions between public and private spheres by gesturing toward utopian models of being and thinking in common that are central to the New Left's political imaginary. In the context of the New Left, the essay film constitutes more than a cinematic genre; it is an attempt to prefigure a new social reality.

THE ESSAY FILM BEYOND THE ESSAY FILM

Most famously associated with the film and video work of Chris Marker, Agnès Varda, Trinh T. Minh-ha, and Werner Herzog, among others, the essay film is often characterized as a kind of hybrid genre, one that brings together avant-garde and documentary cinematic traditions. Drawing on the literary essay, the essay film blurs fact and fiction, history and experience, personal and political, to produce a singular mode of cinematic thinking. Though the notion of cinematic thinking is not original to the essay film, the essay film nevertheless presents a form of enunciation driven by argumentation and reflection that distinguish it from other cinematic traditions.[2]

The essay, much like the novel, is a literary form that is closely tied to the historical development of the modern era. Originating in the late European Renaissance through the writings of Michel de Montaigne, *essais* are often associated with a kind of mobile thinking, as the form's unique brevity allowed easy dissemination. *Essai* in the original French has the connotation of "trial," "attempt," or "test." In other words, Montaigne conceived his essays as a way of trying out ideas, experimenting with form, and thinking through lived experience. This connotation of the term *essai* as a kind of thought on trial emphasizes the process of thinking over the finished product, a characteristic that carries over into the essay film.

Accordingly, Timothy Corrigan argues that the essay is a form of "expressive subjectivity," a kind of thinking aloud that demands "the articulation or projection of an interior self into an exterior world."[3] It is in what Corrigan calls the "encounter between the self and the public domain" that the limits, capacities, and even constitution of that interior self are tested and reconfigured.[4] Similarly, Theodor Adorno argues in "Essay as Form" that the essay lies at the intersection of subjective experience and reflection on larger social, cultural, and historical forces. For Adorno, the essay takes quotidian experience and "opens it up to relation with all of history."[5] In both of these accounts, the essay instigates something like an encounter between the self and the social, experience and history. Corrigan's emphasis on "expressive subjectivity" within the essay film is in accord with the majority of criticism on the genre produced within the past decade, such as Laura Rascaroli's *The Personal Camera: Subjective Cinema and the Essay Film* (2009).[6] In this vein of criticism, it is its inherently "subjective" and "personal" nature that separates the essay film from other documentary forms:

> Just as the first-person presence of the literary essay often springs from a personal voice and perspective, so essay films characteristically highlight a real or fictional persona whose quests and questionings shape and direct the film in lieu of a traditional narrative and frequently complicate the documentary look of the film with the presence of a pronounced subjectivity or enunciating position.[7]

According to both Corrigan and Rascaroli, the epistemological innovation of the essay film comes from its break with a problematic claim to objective knowledge that has troubled documentary cinema.[8] Foregrounding the "enunciating position," the essay film in this account sidesteps the epistemological trap of camera-as-neutral-observer by placing the "I" at the center of knowledge production.

In "Essay as Form," Adorno laments, "the contemporary relevance of the essay is that of anachronism. The time is less favorable to it than ever."[9] Declaring the essay to be anachronistic in 1958, Adorno suggests that the decline of the epistemological method of the essay is concomitant with the ascent of a technoscientific regime geared toward the production of utilitarian knowledge for capital. Corrigan charts a parallel history in which the essay form (while perhaps declining in literature) was taking hold in the cinema, a "predilection" apparent at cinema's inception that begins to flourish in postwar France.[10] Corrigan's rich history of the essay film firmly grounds it within the development of the auteur tradition, which emphasizes a form of creative subjective expression that flows from the crises of postwar subjectivity and is enabled by technological advances such as synchronized sound and lightweight cameras.[11]

In Corrigan's genealogy, the advancement in modalities of authorial expression are encapsulated in Alexandre Astruc's influential 1948 essay "Birth of the New Avant-Garde: The Caméra-Stylo," which laid the theoretical foundation for the advancement of the essay film. A champion of the French New Wave, Astruc declared a new era of filmmaking based on the principles of the camera-pen, a way of imagining cinematic expression as a form of writing. His manifesto embodies the spirit of the auteur tradition by conceiving of cinematic form as the expression of authorial intent, an assumption that would come to characterize European art cinema of the 1950s and 1960s. For Corrigan, Astruc's theory presents the "key terms" of the essay film that foreground and "dramatize cinematic subjectivity."[12]

In contrast to this emphasis on defining the essay film as a strictly personal or subjective form of expression, I aim to show that only twenty years after Astruc's theorization of the camera-pen—during the New Left movements of 1968—this individually authored ideal of thinking and writing through the cinema gives way to a collective expression of cinematic thought. In fact, we can locate a minor tendency within the history of the essay film—starting with Hans Richter's early films during the interwar period—that is far less interested in possibilities of "expressive subjectivity" within the genre than it is in the use of the cinema to address complex conceptual problems. Richter coined the term *essay film* in 1940, arguing that this type of filmmaking provides the possibility for more abstract forms of thinking than traditional documentary:

> In its effort to make visible the invisible world of imaginations, thoughts, and ideas the essayistic film can tap into an incomparably larger reservoir of expressive means than the pure documentary film. One is not bound in the essay film to the representation of external appearances or to a chronological sequence. On the contrary, one must pull together material for view from everywhere and for this reason can jump through space and time: for example from the objective representation of reality to the fantastic allegory. One can represent dead or living, artificial or natural things. Using everything that exists and allows to be invented—just as long as it can serve as an argument for the visualization of a basic idea.[13]

Richter encouraged a generation of documentary filmmakers to liberate the cinematic image from its fidelity to pro-filmic reality and to use the language of cinema to creatively express concepts, ideas, and arguments that reach beyond the immediately visible world. He also urges them to imagine a new form of cinematic temporality, organizing visual thinking not according to the dictates of chronological time but rather in accordance with the logical imperatives of their arguments. Richter cites his own films *Stock Exchange* (1939) and *Inflation* (1928) (discussed in chapter 6) as emblematic of the kinds of cinematic attempts for which he is advocating. Both work to analyze what we might call "concrete abstractions," to use Marx's term, though the language of cinema, and neither presents an "I" that would ground its analysis in the personal domain. They instead develop an analytical language in cinematic form complementary to Sergei Eisenstein's proposal for a cinematic version of Marx's *Das Kapital* that would teach the tools of dialectical thinking to the workers.[14] Situating Richter's early pronouncements on the essay film as foundational to subsequent essayistic practices, we can see that the "expressive subjectivity" and "personal" engagement that Corrigan, Rascaroli, and others find to be essential to the genre is, perhaps, only one tendency within the history of the essay film that evolves alongside, and is inextricably tied to, auteur cinema in France.

It is worth noting that the distinction between the literary and cinematic essays is a simple issue of medium: while writing is generally a solitary activity, the cinema is, most often, collaborative. Though this collaborative tendency was subdued in the auteur tradition, it is actively exploited by New Left cinema. However, there is more at stake in arguing that the cinematic essay is a potentially plural and collective mode of expression. The importance of this distinction comes to the fore if we examine the function of the essay in modernity as a form that mediates public and private spheres. As John Mowitt argues, the essay was born at the moment in which these spheres were being separated and provided a form of expression capable of traversing the newly splintered character of bourgeois experience via a burgeoning print culture. For Mowitt, the essay is a literary form that thus enacts the transformation from feudalism to capitalism by providing a bridge between public and private domains. What Mowitt likens to the "bourgeois displacement of the feudal public sphere" we might also put in terms that have gained currency within recent years, namely, that of enclosure—an enclosure of that which is held in common.[15] "The commons," in this sense, is not only conceived of as a physical location but also refers to shared beliefs, practices, and languages.[16] The essay, then, is a literary form that performs this very enclosure, one that instantiates the division between the personal and the public, while at the same time occupying a liminal space between them.

For Mowitt, the essay's liminal position suggests an almost utopian potential. To understand this utopian potential, Mowitt returns to Lukács's reading of the essay, where he "discovers that the essay is a form fissured by its anticipation of a regime of truth he will later call 'communism.'"[17] The essay's vexed and complicated relationship to the production of the public and private social spheres also points to that which lies beyond them, namely, modes of being and thinking in common that must be excluded from life under capitalism: "[the essay] registers the efforts to grasp the forms of community that may lie beyond a model of society bounded by the very notion of subjectivity contradicted by the genre."[18] In other words, the essay has a singular ability to register forms of common expression that are incommensurate with the binary divisions of public and private so essential to capitalist modernity.

Emerging from a historical moment that saw the crisis of the modern division between public and private spheres, the essay films of the New Left occupy a significant place not only in the history of cinema but within the history of the essay genre itself. Actively working against individual expression, the films that I discuss are not invested in producing private subjective utterances. The latent forms of collective thought and expression that are registered within the literary genre become fully manifest in New Left cinema. They become constitutive of it. In this way, the essay film of the 1960s and 1970s is a cinema adequate to the crisis of modern subjectivity founded on the distinction between public and private (and, implicitly, the separation between productive and reproductive spheres, as I discuss in subsequent chapters). At the threshold of the crises of industrial modernity and the new enclosures of collective, social practice that characterize post-Fordist capitalism, the New Left's essay film expresses modalities of being and thinking in common that point not only to the emergence of a new regime of control that we inhabit at present but also to forms of life that may "lie beyond" these enclosures.

AGAINST "LE PATRON DU SENS": THE
ESSAYISTIC IMAGINATION OF MAY 1968

In the tumultuous postwar period in France, we can trace the coevolution of what I am calling the minor history of the essay film that rejects the model of "expressive subjectivity" alongside the ascent of auteur cinema. This lineage is most apparent in the early cinema of Guy Debord, which appears in tandem with the canonical auteurs of the essay film in France discussed by Corrigan and others. Though his films conform to the genre's distinguishing features, his cinematic work has been almost completely ignored by the extensive literature on the topic. I would surmise that the reason Debord's films have not been canonized within the genre is that the aim of his cinematic project defies the basic presuppositions that inform contemporary theories of the essay film, namely, that it is a cinematic form inextricably linked to the auteur tradition with the objective, like the literary essay, of circulating personal experience in a public sphere. Debord's utter disdain for the project of auteur cinema is apparent in his early films, as Debord directly attacks the sentiment of Astruc's manifesto and the ideology that the cinema should function as a vehicle for subjective expression in *Sur le passage de quelques personnes à travers une assez courts unité de temps* (On the passage of a few persons through a rather brief unity of time, France, 1959). Over a blank white screen, the film lambasts the desire to equate filmmaker and author:

> There are now people who pride themselves on being authors of films, as others were authors of novels. They are even more backward than the novelists because they are unaware of the decomposition and exhaustion of individual expression in our time. . . . There is talk about "liberating the cinema." But what does it matter to us if one more art is liberated to the point that every Tom, Dick, and Harry can use it to complacently express

their servile sentiments? The only interesting venture is the liberation of everyday life, not only in a historical perspective, but for us, right now. This project implies a withering away of all of the alienated forms of communication. The cinema, too, must be destroyed.[19]

Debord's line "the cinema, too, must be destroyed" should be seen not only as a general proposal but also as a direct answer to the French New Wave. Produced two years after Marker's *Lettre de Sibérie* (Letter from Siberia, France, 1957), a film that in the literature signals the birth of the contemporary essay film, Debord's 1959 film, like Marker's, employs innovative use of the soundtrack and voice-over to complicate the conventions of documentary narrative. He does so, however, not to circulate personal or subjective experience;[20] rather, as Sooyoung Yoon shows in her analysis of *Sur le passage,* it is precisely this question of circulation that the film denies: "for the SI [Situationist International], the problem of circulation was linked to a decomposition of communication, a collapse of the back and forth of exchange, a division of labor in the form of a unidirectional imposition."[21] The film takes the methodology of the *dérive,* which allows one, in Yoon's words, "to systematize a different temporality, not that of mobility and speed of circulation, but that of the encounter."[22]

Yoon rightly places the SI's move away from circulation in the context of the increased surveillance, control, and police violence against the Algerian population in France during the Algerian War and argues that the "colonization" of everyday life of which the Situationists speak draws a direct connection between France's colonial legacy and the rise of impoverished forms of life in consumer capitalism. Instead of circulating personal experience in some kind of pseudo-public space (a task that capital has well enough accomplished), Debord's essay films of the SI period produce intensities that unfold through what Thomas Levin has called "the mimesis of incoherence," a détourning of the documentary form to reflect the "fundamental incoherence of reality in late capitalism."[23] Exploring the trajectory of his work gives us access to a contrary formulation of essayistic practices that seeks, in its rejection of the model of the *caméra-stylo,* the production of new intensities that deny the centrality of expressive subjectivity, critiquing it as a form of bourgeois mysticism. For Debord and the Situationists, the aim to destroy cinema as an alienated form of communication is part of a larger project to reclaim everyday life.

Drawing a red thread from the late 1950s through the mid-1970s, Kristen Ross argues that there was nothing "spontaneous" about the events of May 1968.[24] Instead, they were, in part, an outgrowth of political awakening in response to the Algerian War and the intensification of police violence in France that formed the background of Debord's early cinematic works. As I will argue, his anti-auteur sentiments should be seen as part of a broader move during this period to contend with the connection between authorship and authority in Western culture. Debord's development of the essay film as an anti-auteur cinema prefigures the manner in which the genre is taken up a decade later in New Left cinema. While Debord's practice as a filmmaker was on pause between 1961 and 1971, an entire generation of filmmakers associated with the New Wave came to take part in an attempt to undermine the expressive principles of auteur cinema.

Before exploring the particular films and collectives that came out of this turbulent period in France, I want to situate the attempt to decenter cinematic authorship within what Ross identifies as the wider political aims of the May 1968 movement as well as efforts to contain and nullify these aims in cultural memory. In examining efforts to "liquidate" the history of radical social movements by circumscribing them within established social categories, Ross identifies two distinct but related tactics—the "biographical" and the "sociological"—for neutralizing the history of May and leaving the general impression that "nothing happened."[25] The biographical involves personalizing the movement by reducing it to "the individual itineraries of a few so-called leaders, representatives or spokesmen," while the sociological operates by reducing political categories to cultural ones and insisting on the reinscription of social categories and divisions onto a movement that endeavored to reject them.[26] The later maneuver is particularly insidious, as Ross argues, precisely because the "critique of the social division of labor" was so central to the May uprising: "overcoming the separation between manual and intellectual work, refusing professional or cultural qualification as a justification for social hierarchies and systems of political representation, refusing all delegation, undermining specialization—in short, the violent disruption of assigned roles, places, or functions."[27] Within the cinema, as elsewhere, the author came under attack as a paragon of these specialized functions. As I discuss in this section, the author-function enacts both the personalization of collective history and the designation of specialized authority in the dissemination of cinematic utterances. The cinematic experiments that surrounded the events of May were in themselves *essais* in generating cinematic meaning outside the division of labor that auteur cinema necessarily entailed. This involved breaking down distinctions between technical and artistic contributions and identifying the role that cinematic authorship played in furthering the social divisions and hierarchies.

In the years leading up to the events of May, a set of cinematic experiments in collective authorship and the decentralized production took place that anticipated the broad reconceptualization of the role of cinema in society during the uprising.[28] Among the most ambitious of these experiments was the Société pour la Lancement des Œvres Nouvelles (Society for Launching New Works), or SLON, a collective comprising more than 150 filmmakers, which produced the groundbreaking film *Loin du Vietnam*. An omnibus of unsigned vignettes by Jean-Luc Godard, Alain Resnais, William Klein, Agnès Varda, Joris Ivens, and Claude Lelouch, organized and edited by Chris Marker, the film's unique model of production opened up a new space for the articulation of collective essayistic practices aimed at intervening in a political context. *Loin du Vietnam* combines found and filmed documentary footage of Vietnam, pro-war U.S. parades, and antiwar protests in the United States and France. Juxtaposing this footage with staged scenarios and poignant voice-overs, the film articulates a heteroglossia of horror and disgust in response to the Vietnam War, amounting to what Richard Roud described as cinema's *Guernica*.[29] In the disjointed unfolding of its argument, the film grapples with the problems of form and politics, presenting disparate visions of what it means to employ cinema as a form of political intervention in a space far from Vietnam.

Loin du Vietnam's effort to complicate cinematic authorship is underscored in its penultimate vignette, which features Godard sitting behind a 35mm camera on the roof of his Paris apartment. A voice-over vividly describes the scene of a bombing in Vietnam, breaking with the narrative by explaining that if the filmmaker were a "cameraman for ABC . . . that's what I would have filmed." The narrator goes on to explain the impossibility of this scene because he "[lives] in Paris and [hasn't] been to Vietnam." After being denied entry into Vietnam, he was forced to contend with what it means to make films about Vietnam in France:

> I make films. That's the best I can do for Vietnam. Instead of invading Vietnam with a kind of generosity (that makes things unnatural), we let Vietnam invade us. And we are made to realize the place it takes in our everyday life, wherever we are. It makes us understand that Vietnam isn't alone. There's Africa and South America. Then we have to start creating a Vietnam. When Che Guevara says: "Let's make two or three other Vietnams," we can apply it to ourselves. If you're in Guinea, it's against the Portuguese. If you're in Chicago, it's for the black people. If you're in South America, it's for Latin America that is completely colonized. First colonized by the Spanish and French cultures, and today, colonized by the American economy. Creating a Vietnam within ourselves. In France, it was last summer, the massive protests in Rhodiaceta and Besançon and Nazarin are deeply connected to Vietnam.

Juxtaposed with footage of Godard, the camera he sits behind, and close-ups of a Vietcong soldier and a female peasant with her child, this voice-over articulates the correspondence between the sites that occupy the New Left's political imaginary. Godard's statements indicate the ways that Vietnam comes to typify struggles against imperial aggression across the Third World, as indicated by his reference to Che Guevara's address to the Organization of Solidarity with the Peoples of Asia, Africa, and Latin America at the historic Tricontinental Conference of solidarity in 1966, an event identified by Robert Young as the "birth of the post-colonial subject."[30] It what Chris Connery calls the "third-world-centered Sixties," Vietnam and the struggle against new forms of imperial domination that it represented served as a nodal point for New Left political culture in imperial centers like the United States and France, becoming "the relay, the reference point, for worldwide refusal."[31] This was especially true in New Left cinema, as Vietnam was the subject of countless cinematic interventions, including Newsreel's *People's War* (United States, 1969) and Santiago Álvarez's *79 primaveras* (79 springs, Cuba, 1969). The contention "we let Vietnam invade us" performs a full inversion of the expressive subjectivity that seeks circulation in the public sphere by presenting a subjectivity that is disrupted and transformed by an encounter with an external force. It suggests the impossibility of any truth of the "interior," of nation or subject by portraying an interior that is both open and immediately connected to other sites of collective struggle. Godard's well-documented transformation during this period from preeminent auteur to militant is emblematic of a turn in which figures both central and peripheral to the film industry in France came to reject not only the model of artistic expression represented by auteur cinema but also the centralized models of production and distribution that were coordinated and heavily subsidized by the French state.[32]

Statements like Godard's that were arising from New Left cinema complemented and expanded ongoing philosophical and political conversations in France about the nature and origin of thought and the problem of authorship. For example, at the same time *Loin du Vietnam* was experimenting with a new modality for cinematic thinking predicated intrusion and disruption, Gilles Deleuze was formulating a similar sensibility in the realm of philosophy. In *Difference and Repetition,* he develops a nonphenomenological understanding of the nature and origin of thought: "Something in the world makes us think. This something is an object not of recognition but of a fundamental *encounter.*"[33] For Deleuze,

> thought is primarily trespass and violence, the enemy. . . . Do not count upon thought to ensure the relative necessity of what thinks. Rather, count upon the contingency of an encounter with that which forces thought to raise up and educate the absolute necessity of an act of thought or passion to think.[34]

Thought is an invasion from the outside that allows us to think differently. In the case of 1967, Vietnam is the name for this invasion. To make "a Vietnam" inside of oneself is to acknowledge that the self is never a closed interior that confronts an exterior world but an enclosure of that which is always-already exterior, just as the political imaginary of French cinema in this period is in no way circumscribed within the confines of the nation or continent but is part of a global confrontation with imperialism and inequality. New Left cinema opens a space of conflict in which each self-contained entity—including the author—is subjected to an invasion from the outside, which is also, already, a deep interior. This is especially true in France, given its long colonial legacy in Vietnam and across the globe.

Decentering the authorial position, undertaken by even the most notorious auteurs, was a key attribute of experiments in collective cinematic production in the lead-up to May 1968. Take, for example, Les groupes Medvedkine, who conducted a series of experiments in collective production in the Rhodiaceta factories based on the "principles of deprofessionalization, situational contingency, and a conception of cinema as a dialogic relation between the film and the filmed."[35] After making *À bientôt, j'espère* (Until soon, I hope, France, 1968), about the strikes in the Besançon factory, Marker and the Medvedkin Group moved toward a more dialogical and then collective model of filmmaking after the film was criticized by the workers for being too sentimental and ignoring important factions of the struggle, especially women; captured in a video recording of the workers' conversation with the filmmakers. As Paul Douglas Grant highlights in his comprehensive survey of the Medvedkin Group's activities, this dialogic engagement with workers led to a different tone in the group's later works, which "were distinctly moving away from the melancholy representation of the workers' endeavors to a far more polyvocal and formally dynamic view."[36] Trevor Stark likens the practices of the Medvedkin Group to those of the "*rencontre*" that Ross highlights in her assessment of May, encounters among diverse groups that allow for difference within the formation of a new political community. These *rencountres* worked to forge new forms of collective, political enunciation that foreground the link between participation and the democratization of the production of cinematic meaning. Abandoning traditional forms of authorship, SLON distributed 16mm cameras and tape recorders among the workers in an attempt to establish a "collective, non-hierarchical model of production, seeking to abolish the separation between expert and amateur, between producer and consumer."[37] The numerous films coming out of the project often took the form of essay films, such as *Classe de lutte* (1969), which foregrounded both the pedagogy of struggle and horizontalized models for producing and circulating cinematic meaning. As Alberto Toscano writes of SLON and the Medvedkin Group, "the destructive creation of new forms . . . is inseparable from the generation of new communist social relations."[38] These projects were collective *essais,* in the sense of a trial or attempt, to create new forms of collective life through a politics of prefiguration. In each of these cases, the cinematic essay is part of a prefigurative effort to generate "new communist social relations." Realizing the latent forms of expression in the essay identified by Mowitt, these cinematic essays are exemplary of an essayistic politics of the common, collaborative and experimental attempts to make new common forms of sense making.

The question "who speaks, for whom, and how?" of course became central to the discourse of May 1968. Any desire to understand isolated projects or groups, such as the Medvedkin Group associated with Chris Marker, or the Dziga Vertov Group associated with Jean-Luc Godard, must contend with the widespread critique of hierarchies endemic to film culture in France, which was a part of the struggle to disrupt the division between intellectual and manual labor and the centrality of authorship discussed earlier. We should thus be cautious of a mode of criticism that seeks to render legible an individual authorial voice in films that were intentionally anonymous, collective, or both.[39] To do so runs the risk reinscribing of what Michel Foucault identified, in the spirit of 1968, as the "author-function," the "complex procedures" of assigning legal ownership to subjective utterances within a regime of private property constitutive of discursive practices, to the films of the New Left that were explicitly trying to evade such designations.[40] Though it may be impossible to altogether avoid assigning the author-function to various texts, it is essential to recognize the potential cost of this reinscription, being diligent in our efforts not to "liquidate" the radical histories of the period through the techniques of personalizing and categorizing, attaching collective utterances to a few figureheads and nullifying them by assigning them to their proper social functions.

Sylvia Harvey examines the unsettling of cinematic authorship in and around the events of May, discussing an anonymous leaflet circulated in the 1968 film festival at Hyères decrying the festival's fixation on the director as what it calls "'*le patron du sens*' (the boss of meaning)."[41] According to Harvey, "the leaflet attacked the notion of individual authorship and the way in which the festival itself worked to enshrine the value and importance of the director as the sole producer of meaning. It spoke of the cinema of directors as a cinema defending the interests of private property."[42] Epitomizing the anti-auteurist sentiment of May 1968, this diatribe against the "*patron du sens*" suggests that, in the year preceding Foucault's "What Is an Author?," a critique of the "author-function" in the cinema and its association with the regime of private property subtended many of the intersecting conversations around how cinema might be transformed during the upheaval. As is well documented by Harvey, the disruption catalyzed an expansion and intensification of already ongoing conversations around the reproduction of cultural hierarchies between technician and director, producer and consumer, and the role of centralized cultural institutions, most of them run by the state, in governing the production and distribution of film. Following the major student-worker demonstrations of May 13, a special Cinema Commission was set up and a number of illegal screenings of "agit-prop" documentaries were coordinated, "in *lycées* (secondary schools) within and outside Paris, in various university buildings and in a number of factories."[43] The radical conversations around film culture culminated in the establishment of the Estates General du Cinéma, which was formed after a meeting between the film technicians union and the editors of *Cashiers du Cinéma* in a Sorbonne building that was occupied by film and photography students. An explicit reference to the Estates General of the 1789 revolution, the EGC organized a series of proposals to transform the French film industry. According to Harvey, the EGC was not a homogenous body with a coherent position; "rather, it was the site of those same tensions, conflicts, and contradictions which characterized the rest of French society in the month of May."[44] With participants including technicians, critics, students, and some well-known auteurs, the EGC presented a series of diverse proposals, among them calls to create radically alternative screening spaces and to reverse the role of spectator and producer.[45] Overall, the proposals put forward by the EGC promoted the idea of abolishing film structures run by the state and a "genuine decentralization of culture."[46] While the EGC sponsored a number of film projects, including *Cinétracts*, it also provided a forum to reject not simply bourgeois film content or ideology but an entire system of Keynesian management of artistic production by the state, characterized by centralization and hierarchy, which upheld the system of auteur cinema. Thus the move toward collective production was consubstantial with the reimagination of the role of cinema within French society.

With this historical context in mind, it is possible now to return to the essay films of the New Left in France produced during the crucible of the late 1960s, understanding them not as a seamless advancement of the principles laid out in Astruc's manifesto but rather as a rupture in authorial enunciation that was part of a larger challenge to established film culture. Perhaps the best-known example of cinematic experimentation that co-alesced during the events of May was the *Cinétracts* project, a series of silent, uncredited documentary and short essay films (also characterized as 'pamphlet films').[47] All edited in camera, each *Cinétract* was composed of one hundred feet of film made for immediate distribution, sold at cost, and screened in a variety of settings, including student assemblies and factories during and after May.[48] In this case, experimentation in collective filmmaking strategies was inextricable from the production of new networks of distribution and new venues and circumstances of exhibition. The *Cinétracts* project was enabled by the existing collective infrastructure of SLON but developed a system for rapidly producing and disseminating political tracts, or leaflets, by way of the cinema—a model that characterized many of the agit-prop films made in the midst of the May events. The tracts, varying from three to four minutes in length, are silent and composed almost entirely of still images and text. Some are more straightforward in their documentary approach, dramatizing confronta-tions with the police, while many employ text and intertitles to generate complex arguments about state violence, the division of intellectual and manual labor, the problem of democracy, knowledge, and the perceived political alliance between the May and Third World struggles embodied by figures like Che Guevara and Mao Zedong. Many stills and techniques are repeated in different tracts, and thus they develop an ongoing visual and conceptual conversation between individual tracts as the events of May unfold. As was characteristic of many essay films of the New Left, popular media, such as advertisements, illustrations, and journalistic photographs, are inserted among the stills, providing common reference points and a visual language that critiques both pop culture and popular representations of the May uprising and of the Left in general.

As a body of works, the *Cinétracts* project amounts to an internally differentiated essay that examines both the politics of the confrontation and the poetics of the encounter. The politics of confrontation come through in Eisensteinian-style montages that examine the clashes between protesters and the police, using techniques that enliven the still images like panning, tilting, or zooming within the frame to create dynamic narratives that do more than simply replicate the unfolding events. They elaborate on a deeper confrontation between a homogenous, violent state and a new formation of dissent. A bird's-eye-view shot of protesters transporting paving stones by way of a human chain serves as a refrain for several of the tracts, emphasizing the horizontalized networks of self-organization that took shape in the streets in contrast to the implementation of state power, which is characterized as hierarchical and uniform, embodied in the figure of the police. In both the text and the images, the subject of enunciation is not *je* but *nous* or the impersonal *on*. The repetition of images and themes among the tracts gives the impression of an experience that is impersonally distributed and collectively shared. The dialectic of the essay negotiates the complicated and variegated process of delineating "us" and "them" as the events of May transpired.

At the same time, the tracts develop a poetics of encounter, creating a visual and verbal language that brings into conversation the various cultural, political, and geographic tensions that come to constitute this internally differentiated *nous,* particularly when addressing the crucial, yet fragile, alliance between students and workers. Recognizable authorial signatures are evident within many of the tracts (particularly those attributed to Marker and Godard), but as in "Tract 14," these signatures are literally put under erasure, locating directors as one of "les forces d'order" (the forces of order). In this tract, stills of police brutality are juxtaposed with handwritten intertitles, one in which the word "réalizateurs" (directors), along with other forces of order, such as doctors and architects, is struck through. The director becomes one of the forces of order that Jacques Rancière would call the "the police," who, in Ross's reading, "become the name in his [Rancière's] view for everything that concerns the distribution of places and functions, as well as the system that legitimates that hierarchical distribution."[49] *Cinétracts* is indicative of the simultaneous project of reinventing the militant image and rejecting the author's role as "le patron du sense" that characterizes the essayistic imagination of May 1968. As mentioned before, the essayistic practice of New Left cinema should be understood as a means of cinematic thinking that harnesses the cinema's unique capacity to produce arguments, analyses, and affects through a time-based audiovisual medium. The cinematic projects surrounding May 1968 represent an *essai* in the sense of a trial or attempt to effect a politics of prefiguration that endeavors to undermine divisions between public and private, mental and manual, and the author-function they buttress.

THE ESSAY FILM, DECENTERED: *HORA DE LOS HORNOS* AND THE DIALECTIC OF DEPENDENCE

Nora Alter argues that the essay film appears at moments of historical crisis—both political and representational—but insists that "the function of the essay is not therapy or healing the wounds produced by the upheavals of the day, but crisis diagnosis enabling and encouraging future social and cultural transformation."[50] Though Atler does not address the crises of the late 1960s, it is worth exploring her suggestion by inquiring what the essay's ubiquitous use in films closely tied to radical social movements across the globe tells us about its capacity to both diagnose and further social and cultural transformation. I argue that at this moment of crisis, the essay film emerges as a *necessary* form. As Christopher Connery (following Jameson) insists when periodizing the 1960s, "history as necessity is far from determinism: it is, in an important way, its opposite. What 'had to happen' was the fact of an entire combination, the totality of forces, whose interrelations consisted of lag, disjuncture, and unexpected openings."[51] The essay film, itself composed of "lag, disjuncture, and unexpected openings," becomes an adequate form to historical crisis.

Working to undermine the thesis that the essay film is intrinsically tied to the evolution of auteur cinema, my effort to this point has been to

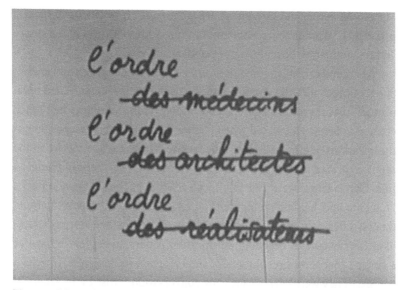

Figure 2. Film still, the order of directors put under erasure, *Cinétracts* (1968).

trace a minor history of the genre, understanding it to be not a tool for the circulation of internal experience but a modality of cinematic encounter with the capacity for generating historical, political, and theoretical analyses. In the case of France, the proliferation of the essay film outside of the auteur tradition was intimately connected to struggles within and beyond its borders, articulating solidarities that were facilitated by the interpenetration of New Left social movements. To imagine the essay film as a genre that is developed in France (or Europe) and then is disseminated globally neglects the manner in which the global imagination of New Left social movements and conversations among them were inflected in the contemporaneous, yet different, manifestations of the genre. In fact, while numerous militant filmmakers in France during this period identify as essayists, perhaps the most developed conversation on the essay film in the late 1960s and early 1970s was taking place in Latin America. In this section, my aim is to further decenter the New Left's essay film, arguing that it is intrinsic to the "third-world-centered Sixties," the anti-imperialist politics emerging from the Tricontinental context that found its inspiration in global militancy. Through a reading of the groundbreaking film

Hora de los hornos and its context, we come to see how cinema became a powerful tool for enabling encounters among different sites of resistance and disseminating novel forms of political analysis.

As argued earlier, the cinematic upheaval in France grew from a series of encounters with the outside, new forms of political alliance and organization that characterized the New Left. Never in a vacuum, the French context is better elucidated when analyzed alongside contemporaneous theorizations of cinematic resistance coming from Latin America in the 1960s, captured in essays such as Glauber Rocha's "Aesthetic of Hunger," Julio García Espinosa's "For an Imperfect Cinema," and Fernando Birri's "Cinema and Underdevelopment."[52] Each of these filmmakers argue, though differently, for an anti-imperialist aesthetic that rejects the dictates of industrial cinema based on European or American models in favor of a cinema that serves revolutionary aims relevant to the Latin American context. They were part of a growing conversation across Latin America, particularly in countries with leftist governments like Chile and Cuba, about what a cinema of liberation might entail. Synthesizing and furthering these ongoing conversations, Solanas and Getino's famous 1969 essay "Towards a Third Cinema: Notes and Experiences for the Development of a Cinema of Liberation in the Third World" advocates for a cinema that is neither Hollywood nor auteur but a collective practice modeled on guerrilla warfare. In it, they argue that cinema, one of the most effective means of mass communication, must be seized and employed in the struggle against imperialism as a crucial weapon in the "decolonization of culture."[53] Proclaiming the camera to be a gun in the struggle against imperialism, the authors insist that audience participation and engagement are essential elements of militant cinema and cite international cinematic collectives, including the U.S. Newsreel collective, student collectives in Italy and Japan, and the Estates General du Cinéma in France, as models for third cinema.[54] For Solanas and Getino, third cinema need not originate in the Third World; rather, the authors insist that cinematic insurgency can irrupt anywhere, as long as it takes place outside of channels they identify with "the System." The lack of geographic specificity in Solanas and Getino's definition contravenes the way third cinema has been defined within the U.S. academy in the past three decades, which has, for the most part, interpreted it as a phenomenon located solely in the Global South and included films and movements that share many of the tendencies of auteur cinema.[55]

"Towards a Third Cinema" became a seminal text for the emergent ciné-geography of New Left cinema, and, in October 1969, the journal *Tricontinental* published an abridged version of the essay in Spanish, Italian, French, and English.[56] Further evidence of the mutual and on-going exchange among New Left cinematic movements prompted by third cinema is found in the conversation between Solanas and Godard, "Solanas por Godard, Godard por Solanas."[57] Originally published in 1969, the conversation came after the distribution of Solanas and Getino's *Hora de los hornos* in Europe and the United States and is as much a draft of a manifesto for a new form of cinema as it is a negotiation of their positions as filmmakers, challenging the status of "second cinema" and the colonial and cultural debts between Argentina and France. Godard, who disavows his own status as an auteur, speaks of his own career not in terms of continuity but in terms interruption—the life of an artist put on trial by the forces that sought to realign the Left globally.[58] In this light, Godard's "third-world turn" (as it has been called) might be conceived of less as a turn by Godard himself than as the result of a larger political reconfiguration of revolutionary subjectivity inspired by the struggles against imperialism in Vietnam, Latin America, and elsewhere as they entered the first world.[59]

Solanas opens the conversation with Godard by describing *Hora de los hornos* as "an ideological and political film-essay." He goes on to nuance this definition by arguing that "the *Hour of the Furnaces* is also a film 'act,' an anti-show, because it denies itself as a film and opens itself to the public for debate, discussion and further developments. Each show becomes a place of liberation."[60] He thus puts into play the sense of the word *essai* as a trial, a space for testing ideas which is also a space of collective engagement and critique. What it means for *Hour of the Furnaces* to deny itself as a film is precisely to deny itself as a whole, as a closure of representation. For Solanas, the essay film is meant to unsettle bourgeois practices of film spectatorship to create a new level of engagement with the film as a process indistinguishable from life, both materially and historically:

There are pauses in the film, interruptions so that the film and the topics presented can pass from the screen to the theater, that is, to life, to the present. The old spectator, the subject who beholds, the onlooker, according to the traditional film that developed the bourgeois concepts of the arts in the 1800s, that non-participant, becomes the live protagonist, a real actor in the story of the film and in the history itself, since the film is about our contemporary history. And it is a film about liberation, about the unfinished stage in our history; it cannot be anything but an unfinished film, a film open to the present and the future of this act of liberation.[61]

In Solanas's conception of the essay film, personal experience is also collective and active—a force intended to transform both the cinematic text and the history in which it intervenes. In a way that anticipates contemporary practices of participatory cinema, the film acts as a pretext for collective engagement and authorship. Because the act of filmmaking is so entrenched within collective, political practice, an essay film on the topic of "liberation" cannot be considered complete until the social movement seeking that liberation has achieved its objectives. It is part of a project that is ongoing, a text constantly modulating with the currents of the history in which it participates. Produced and shown clandestinely within the heart of a military dictatorship, *Hora de los hornos* worked to challenge the conventions of passive spectatorship by creating a situation in which the viewer was forced into a politicized position through the very act of viewing the film, as both the filmmakers and the spectators participated in these film acts at great risk. The essay thus opens itself to collective engagement and critique as workers, students, peasants, intellectuals, and revolutionaries all act as collaborators, or even accomplices, in its production.

If Lukács located a tendency toward communism in the essay form, the essay films such as *Hora de los hornos* endeavored to realize it. Transforming the assertion that the cinema be a medium of thought for the individual filmmaker into a demand that it become a collective mode of insurgency, the conversation between Solanas and Godard is a reinterpretation of Astruc's notion of the camera-pen in response to the global uprisings of 1968. The conversation produces a novel conception of cinema, one that must move through and reject individually authored cinema, as is figured in Godard's Maoist self-critique, to arrive at an understanding of cinematic insurgency centered in the Third World and manifested through the essay as a creative, insurgent, and collective form of resistance. If the crisis of 1968 was characterized as a rupture in closed forms of social organization and representation, then the essay is the formal corollary to this crisis—both the form of crisis and the crisis of form.

Solanas and Getino's conception of third cinema and the militant essay film is best understood through their work as filmmakers, particularly in building a militant cinema form and infrastructure in the production of *Hora de los hornos* during 1967–68. Like many of the films discussed in this book, its political intervention was inseparable from the alternative channels of distribution and exhibition through which it traveled. Produced clandestinely under the military dictatorship of Juan Carlos Onganía, installed in 1966 amid growing student and worker unrest, Solanas and Getino recount how *Hora de los hornos* circulated through an underground network of distribution and exhibition through the group Cine-Liberación that coordinated screenings for "25,000 participants" in 1970 alone and was "tightly linked to work of the political organizations" across Argentina.[62] Modeling cinematic production on guerrilla warfare, Solanas, Getino, and the Cine-Liberación group to which they belonged sought to use the medium as a means to build solidarities among anti-imperialist movements, and their experiments with collective authorship and production engaged workers, students, peasants, intellectuals, and revolutionaries in the process.

Hora de los hornos develops its critique of neocolonialism by examining everyday violence in Latin America, layering moving and still images, found footage, text, and sound to imbricate all facets of life into a total system of domination and subjugation that amounts to what Mark Wayne characterizes as "one huge rejoinder (a favorite word of Bakhtin) to Argentine society."[63] The film does more than critique its immediate national context, however. As a "strategic essay film," according to Getino, "the validity of its analysis must remain relevant for months or years and [it must] be able to cross national boundaries."[64] The militant essay film is tailored to an immediate political situation, while at the same time building an enduring analysis that resonates internationally. Following the minor history of the essay film I have been working to outline, Getino insists that the essay film be judged on the "validity of its analysis," not its capacity for personal reflection. The analytic force of the strategic essay is demonstrated in the devastating critique of neocolonialism presented in *Hora de los hornos,* a film that, in line with Hans Richter's original conception of the essay film, tackles abstract concepts and problems through the language of cinema.

Advancing a pan–Latin American political project within the context of a Tricontinental perspective, the opening sequence of *Hora de los hornos* is set to the tempo of indigenous music and is composed of footage of police brutality and protest, intercut with text bursting onto the screen, repeating words like "liberation" and "power," and quotations on colonial liberation and violence from Frantz Fanon, Aimé Césaire, Fidel Castro, and others. In this opening sequence and throughout its first section, "Neo-colonialism and Violence," the film presents the overarching thesis that "Latin America is a continent at war" and is composed of twelve chapters with titles such as "History," "Culture," "Ideological Warfare," and "The System." Each of these chapters addresses a different aspect of the thesis, expanding the definition of war and its frontiers to incorporate the unspoken forms of imperial violence running through collective life and daily experiences. For example, in the section "Daily Violence," the sound of the siren grows louder and more ominous as the sequence cuts to footage of people running through the city with what sounds like gunfire enveloping the scene, giving us the impression that we are viewing a war zone. It soon becomes apparent, however, that this is footage of people running through the rain (perhaps on their way to work). At the same time, what sounded like gunfire is revealed in the next sequence to be the sound of workers punching a time clock. Only through the juxtaposition of sound and image is this sequence able to take quotidian experiences and produce what appears to be a scene of war. Sound, in this instance, communicates the idea that wage labor is a form of daily violence visited upon the people and that the punctuation of time by work imposes a visceral terror on those who endure it. In *Hora de los hornos,* the sounds of quotidian life—popular music, a plane landing, the punch of the time clock—become emblems of violence and calls to revolutionary action. These calls would have been all the more urgent to viewers seeing the film in covert screenings, at their own risk. In this way, *Hora de los hornos* sought to reshape the concept of cinephilia by inducing, rather than stifling, political participation through spectatorship; the film was intended as a provocation to its viewers, who were, in turn, interpellated as participants in the film's revolutionary project.[65] In a revolutionary cinema, the love of the image is not the desire for a "life beyond," as Debord argued, but an understanding of the image as a material force in the world that sees the spectator as a participant in shaping that image.

Hora de los hornos engages in nothing less than a total critique of the bankruptcy of life under the neocolonial regime, portraying a society whose accumulated debts to imperial powers have outstripped its capacity to function, producing a permanent condition of indebtedness. In the "History" chapter, a voice-over contends that the oligarchies of Argentina were the product of three factors: "English gold, Italian hands, and French books." The film illustrates how cultural and economic debts are two sides of the same crisis of national identity and attends to the violence of cultural imperialism, arguing, in the vein of the movements for national liberation across the globe, for the development of a national culture in a form and language indigenous to Argentina. While tracing Argentina's colonial legacy, *Hora de los hornos* also examines a shift away from this oligarchic system, illustrating that neocolonial violence now trades in only one currency: "Yankee dollars." Cultural imperialism and global financial systems had been melded into one and the same substance, a system of domination and control enveloping every aspect of social, economic, and political life.

In the chapter titled "Dependence," *Hora de los hornos* expands its thesis on debt and cultural imperialism by engaging early postcolonial theories of dependency put forward by Latin American structuralists such as Raúl Prebisch and Juan Noyola, later popularized in the world-systems theory of Immanuel Wallerstein. Throughout the 1960s and into the 1970s, dependency theory took hold in Latin America and elsewhere as a rebuttal to the modernization theory of development, which posited successive stages through which nations pass on the path to industrial wealth. Introducing terms that have become indispensable to analyzing global inequality among nation-states, dependency theory argued that the wealth of the First World—"core" countries in the global capitalist system—was generated through the systematic underdevelopment of countries on the "periphery." Brazilian social scientist Theotonio Dos Santos wrote prolifically on dependency theory while in exile in Chile from 1965 to 1973 before being exiled again to Mexico after Pinochet's coup, arguing that the "new dependency" characteristic of global imperialism is predicated on the industrial and technical underdevelopment of peripheral countries, primarily through the mechanisms of financial control by way of foreign debts. The model of dependency, characterized by the continuous reproduction of "backwardness, misery, and social marginalization" within peripheral countries, perpetuates and expands debt and is thus "superexploitation."[66] With close affinity to Lenin and Luxemburg, as well as contemporaneous analyses like Kwame Nkrumah's theory of neocolonialism, dependency theory foregrounds the asymmetrical power relations in finance that drive the imperialist production of global inequality.[67] It offered a structural analysis of global inequality that bolstered, while also being fed by, the wave of anti-imperialist revolutionary activity sweeping the continent.

Over a panning shot of the harbor of Buenos Aires, the "Dependence" chapter commences with a quotation from 1544 by Sebastián Caboto, an early Italian explorer: "Those who live in rural areas say there are mountains where they mine endless gold." The camera then slowly pans to reveal the immensity of the city accompanied by a voice-over that delivers a sharp critique of the debt economy imposed on Latin America:

> Loans, investments, have always been a part of the same political subjugation.... So called imperialist aid is an aid that always costs he who receives it more than he who gives it. For every dollar invested in Latin America, imperialism gets back four.

Soft female vocals then begin to play over an extended montage of sheep and cattle being delivered to a slaughterhouse, hung upside down, their throats slit or the back of their necks pummeled with a sledge hammer, skinned and bled out as their carcasses move along an assembly line.

Often discussed as a citation of Sergei Eisenstein's *Strike* (USSR, 1925), the footage of industrial agribusiness, one of Argentina's most lucrative industries, is paired with popular advertisements of white models extolling the virtues of consumer society. Interspersed throughout the sequence are intertitles explaining the basic theses of dependency theory—"every day we export more and get back less," "Argentina's foreign debt is six billion dollars," and "the foreign monopolies and their local allies control almost all the national economy"—and listing the industries that are under foreign control. Paired with footage from the slaughterhouse, these figures of debt illustrate a body politic that is literally bleeding out its capacities. Juxtaposed with advertisements promising a better life through consumption, these figures indicate that culture, like the national economy, is bankrupt. *Hora de los hornos* offers a critique of the spectacle and finance capitalism as dual mechanisms mining human (and nonhuman) resources for the promise of infinite riches, the endless gold in the mountains of

Figure 3. Film still, slaughterhouse scene, *Hora de los hornos* (1968).

Figure 4. Film still, advertisement, *Hora de los hornos* (1968).

which Caboto speaks that characterized the colonial project of primitive accumulation at its inception. Contradicting the linear and teleological temporal framework of modernization theory, the elaboration of dependency theory in *Hora de los hornos* testifies to a different kind of temporal experience: that of debt and indebtedness. The mechanisms of social reproduction that constantly reinforce social hierarchies predicated on a system of debt induce the experience of a collapsed futurity, one in which "development"—representing the potential for a different future—is foreclosed. Exploring this temporality, *Hora de los hornos* expands the theoretical framework of dependency theory to analyze the role of systems of social reproduction—art, language, education, media, folklore, and so on—as sites that propagate and reinforce dependency and underdevelopment. This sequence conveys the affective dimensions of the indebted position, the attachment and striving for a better life figured by the advertisements and experience of being bled dry that accompany such attachments, a kind of "cruel optimism" in the words of Lauren Berlant.[68] Beyond the economism of most dependency theorists who saw culture as little more than "perfume,"[69] the practice of third cinema reflected in *Hora de los hornos* (with a significant debt to figures like Frantz Fanon and Fernando Birri) takes culture to be inextricable from any discussion of dependency. As Solanas and Getino write in "Towards a Third Cinema," "the culture, including cinema, of a neocolonized country is just the expression of an overall dependence that generates models and values born from the needs of imperialist expansion."[70] Rather than simply translating the concept of dependency into the cinema, *Hora de los hornos* expands an analysis of the violence of neocolonialism, impressing upon the viewer complex arguments within an affective register.

Hora de los hornos later reinforces the affective character of this in-debted position in the chapter "Ideological Warfare," whose opening consists of a mobile shot of a street scene that meanders through crowds as they enter movie theaters and shops. A voice-over contends that "the war in Latin America is waged principally in the minds of men.... For neocolonialism, mass communication is more powerful than napalm." As a woman stops to watch several television screens in a shop window, the voice-over continues, "Ideological frontiers have replaced conventional ones," and the ideological frontier appears as a mobile and open bound-ary. Undiagetically, "I Don't Need No Doctor" by Ray Charles begins to envelop the scene as the camera wanders into a record shop where young people peruse the records as they tap their fingers and bob their heads. The sequence cuts between different angles of the scene, focusing on one man who is particularly taken with the music, the shot lingering on him as his body convulses while he shops. This relatively simple sequence is, argu-ably, one of the most disturbing in the film, as pleasure and consumption are revealed to be deeply political. The nondiegetic music is edited with the footage in a way that does not exactly sync with the man's gestures, introducing an interstice between image and sound that turns his undula-tions into almost repulsive expressions of submission. As this sequence reveals, the ideological frontier in imperialism operates on an affective, precognitive level, turning moments of consumption into moments of production—the production of neocolonial subjectivity.

"Everyday life is a colonized sector."[71] Guy Debord made this argu-ment in 1961 (drawing on the work of Henri Lefebvre) with reference to the expansion of consumer culture in industrial societies. Amid the

Figure 5. Film still, man enjoying music while shopping at a record store, *Hora de los hornos* (1968).

ongoing Algerian War of Independence, and a few months before the massacre of dozens of Algerians in Paris, Debord casts the struggle over daily life—and the struggle against the spectacle—within terms inspired by anticolonial movements. *Hora de los hornos* takes Debord's analysis further. For it, colonization is not a metaphor but an active and ongoing process of historical domination that penetrates every aspect of life. Rather than representing a new, abstract mode of production that Debord identifies as "the spectacle," *Hora de los hornos* understands the colonization of daily life to be the ever-increasing expansion and intensification of imperialism. This daily violence, for *Hora de los hornos,* is inseparable from imperialist mechanisms of finance that feed the continuous cycle of dispossession and serve as a source of unending crisis. *Hora de los hornos* is less concerned with the alienation inherent in the commodity form than it is with a cultural imperialism that forms subjects through modes of expropriation that are integrated into the violence of imperial finance.

In its foresight, *Hora de los hornos* anticipates the massive bleeding out that Argentina—along with a host of other underdeveloped nations—would be subjected to as neoliberal laboratories established during 1970s, leading to ongoing decades of foreign debt and structural adjustment culminating in the 2001 financial crisis and default.[72] At the same time, it analyzes the affective, economic, political, and historical dimensions of the experience of indebtedness prior to the apparent rise of forms of neoliberal governance, identifying salient aspects of debt as a technology of power, the acknowledgment of which has become widespread in the aftermath of the 2008 financial crisis.[73] In doing so, it combines its more robust cinematic theorization of the "colonization of everyday life" by capitalism with an early recognition of what Randy Martin called the "financialization of daily life" in reference to the production of financialized subjectivities in the neoliberal era.[74] However, it goes beyond each of these theories by locating its critique in a politics of Third World liberation. *Hora de los hornos* thus achieves the objectives of the strategic essay film set forth by Getino, presenting an enduring analysis of neocolonial violence within an internationalist horizon.

Hora de los hornos ends, as one might suspect, with a call to revolutionary action. "The Choice," its final chapter, opens with a relatively long sequence of a peasant funeral, panning over the faces of the grievers. A voice-over laments, "The people of Latin America are condemned peoples; neo-colonialism does not permit them to choose their own life or their own death. Life and death both bear the mark of daily violence." The voice-over then iterates numerous statistics of the millions of preventable deaths caused by disease and hunger in Latin America. Abruptly, the segment cuts to footage of Che Guevara's corpse, as people pass by his dead body. The voice-over draws out the contrast: "For the man who dies in an act of liberation, death is no longer an end. . . . He who chooses his own death is also choosing his own life." In the last segment, which shows a photographer straddling Che's dead body in the moment right after he has taken a photograph, we are told, "He is already life and liberation itself." The voice-over continues: "In his revolutionary action, the Latin American recovers his existence." The sequence ends with the famous photograph of Che's lifeless face, which remains on the screen for nearly three minutes.

Figure 6. Film still, photographer after he has taken a picture of Che Guevara's corpse, *Hora de los hornos* (1968).

What I want to highlight about this last segment is not only the long resurrection of Che's still image but also the footage that precedes it. By ending with an image of the photographer standing over Che, we understand that he has just taken the picture we are seeing; the photographer becomes the midwife of this life after death. The act of the photographer is made to stand in for the act of the essay filmist, the one who makes the "transient eternal," in Adorno's words. *Hora de los hornos* ends with a soulless image—a corpse—to imbue it with new life, transforming Che's death into an affirmation of struggle and resistance. Just as a death met in an act of liberation is not an end, the image is not a simple death or present absence. Instead, through the process of the "film-act," the cinematic image opens itself to life, and, just as the Latin American revolutionary, it "recovers its existence."

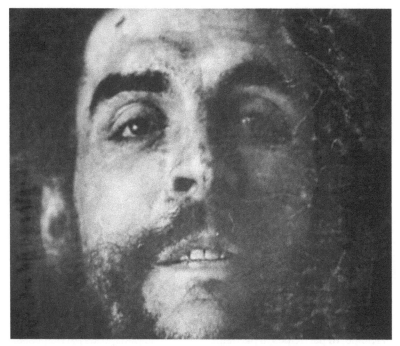

Figure 7. Film still, photograph of Che Guevara's corpse, *Hora de los hornos* (1968).

THE FILM-ACT AND THE POLITICS OF PARTICIPATION

The sequence featuring Che's dead image is emblematic of the ways that *Hour of the Furnaces* attempts to force its spectator to refuse a relationship to culture conditioned by passivity and consumption, as each spectator is called on to make a choice, to take a position on a side of the ideological line that the film is drawing. For Solanas and Getino, enabled by the film-act, "*the spectator made way for the actor, who sought himself among others.*"[75] In other words, if the spectator is individuated in the act of media consumption, then it is only by activating politics, struggle, and thought that she can again enter a space of collectivity. The essay film becomes the conduit for a new, collective cinema of insurgency that sets out to perform a creative destruction of cinematic form. For New Left cinema, the essay as a trial produces—in Solanas and Getino's words—"a cinema fit for a new kind of human being," a human being who is not defined by the same divisions of interior–exterior, public–private, that constitute the modern subject but is a subject with a new capacity to think and act in common.[76]

The decentralized, participatory cinema characterized by the New Left's essay film is, without question, tied to a broader turn toward participatory, relational aesthetics in the 1960s and 1970s. In *Artificial Hells,* Claire Bishop undertakes a critical history of participatory practices in what she calls the "social turn" in contemporary art, and the emergence of these practices in 1960s France and Argentina are among two of the extended case studies examined in the book. In the case of France, Bishop evaluates the assumption that participation is intrinsically linked to democracy that motivated artists at the time. Looking at the SI and their relationship to more mainstream participatory artists and movements, like the Groupe de Recherche d'art Visual and Jean-Jaques Lebel, Bishop argues that the theory of participation coming out of France was "founded on a binary of active and passive spectatorship."[77] She critiques this position with a poster made by the Atelier Populaire in 1968 that reads "je participe, tu participes, il participe, nous participons, vous participez, ils profitent" (I participate, you participate, he participates, we participate, you participate, they profit).[78] A riposte to the sentiment behind the May 1968 graffiti "To be free means to participate," the Atelier Populaire poster stands in for Bishop's broader critique of the automatic coupling of participation and democracy.

In the case of Argentina, Bishop examines how different approaches to participatory practices functioned to make "social sadism made explicit," producing happenings that threw the violence of life under dictatorship into relief.[79] Of the Argentine examples she cites, the Rosario Group's Ciclo de Art Experimental (Cycle of Experimental Art, 1968) and Augusto Boal's influential *Theater of the Oppressed* relate most closely to the development of participatory practices in third cinema:

> If the artists in Rosario produced coercive situations that functioned as poetic analogues for political repression (inflicting restriction on the viewer as a wake-up call to his/her oppression by the Onganía dictatorship), Boal connected this oppression more explicitly to the economics of

class inequality. His Invisible Theatre was aimed at training the public to be more conscious of class difference and to provide them with a forum for articulating dissent.[80]

Bishop traces these political and aesthetic inclinations to León Ferrari, who wrote, "Art will neither be beauty nor novelty; art will be efficacy and disturbance. An accomplished work of art will be that which, in the artist's environment, can make an impact similar to the one caused by a terrorist act in a country struggling for freedom."[81]

As is evident, participatory cinema in the context of the New Left in both France and Argentina was tied to a broader conversation on participation within the visual arts and performance in each context. In France, the association of participation with democracy informed the Medvedkin Group's attempts to democratize the means of cinematic production, while the Estates General du Cinéma worked to decentralize film culture and separate it from the institutions of auteur cinema. Similarly, the theory and practice of third cinema resonate with participatory performance art being developed in the Argentine context. These similarities are evident in the former's camera-gun metaphor that imagines cinema as a weaponized tool, as well as its themes of quotidian violence and the confrontational, if not coercive, situations generated by each film-act. But while the principles of collective production, audience engagement, and the implicit attempt to overcome the separation between art and life run through all of the aesthetic projects discussed herein, the New Left's essay film is nevertheless distinct from the participatory practices that Bishop traces in *Artificial Hells*. Cinema, as an industrial art, has a complex and often ambivalent relationship to performance and art practice in general. The New Left's essay film plays a different role predicated not only on producing situations to induce audience participation but also on generating new analytical frameworks and arguments that contend with complex and often abstract societal processes and phenomena and circulating these by way of an archival, audiovisual medium. Thus the New Left's essay film is as concerned with the problem of forging alternate channels for the distribution of meaning and information throughout society as it is with creating new participatory models beyond the hierarchies implied in auteur cinema. New Left cinema was responding to the centralization of mass culture within the industrial era by generating new channels of media distribution. The critique of film and video, archival and broadcast media, cannot be reduced to the terms used to critique theater and performance, though there are invariably overlapping histories that tie the tendency toward collective authorship and participation in the cinema to larger trends within the world of art.

There are more fundamental problems, however, with the ways that participatory practices were framed in New Left cinema. For example, Jacques Rancière takes issue with theories of spectatorship that conceived of it as a passive activity and the manner in which the artist must overcome that passivity by generating didactic work that forces the viewer into a position of activity. Critiquing Debord's conception of the spectacle (defining it as an inheritor of Brecht's theater), Rancière disputes the division between activity and passivity, arguing that the individuated spectator is, inherently, an active position: "every spectator is already an actor in her story; every actor, every man of action, is a spectator of the same story."[82] Thus the false binary between passivity and activity that undergirds the theories of participation in the 1960s undermines the open-ended experience that defines, for Rancière, the "aesthetic regime of art," which is inherently "disavowed" by socially engaged art.[83]

Though I am sympathetic to Rancière's concerns about the underlying assumptions and dichotomies that inform the turn toward socially engaged, participatory art, I also find that he fails to interrogate why these theories and practices appear at the height of industrial modernity as a response to mass culture. The politics of spectatorship and aesthetics are not transhistorical phenomena but immanent to a set of material circumstances. As Jasper Bernes argues, the turn toward participation in both the artistic and literary worlds was part of a broader "qualitative" critique of work in the industrial era, what Luc Boltanski and Eve Chiapello have called the "artistic critique of capitalism" that manifested in the movements of the 1960s.[84] In addition to responding to the character of work in the industrial era, as Bernes suggests, I would argue that New Left cinema also endeavored to overturn the structure of the spectacle in the industrial era, creating decentralized, nonhierarchical, participatory models of collective authorship. While Rancière might be correct that the ontological division between "active" and "passive" spectatorship is suspect, we can certainly analyze the ways that the division between producer and consumer of media in the Fordist era involved a clear separation of the means of production. The goal of New Left cinematic movements was to reclaim the tools and channels of cinematic production, while undermining the regime of private property that upholds them, namely the "author-function," which consistently reinscribes cinematic utterances within the domain of the personal. Therefore we cannot so easily discount the political aims of New Left cinema as they attempt to overcome cultural hierarchies—between producer and consumer, core and periphery—responding to and enacting a politics inspired by struggles for Third World liberation. This aim, rather than naively perpetuating false binaries, engenders what Alberto Toscano calls the "communism of the senses," in which the aim of the avant-garde art (Vertov being a historical touchstone) is guided by "the need to anticipate communist social relations (of production, distribution, and consumption—as well as collaboration) within art-making itself, to make the fashioning of new *aesthetic* relations simultaneously into the eliciting of *new social and political* relations."[85] The New Left's essay film conducts this prefigurative politics in its drive to overcome the public–private divide and produce analyses and affects in common, "a cinema fit for a new kind of human being."

However, in looking at the legacy of this cinema, we should also ask what became of these new, revolutionary demands and aspirations. While the cinema of the New Left opened radical practices that endure in leftist media culture today, it also prefigured possibilities for capitalist reappropriation that have come to define the present. Indeed, it is precisely the demand for participation, and not passivity, that characterizes contemporary capitalist culture. As Bernes contends, the critiques of capital in the postwar era "became a significant force behind the restructuring of capitalism, by providing important coordinates, ideas, and images for that restructuring."[86] Furthermore, one could argue that the hierarchies between spectacle and spectator, media producer and consumer, that the New Left sought to overcome have been realized, but not in the ways that New Left practitioners foresaw. In evaluating this new cinema of insurgency, it is perhaps only in retrospect that we come to see the ways that a film such as *Hour of the Furnaces* runs up against the limits of its own presuppositions about both the subject of cinema and revolutionary change by advocating for the very forms that come to define media production in postindustrial capitalism. This failing, or the inevitability of appropriation, however, cannot completely define the New Left's essay film, whose plurality and tendency toward common forms of enunciation ultimately exceed attempts to contain them. For example, the durability of the political critique in *Hora de los hornos* is manifest in its capacity to present complex arguments regarding the relationship between imperialism and forms of indebted and bankrupt life that have only been expanded and intensified since its production. If, as Solanas argues, a militant film cannot be complete until the social movement it is a part of achieves its objectives, then we might argue that *Hora de los hornos,* along with many essay films of the New Left, remains incomplete. Nevertheless, the New Left cinema inaugurates an era in which political struggle takes place within the domain of the image more than ever before. The myriad ways that the New Left's essay film attempted the common production of meaning and affect beyond existing categories and hierarchies will remain central in what is to follow.

2

Toward a New Mode of Study

THE STUDENT NEW LEFT AND THE OCCUPATION OF CINEMA

The student graduates. But not all of them. Some still stay, committed to black study in the university's undercommon rooms. They study without an end, plan without a pause, rebel without a policy, conserve without patrimony. They study in the university and the university forces them under, relegates them to a state without interests, without credit, without debt that bears interest, that earns credits. They never graduate. They just ain't ready. They're building something down there. Mutual debt, debt unpayable, debt unbounded, debt unconsolidated, debt to each other in a study group, to others in a nurses' room, to others in a barber shop, to others in a squat, a dump, a woods, a bed, an embrace.[1]

— STEFANO HARNEY AND FRED MOTEN,
The Undercommons: Fugitive Planning and Black Study

The figure of the student is indelibly seared into the audiovisual archive of the New Left. Images of her protests and occupations, posters and screams, have become shorthand for a whole set of myths about the 1960s: the idealism of youth, the emptiness of middle-class protest, and the tenuous and short-lived alliances of an embattled Left. Despite attempts to trivialize them, student movements in India, Thailand, Mexico, Turkey, Egypt, and Nigeria (to list only a few) that erupted in 1968 in tandem with disruptions in industrial centers like the United States, Western Europe, and Japan became what George Katsiaficas describes as "a force of international relations."[2] The rapid expansion of higher education in the postwar era enfolded a much larger section of the population into the university system than in previous generations. An unintended consequence was a social force that could analyze and resist the role of the university in

69

imperialist ventures, its production of specialized labor for capital, and the ways that its knowledges participated in the reproduction of manifold forms of inequality. Coinciding with the Keynesian era of demands for full employment, Nick Mitchell suggests that the swelling of the student population in the postwar period was an implicit strategy to contain and manage a significant portion of the population that would otherwise be seeking jobs and that the best analogy for the university in the postwar era might not be a "factory" but rather a "warehouse" for the industrial reserve army.[3] This interpretation of the student in the postwar era positions her not only as a "force of international relations," as Katsiaficas suggests, but as a force of capital relations as well.[4]

As a global force, student movements played a principal role in redefining what constitutes valid academic knowledge. Scholars such as Roderick Ferguson have argued that student struggles for ethnic and women's studies in the United States gave birth to interdisciplinary knowledges grounded in difference. For Ferguson, it was through these struggles that "the agencies and processes of life, labor, and language would be subjected to an unprecedented scrutiny that sought to determine their constitution through historical particularities rather than transhistorical universalities."[5] Furthermore, the interdisciplinary knowledges being formed within student movements integrated traditions of thought connected with anti-imperial struggles. For example, student movements in the United States, such as the Lumumba Zapata movement at the University of California, San Diego, took up theories of internal colonialism as a way of "imagining institutions not only as sites for addressing racial exclusions but as locations for illuminating formations from multiple geographical terrains."[6] The "imaginative geographies" that informed the New Left student movements were critical to generating alternative epistemological paradigms.

We can read in the often raucous cinematic artifacts of New Left student movements these efforts to create new, situated knowledges. Across the United States, Latin America, Europe, Africa, and Asia, New Left student movements both inspired and participated in the production of films that worked to articulate these new forms of knowledge and modes of inquiry not only in their form and content but also by forging alternative methods of production, distribution, and exhibition characteristic of

New Left cinema in general. As discussed in the previous chapter, these cinematic movements often actively rejected auteur cinema and developed collective models of filmmaking as a political gesture in a broader attempt to overcome the implicit forms of authority and hierarchy that auteur cinema was thought to engender. Within student movements, this was an international phenomenon, as numerous student films that followed student uprisings employed collective approaches to production, including *El Grito* (The scream, Mexico, 1968) and *Cinegiornale del moviemento studentesco* (Cinema journal of the student movement, Italy, 1968).

While locating the centrality of the student in defining the New Left's "expanded base of revolution," this chapter centers on the ways that New Left student movements extended beyond the student and the university and engaged with film as a new mode of study that fostered capacities for being and thinking in common. The student movements examined here serve as an entry point into a broader discussion of struggle and epistemology within New Left cinema. In the two cases addressed in this chapter, New York Newsreel's *Columbia Revolt* (United States, 1968) and Ogawa Pro's *Nihon kaiho sensen—Sanrizuka no natsu* (The battlefront for the liberation of Japan—summer in Sanrizuka, Japan, 1968), tensions around New Left cinema's capacity to incite new epistemological frameworks and forge new encounters and collectivities come to the fore. Highlighting the New Left's imaginative geographies, each of these films is situated within a social movement that uses a language of anti-imperialist struggles in the defense of both university and extra-university spaces. Furthermore, these spaces were figured as commons under threat, each film dramatizing struggles against enclosure by either the university or the state. Like the movements from which they were born, *Columbia Revolt* and *Sanrizuka no natsu* demonstrate how new knowledges are fashioned through radical and collective modes of study, thus realizing Mario Tronti's assertion that "knowledge comes from struggle" in cinematic terms.[7]

CINEMATIC STUDY

When referring to New Left student cinema as a mode of study, I use the term *study* in its broadest sense, constituting what Moten refers to as a "speculative practice" or a "common intellectual practice" that is not necessarily geared toward an end and is often not recognized as valid by authoritative academic standards.[8] In fact, the knowledge produced by study in the university's "undercommons" is frequently deemed to be "conspiratorial, heretical, criminal, amateur," according to Harney and Moten.[9] Their understanding of study as a practice emphasizes common inquiry, "where the text is open enough that instead of being studied, it actually becomes an occasion for study."[10] Rather than studying *some thing,* a thing in the world becomes an incitement to a collective act of exploration. Thus the practice of study veers away from the empirical to emphasize the creative activity implied in knowledge production.[11]

This "speculative practice" of study, I argue, is the epistemological orientation of the New Left's essay film. Cinematic studies, in the examples I discuss in this chapter and throughout the book, are an occasion for a new kind of sociality generated through cinema. Cinematic study, in this sense, builds on the essayistic politics of the common discussed in the previous chapter, refining the implications of thinking cinema as a manner of inquiry, a starting point for collective exploration that tests ways of apprehending the world and living within it. Like the essay films discussed in the previous chapter, the films coming out of New Left student movements are attempts to produce collective enunciations and participatory modes of communication, while at the same time often arriving at ways of knowing that might at first appear "heretical, criminal, [or] amateur." In the spirit of Cuban filmmaker Julio García Espinosa, New Left cinematic study is not "impartial" but "imperfect."[12] An "imperfect cinema" is one that undoes hierarchies between amateur and professional, understanding creative experimentation through cinema to be an integral part of revolutionary struggle in the Third World. For García Espinosa, "imperfect cinema is an answer" to a cinema that strives to be technically masterful and ideologically and artistically impartial, "but it is also a question which will discover its own answers in the course of its development."[13] In other words, rather than creating neutral and professional documents of an unfolding struggle, "imperfect cinema" takes cinema to be a starting point for a new set of questions and problems to arise "in the midst" of struggle and life.[14] It is a question in the sense that it is an occasion to struggle, imperfectly, and to create a cinema that is intrinsic to that struggle. In his utopian speculation on the unraveling of hierarchies between high and low cinema, García Espinosa concludes his essay by arguing,

> The future, without doubt, will be with folk art, but there will be no need to call it that, because nobody will call it that, because nobody and nothing will any longer be able to again paralyze the creative spirit of the people. Art will not disappear into nothingness; it will disappear into everything.[15]

Working though these problems in Cuba, a newly communist country at the time, García Espinosa imagines a cinema of the people that participates in the general withering away of the artistic divisions upheld by bourgeois society.

Cinematic study, in its imperfect form, seeks the disruption of given categories and divisions, especially those that separate high from low, professional from amateur, art from life. In doing so, the practice also resonates with what Kristen Ross has called "communal luxury" in reference to the Paris Commune. Communal luxury is, for Ross, among other things, "the project of making art *lived*—not superfluous or trivial, but vital and indispensible to the community."[16] By undermining set categories and integrating art and life, Ross explains that "at its most speculative reaches, communal luxury implies a set of criteria or system of valuation other than the one supplied by the market for deciding what a society values, what it counts as precious."[17] The capacity for the communards to generate new systems of value stemmed from their epistemological orientation, which, as I discuss later, privileged open exploration not dissimilar from the idea of study as a "speculative practice": "anything that can be laid hold of can become a starting point for emancipation."[18] In the case of the collectives discussed in this chapter, cinema was this point of departure, a place from which to endeavor to create forms that assemble, in a prefigurative manner, a new set of values and a world in which these values are shared.

It is important to underscore that these values are in no way neutral. Like the Paris Commune in Ross's account, the epistemological inclinations of the films addressed in this chapter are entwined with the tactics of occupying and barricading spaces. A central task of this chapter will be to unpack the concept of cinematic study as a modality that generates situated, partial, and imperfect knowledges that are framed through a constituent antagonism. By cinematically rendering affective dimensions of living behind the barricades, using formal strategies that situate the camera as an implement of struggle rather than a neutral observer, both *Columbia Revolt* and *Sanrizuka no natsu* build on new forms of knowledge and systems of valuation that materialize in these spaces of collaboration and contradiction, generating affects and amplifying antagonisms. In doing so, the chapter examines how cinematic knowledge within the New Left was formed in and through antagonism—an antagonism that transmuted collective experiences of dispossession. In this antagonistic mode of study, struggles facilitated the accumulation of mutual debts, debts that are inverse of the financial debts accrued by the student in the neoliberal era.

COLUMBIA REVOLT: STUDY AND THE BARRICADE

Columbia Revolt opens with a homily on the "modern university":

> The modern university is the cradle of the nation's future. Today it not only preserves and transmits knowledge and values, it serves more and more as a center of research and innovation. It has been called the chief energizing and creative force in our entire social system. The modern university is the cradle of the nation's future: *this be so.* Let us not underestimate the task we face. Meanwhile the explosive growthage still increases the demands upon us. The underdeveloped peoples look to us for training and guidance.

Attributed to Columbia president Grayson Kirk and delivered in a grave tone characteristic of the "voice of god" narration in mid-century documentary, the voice-over is accompanied by ceremonious organ music and booms over footage of marble columns and statues that line the halls of the university. This lecture, however, is interrupted by the sound of a machine gun and the rapid fire of the Newsreel logo on the screen, unsettling the imperious proclamation "*this be so*" with a militant affront to the university and its claims to both truth and futurity. In the following sequence, the neoclassical architecture and authoritarian tone of the intro are juxtaposed with footage of rigid, modern university buildings and unattributed voice-overs of students and activists speaking about the increasing militarization and corporatization of the university. These anonymous voice-overs, which Jonathan Kahana has described as "voice-offs," are characteristic of the early Newsreel style, indicating an antiauthoritarian, situated knowledge taken from interviews with participants.[19] The aural politics of Newsreel films, particularly the use of the voice-off, breaks with the "omniscience and objectivity" of the classic voice-over and is partial, according to Kahana, in both senses of the word: it is politically charged and made up of a cacophony of nonindividuated voices.[20] In its rejection of the idea that any one voice could represent the totality, the voice-off functions as the primary formal mechanism for foregrounding difference in the film by displacing universalizing claims to truth with disparate perspectives. Refusing the purported neutrality of the university and the knowledges it produces, *Columbia Revolt* expresses an antagonism between universality and difference through voice-offs that both narrate and analyze the events that unfolded at Columbia University and surrounding areas in April and May 1968. As I explore in this section, the tactic of the barricade employed in the course of these events, centrally featured in and constitutive of *Columbia Revolt,* allows the film to build on this fundamental antagonism, expressing a profound partiality that allows it to arrive at new knowledges and values.

Columbia Revolt was among the first cinematic interventions of the early Newsreel collective—a film that would reveal both the strengths and shortcomings of early New Left cinema in the United States. Along with San Francisco Newsreel's *Black Panther: Off the Pig!* (United States, 1968), *Columbia Revolt* became a mainstay of the underground cinema scene in the United States, its screening prompting not just conversation and debate but actual campus uprisings, such as the burning of an ROTC center at the State University of New York, Buffalo by the film's audience immediately following its exhibition.[21] As Robert Kramer of the New York Newsreel insists in an often-cited statement, the objective of Newsreel's films was to create "a form of propaganda that polarizes, angers, and excites for the purpose of discussion—a way of getting at people, not by making concession to where they are, but by showing them where you are and forcing them to deal with that, bringing out all their assumptions, their prejudices, their imperfect perceptions."[22] Tools for organizing solidarities, Newsreel's early films offer a rough style that intensifies the "political mimesis" that underlies the film's portrayal of struggle. In his critique of *Columbia Revolt,* Michael Renov asserts that the film's analysis is "muted in comparison to the spectacle of community and solidarity it offers."[23] While underscoring its capacity to generate affective solidarities, I want to resist characterizations of the film that cast it as a form of amateur cinema whose capacity for analysis is "muted." Following Kramer's statement on Newsreel, it is the confrontational style of films like *Columbia Revolt* that drives their analysis, though rough, imperfect, and partial.

Newsreel's collective production methods and its independent distribution and exhibition practices were paradigmatic of New Left cinema in the United States.[24] Following groups that worked to horizonalize cinematic production elsewhere, the collective had its origins in both participatory democracy and radical education, one of the group's early catalysts being a cinema workshop offered by Allan Siegel at the Free University of New York.[25] Screenings of Newsreel films took place in "churches, union halls, campus dorms, and public parks" and became opportunities for organizing through audience participation and dialogue.[26] Furthermore, Newsreel's distribution and exhibition of its own films was only one aspect of the group's cinematic ambitions. As Cynthia A. Young demonstrates, Newsreel created an international network for the distribution of films from liberation struggles in Asia, Africa, and Latin America that were otherwise unavailable in the United States: "Newsreel's distribution network served as a critical pipeline ferrying the strategies, philosophies, events, and people that helped build a Third World anticolonial common sense."[27] Films like *Columbia Revolt,* then, must be understood within the overarching leftist cinematic infrastructure that Newsreel was developing—one that shared many organizing principles and strategic tendencies with collectives discussed throughout this book.

With regard to its immediate prehistory, I find it essential to situate *Columbia Revolt* within the radical turn taken in U.S. student activism at the time. In her popular account, published in 1969, of the Columbia protests and occupations, Joanne Grant identifies what she calls the "Columbia pattern of protest," a form of student revolt that marks a break from earlier student protests, the latter typified by the 1964 Berkeley free speech movement. Grant locates "black separatism, student occupations of buildings, student and community participation, police battles, reluctance to negotiate, [and] rebel demands for amnesty" as the hallmarks of the new campus activism.[28] Though often characterized as an escalation of campus protests against the Vietnam War, the clash at Columbia was inseparable from the increasing black militancy and its effects on the student New Left in the United States, linking imperial struggles abroad to domestic struggles against racial oppression. At the same time, the Columbia protests were symptomatic of resistance to the university's role in reproducing the white-collar workforce. These sentiments are evident in a communiqué put out by Students for a Democratic Society (SDS) that tried to correct the portrayal of the protests in popular media as "youthful outbursts" or simply "general student unrest due to the war in Vietnam":[29]

> But in reality, striking students are responding to the totality of the conditions of our society. . . . We are disgusted with war, with racism, with being a part of a system over which we have no control, a system which demands gross inequalities of wealth and power, a system that denies personal and social freedom and potential. . . . The university can only be seen a cog in the machine, a factory whose product is knowledge and personnel (us) useful to the functioning of the system. The specific problems of university life, its boredom and meaninglessness, help prepare us for boring and meaningless work in the "real" world.[30]

Recalling simultaneous statements being made by Parisian students during the events of May 1968, SDS links the "meaninglessness" of life within the university—alienated study—to the alienation of work beyond the university. At the same time, the students trace connections between their own alienation and the university's role in a broader system of oppression: "the policies of the university—expansion into the community, exploitation of blacks and Puerto Ricans, support for imperialist wars—also serve the interests of banks, corporations, government, and military represented on the Columbia Board of Trustees and the ruling class of our society."[31] The university itself becomes an object of and occasion for study, a site of contestation in the production and reproduction of alienation, inequality, and war.

The radicalization of the student New Left between 1964—the start of the Berkeley free speech movement—and the Columbia insurrection in 1968 was, in large part, inspired by the transition taking place in struggles for black liberation, which morphed from civil rights to Black Power when formative groups like the Student Non-violent Coordinating Committee and the Congress of Racial Equality began to reject "interracial liberalism."[32] In the United States, the student New Left came out of the civil rights movement, and it is no coincidence that a "new pattern" of student protest would arise at Columbia, a university situated next to Harlem, a center of the growing Black Power movement. As is suggested in SDS's communiqué, the Columbia conflict between students and administration was catalyzed by the intensification of hostilities between Columbia and the surrounding Morningside Heights and Harlem neighborhoods. Tensions between Columbia and the black community that had been growing for years came to a head in the aftermath of Martin Luther King Jr.'s assassination and the riots that ensued only a few weeks before the Columbia strike. In the name of "urban renewal" and crime reduction, Columbia had been in the process of evicting primarily black tenants from its vast real estate holdings in Morningside Heights.[33] The focal point of the Harlem community's protests against Columbia became a gym that the university planned to build in Morningside Park, a small green space that separated Columbia and Harlem. In the years leading up to the Columbia protests, the plan for the private gym built on public land, which would have a separate entrance and facilities for community members in the basement, galvanized the increasingly militant Harlem community, whose leaders, such as H. Rap Brown, articulated the grievances of the community through the language of Black Power.[34] For Brown, blacks' status as a colonized people was unambiguous: "there is no difference between Harlem and Puerto Rico, or Harlem and Vietnam, except that in Vietnam people are fighting for their liberation."[35] As Young argues in her assessment of the birth of a Third World consciousness within the United States, the internal colony became a key political concept for building both real and imagined political solidarities within black communities in the late 1960s.[36] Drawing on the thesis that Harlem represented an internal colony of the United States, local activists figured the gym as an "invasion" of their community—linking white supremacy and imperialist strategies at home with those abroad.[37] A pamphlet entitled "Gym Crow," most likely produced by Columbia students aligned with the Student Afro-American Society (SAS), presented a carefully researched case against the gym that gave ammunition to the struggle to thwart its construction, providing a pithy slogan that signaled the project's connections to white supremacy.[38]

Like the larger student movement, *Columbia Revolt* draws inspiration from the escalation of struggle by the black community to define militancy through cinema. In an often chaotic and contradictory manner, *Columbia Revolt* works to underline the disparity between the university's ideals and its reality by foregrounding the struggle against the gym. The body of the film opens with the gym's fenced-off construction site, accompanied by voice-offs from members of the Harlem community filmed prior to the events of late April. "This country went up on violence and this country's going down on violence; as a house go up, a house must come down," states a distinctly African American female voice (one of the few such voices we hear in the film). In a crucial moment that sets the stage for what is to follow, the sequence cuts to footage of a black man, lying in the blade of a large bulldozer while defiantly smoking a cigarette, and a black woman, sitting in front of the tread of the same machine. These protesters visualize the militant posture of the community against the encroachment of Columbia. Their unwavering affect stands in stark contrast to their corporeal vulnerability in relation to the heavy machinery. Using their bodies as instruments of obstruction in a larger strategy of refusal, these protesters demonstrate that it was the Harlem community that was both under assault and taking the greatest risks in the intensification of the conflict with the university. Though the vast majority of *Columbia Revolt* concentrates on the actions of the white students and is largely told through their voices, this sequence stands out as a brief acknowledgment of the prehistory of the Columbia protests that places the Harlem community at the forefront of the struggle.

The preceding sequence foretells the centrality of the militant tactics that would come to shape the disruptions of April and May at Columbia University. The SDS are often given credit for escalating protest, but it was the Harlem community and black Columbia students who led the

Figure 8. Film still, Harlem community member protesting construction of gym, *Columbia Revolt* (1968).

charge by rejecting the tactic of an integrated, nonviolent sit-in character-istic of the Berkeley free speech movement. Instead, the black leadership barricaded Hamilton Hall, which they renamed "Malcolm X University," and demanded that the white students leave (due to their disorganiza-tion, internal divisions, and unwillingness to barricade the building) and let the black students and members of the community take charge in the struggle against the gym.

While *Columbia Revolt,* like the larger protest, ultimately arrives at its militant position by way of the tactic of the barricade, it conveys an am-bivalence toward the black leadership that instigated it. The "black–white split," as it is named in the film, is presented in *Columbia Revolt* through an account of a member of SDS in a moment of self-critique as he narrates the series of events that led to the split over footage of SAS leaders such as Cicero Wilson, Ray Brown, Bill Sales, and Ralph Metcalfe Jr., all of whom go unnamed in the film, unlike Mark Rudd, then SDS president, whose leadership is mentioned at several points. This voice-off (a turning point in the film) functions as an affirmation of the tactics of SAS and the Harlem community in escalating the confrontation. Nevertheless, it simultaneously robs the black leadership of a voice at the moment of the clearest assertion of their power. By featuring the images, but not the voices, of the black leadership, this scene reproduces the worst racial hierarchies that plagued the student New Left, begging the May 1968 question, *Who speaks? For whom? And how?* Despite its desire to disrupt the discourse of the university by designing the production of the film around the principles of participatory democracy and collective critique, *Columbia Revolt* ultimately falls short by consistently presenting an account of the events from the perspective of the white (primarily male) participants, whose voices crowd out those of the black students and community participants whose militant leadership and tactics precipitated the radical turn of events. The voices heard on-screen reflect the complexion of the early New York Newsreel at the time, whose primarily white, male leadership replicated the hierarchies in the organization of cinematic meaning that the group purportedly sought to undermine. These contradictions within early Newsreel have been well documented and eventually led to the formation of the Third World Newsreel in the early 1970s.[39] As Bill Nichols has argued, the Newsreel collective operated as a kind of barometer for the Left in the United States, and the contestation over the production of radical cinematic meaning that played out in the Newsreel is an index of larger struggles within the New Left itself, a point that is thrown into relief in the following chapter.[40]

    It would be easy to dismiss *Columbia Revolt* offhand due to its inability to deal with difference at crucial moments, but to do so would be to miss the importance of the struggles of the black community and the ways they become constituent of the film. Despite its failure to give voice to the black leadership, *Columbia Revolt* foregrounds the black leadership's tactical innovation, contending with the construction and consequences of the barricade in occupying and reclaiming university territory. It does so by focusing on the importance of building and maintaining the barricades and emphasizing how new possibilities of being-within-struggle were magnified behind the barricade walls. A sequence documents the process of building the barricades at Hamilton Hall, using water cannons,

Figure 9. Film still, students occupying Hamilton Hall looking out at the crowd gathered outside, *Columbia Revolt* (1968).

chairs, and other furniture to prevent a surprise takeover by the police, while another voice-off recounts groups of Harlem high school students, mothers, and other sections of the black community marching on Columbia. In a shot taken from the interior of the building while H. Rap Brown (with Stokely Carmichael by his side) reads the students' demands to onlookers and the press in front of Hamilton Hall, the silhouettes of three black Columbia students look down on the crowd assembled outside. This shot conveys the power of the barricade as a tactic, creating a dynamic that temporarily displaces the spatial, and racial, order of everyday life at Columbia University. In scenes that anticipate the militant struggles for ethnic studies that would emerge in places like San Francisco State (captured in San Francisco Newsreel's *San Francisco State on Strike* in 1969), Cornell University, and numerous campuses across the country, the display of black militancy in reclaiming university spaces and connections with the larger black community engendered a broader claim to knowledge production and dissemination.[41] In defending the commons,

Morningside Park, and the surrounding community, a space for an alternate commons is forced opened within the institution or, better, within its undercommons. This alternate commons is the knowledge, experience, and history of the black community.

In these scenes from Hamilton Hall, *Columbia Revolt* underscores how the epistemological grew from the tactical, generating a situated knowledge made possible by the act of occupation. In a voice-off, we hear a student reflecting on tactical transition from sit-in to barricade: "we realized that our strength was in our militancy, in holding those buildings. It took the example of the blacks to move us." In the following scene, a voice-off recounts one of the most controversial moments of the Columbia protests, in which occupying students took over President Kirk's office and went through his files. In them, they discovered ample evidence of Columbia's links to the Institute for Defense Analysis and its plans to take over the surrounding neighborhood, further displacing the black and Puerto Rican communities, findings that were disseminated in mimeographed dispatches during the occupation. Enabled by the barricades, this radical form of study took the university itself as an occasion for that study. Generating and distributing knowledge in the course of the occupation was a form of political power, the revelations themselves being less important than the collective process of study and antagonism that brought them to light.

The production of *Columbia Revolt* was modeled on the collective study already at work within the occupation, implicating the filmmakers as participants. With cameras in each of the occupied buildings, Newsreel, the only media outlet with such access, was able to capture the occupations from the perspective of the striking students.[42] In a sequence that depicts the building and securing of barricades, a voice-off explains that they had become "politically and strategically" necessary. *Columbia Revolt* as a whole is a testament to this political and strategic necessity, affirming the barricades by actively participating in their construction and maintenance. According to Newsreel member Roz Payne, cameras were used "as weapons as well as recording the events. Melvin has a W.W.II cast iron steel Bell and Howell camera that could take the shock of breaking plate glass windows."[43] Militant study through cinema in the case of *Columbia Revolt* necessitated transforming the camera into a tool of the barricade, one that could communicate antagonisms by producing distinctly situated knowledges. Like the mimeographed dispatches from the occupation, *Columbia Revolt* is the product of collective participation in the occupation rather than an objective document of it.

Perhaps the most memorable sections of *Columbia Revolt* are those that deal with the affective dimensions of life behind the barricades, exploring intensities formed in communal existence, as captured in the voice-off of a participant: "the life of the commune was a group of people who were incredibly close to each other on no other level but the level of struggle." The film reflects on the possibility of redefining self, home, and family within the occupation. Over a sequence of a milk carton being passed around, a voice-off recounts, "There was a total collective feeling. No one particularly cared about his individual feelings, because you never experienced them. Everything was experienced in the most collective sense that I've ever known. This was one of the new experiences for most people in the strike, a kind of electric awakening." In an emphatic tone, a participant asserts, "People are living here, it's a home. *It's a home.* I've never been so comfortable on this campus." Scenes of people drumming, dancing, forming a limbo line, and getting married in the organized chaos of the occupied buildings impart a joyful and collaborative mood in these spaces. "We chose to be married at home and with our family," states a voice-off of the bride. *Columbia Revolt* does not linger on the commune but reasserts antagonism by interrupting cheers from the wedding crowd with the sounds of police sirens and the inevitable breaking of the barricades. In this sequence, we find an unspoken blurring of the "black–white split" discussed earlier. The moments in which the film asserts a new definition of home and family also suggest a camaraderie among different factions of the strike. In these scenes, *Columbia Revolt* attests to García Espinosa's belief that imperfect cinema can and should be a cinema of enjoyment: "the struggle requires organization—the organization of life.... And in life, as in the struggle, there is everything, including enjoyment. Imperfect cinema can enjoy itself despite everything that conspires to negate enjoyment."[44] These collective forms of life and cinematic knowledges stand as an affront to

Figure 10. Film still, marriage ceremony in occupied building, *Columbia Revolt* (1968).

forces that seek to undermine enjoyment, especially in political struggle.

Despite its limitations, in conducting a new mode of study by way of a cinema that activates and participates in struggles to redefine the university, *Columbia Revolt* served as a catalyst for student uprisings in the United States and globally by exploring the epistemological and affective values discovered, however briefly, in life behind the barricade. Instigated by the dispossession of the black community by Columbia (within the broader context of U.S. imperialism), the tactic of the barricade opens the occupiers to what Judith Butler and Athena Athanasiou would argue is a different, more fundamental experience of dispossession that follows from a basic "dependency and relationality."[45] This latter form of dispossession "establishes the self as social, as passionate, that is, as driven by passions it cannot fully consciously ground or know, as dependent on environments and others who sustain and even motivate the life of the self itself."[46] The experience of the commune the participants described was one that allowed them to touch, momentarily, on a form of existence where dispossession—a fundamental debt to and dependency on others— could be experienced as freedom rather than imposition. This experience of dispossession is the starting point for a creative exploration of a new set of values, of "communal luxury."

REMAPPING CINEMATIC STUDY IN *SANRIZUKA NO NATSU*

While the emphasis on alternate forms of production, distribution, and exhibition were simultaneously developing in Latin America, Europe, and the United States in the years leading up to upheavals of 1968 and the publication of Fernando Solanas and Octavio Getino's "Towards a Third Cinema," some of the most innovative theorization and infrastructure of independent New Left cinema was being cultivated in Japan under the auspices of the Jeiso collective. Coming out of a rich culture of independent and avant-garde filmmaking, the group was centered around Ogawa Shinsuke, a charismatic figure who, along with prominent filmmakers like Tsuchimoto Noriaki, abandoned mainstream filmmaking in the midst of a radical transformation in Japanese documentary cinema taking place in the mid-1960s. Embodying an undercurrent in Japanese cinema, Ogawa rejected both commercial cinema and the centralized hierarchies that characterized the documentary cinema associated with the Japanese Communist Party (JCP).[47] Ogawa quickly connected with the student movement in Hanai and formed the Jishu Joei Shoshiki no Kai (Independent Screening Organization), or Jeiso, in 1966. Largely unknown in the United States to this day, Jeiso's early films, such as *Seinen no umi* (Sea of youth, 1966), *Assatsu no mori* (Forest of pressure, 1967), and *Gennin hokusho-Haneda toso no kiroku* (Report from Haneda, 1967), galvanized the Japanese student movement in the late 1960s. During a tumultuous period of student uprisings and occupations, Jeiso's early films seized upon the energy of the student movement and, like Newsreel, used cinema to spread news of insurgency as well as insurgency itself.

As Abé Mark Nornes chronicles in his definitive account of Oga- wa's career, Jeiso (renamed "Ogawa Pro" in 1968) redefined movement filmmaking in several ways. First, the collective developed an elabo- rate, independent distribution and exhibition network that emphasized audience participation and engagement: "Ask an Ogawa Pro member about its 'film movement' and he or she would assume you are talking about the screenings, not the film. The real activism of the collective centered on the reception context."[48] As spaces for networking among different segments of the New Left, especially the student movement, screenings were held across Japan in nontraditional spaces, "from urban art houses to rural gymnasiums to homemade theaters."[49] Second, a method of collective research and production was systemized for each film, in which various working groups—such as screening, production, investigation, and theory—were engaged in carrying out every aspect of production, distribution, and exhibition collectively.[50] The organization of Jeiso was remarkably similar to the cells in the "*film-guerilla* group" described by Solanas and Getino in the "Implementation" section of "Towards a Third Cinema."[51] In addition to networking among the New Left in Japan, the collective developed connections with international New Left organizations, including the Black Panthers, whose minister of propaganda, Elbert Howard, visited the Ogawa Pro in 1969.[52] The organization also made connections with New Left film collectives in the United States and France, including Newsreel, and produced dubbed Japanese versions of *Columbia Revolt* and *Black Panther*.[53]

While incorporating aspects of international New Left cinema into their practice, the group's approach to cinematic inquiry was largely influenced by the theory of avant-garde documentary developed by the New Left filmmaker and theorist Matsumoto Toshio. Matsumoto rejected naturalism and called for a "new realism" that would "unify the documentary and the avant-garde" by way of a dialectical engagement between what he identified as the "inside," the subjectivity of the filmmaker, and the "outside," the world conceived of as active rather than inert.[54] For Jeiso, this approach manifested in the active engagement with the student movement in the production of *Assatsu no mori*, which included conducting research by making trips to numerous Japanese universities and political organizations.[55] Following Matsumoto's imperative, as Nornes puts it, the Jeiso collective's "experimentation with documentary style asserts the subjectivity of the filmmakers in the tissue of the image and sound."[56] Rejecting the notion of a neutral camera, Matsumoto's understanding of documentary subjectivity produces cinematic utterances that, like those of the Newsreel collective, are partial in nature. Jeiso's theorization of collective, subjective engagement through cinema demonstrates their attention to the epistemological consequences of using cinema as a form of social engagement and occasion for radical study, as I discuss later.

The subjects of Jeiso's cinematic explorations closely followed the Japanese student movement, beginning in the universities before expanding beyond them. Just as the struggle around "Gym Crow" drew connections between the local displacement of black communities and imperialism, the Japanese student movement's antagonistic view of the Vietnam War drew connections between U.S. imperialism in Vietnam and imperial and capitalist legacies domestically. These issues converged in the struggle against the construction of the Narita Airport outside of Tokyo, which would become one of the most protracted battles of the long 1960s, continuing for more than a decade and involving an estimated 750,000 to 1 million people.[57] The conflict began with farmers being displaced by the construction of the airport, opposing the initial purchase of their land by the government and forming a coalition of villages united under the name of Hantai Dōmei. Resistance to the airport soon became the focal point of the Japanese New Left, particularly the student movement. As David Apter and Nagayo Sawa demonstrate, the intensity of the struggle against Narita Airport grew out of a legacy of New Left activity in Japan centered on resisting U.S. imperialism, particularly the construction of U.S. airbases, which culminated in 1960 with the AMPO (Anti-U.S.-Japan Security Treaty) movement. With the help of New Left student organizations like Zengakuren (a group that had officially split from the JCP in 1958), militants framed the airport struggle through anti-imperialist language.[58] The militants' defense of the farmland was not informed by a nostalgic pastoralism but rather understood the displacement of the farmers as "part of the process of world capitalism, a form of primitive accumulation" that was intended to "create both an authentic proletariat and an industrial reserve army."[59] In short, the Japanese New Left understood the struggle against the airport as a struggle against enclosure, connecting peasant struggles against proletarianization in Asia and elsewhere with the accelerated industrialization of Japan in the postwar period.[60] The resistance to the airport demonstrates how the New Left Japanese student movement drew inspiration and tactics from anti-imperialist struggles globally, aligning themselves with peasants and others who constituted the New Left's "expanded base of revolution." With the participation of antinuclear movements and the burgeoning movement against the tragedies of industrial pollution in Minamata (explored in depth in the documentaries by Tsuchimoto Noriaki), the struggle over the construction of the airport combined a Marxist critique of what David Harvey has called "accumulation by dispossession" with a nascent environmentalism.[61]

The Ogawa Pro collective's sustained involvement in the the Narita Airport struggle, which lasted nine years and yielded seven films, paralleled the trajectory of the Japanese New Left from the late 1960s through the 1970s. When the collective shifted their focus to the Narita struggle in summer 1968, they documented the escalation of the conflict around the preliminary survey of the land, as the first major wooden barricades were constructed and basic weapons, such as bamboo spears and even buckets of human feces and urine, were employed to halt the surveyors' activities.[62] Against the purported impartiality of the documentary image, *Sanrizuka no natsu,* the first film Ogawa Pro produced about the conflict, makes clear the ways that the collective actively participated in life behind the barricades and shot the conflict from the perspective of the farmers and protesters, with ample footage of the filmmakers engaged in struggles with the police (at one point a cameraman is even arrested on film). In documenting the battle against the enclosure of the farmland, the collective became deeply entwined in life behind the barricades. According to Adam Bringham, "Ogawa and his collaborators entirely redefined and re-conceptualized discursive filmmaking by becoming one with their subjects, by conceiving of the documentary form not as a record and thus closed reality, but as a continuous, unfolding, and mediated process."[63] In attempts to overcome the partitioning of art and life, process and product, the collective became intimately involved in the lives and struggles of the villagers. Much like the Newsreel, however, the collective exhibited its own internal struggles with difference, particularly around gender, and reproduced some of the most lamentable internal divisions of labor. While female farmers are given a strong voice within *Sanrizuka no*

Figure 11. Film still, hand-drawn map planning protest against construction of Narita Airport, *Sanrizuka no natsu* (1968).

natsu and other films in the series, the internal structure of the collective most often relegated women to domestic labor.[64] Like so many New Left social movements, women were often assigned the task of reproducing the conditions in which radical politics, in this case, filmmaking, could take place.

Episodic in nature, *Sanrizuka no natsu* partakes in a series of events that occurred in the battle over the initial land survey, and the film shares a sense of urgency and roughness with *Columbia Revolt*. Rather than using voice-offs, the film privileges a cinéma vérité style, emphasizing the narration of events by the farmers themselves.[65] However, the use of sound in the film is far from neutral. In the opening sequence, an exterior shot shows a field being battered by a rainstorm. The bucolic beauty of this shot is interrupted by the sound of a rhythmic drumbeat, which we come to discover in the next sequence originates from villagers striking steel drums as a call to action to the surrounding residents, signaling an invasion by the police and the land surveyors. In this sequence and throughout, sound in *Summer in Sanrizuka* builds toward dissension, framing the land and its inhabitants through conflict.

The sequence cuts to an interior close-up of a hand-drawn map being discussed and edited by the resistance. In scenes that serve as refrains throughout the film, we observe farmers strategizing battle plans, mapping out barricade locations, and communicating with each other over walkie-talkies. In contradistinction to the knowledge of the space being produced by the land surveyors, who are shown throughout the film using purportedly neutral tools of measurement, *Sanrizuka no natsu* charts out a space that is apprehended by way of a fundamental antagonism. In essence, the film draws two maps: one whose knowledge is produced by an imperialist consensus and applied to the land without regard to its material history and a second whose understanding of the same space is creative, in process, and determined by conflict. The primary struggle depicted in the film is between these two ways of rendering the land. Victory depends on not only halting the survey but also delegitimizing the knowledge produced by it, a knowledge that depends on an a priori violence that the struggle renders visible.

In one of the few formal interviews in the film, a leader of the Hantai Dōmei draws an explicit connection between the struggles of the peasants in Vietnam against the United States and the militant tactics of the Japanese farmers against the dispossession of their land. The interview is intercut with footage of a large-scale clash with the police, which includes both long, static shots and jittery, handheld close-ups of protesters being beaten and arrested by the police. The sequence reaches a crescendo with a shot of protesters being pummeled by water cannons. Formally replicating the shot of the field battered by rain in the opening sequence, this protest sequence further reinforces the idea that the embattled landscape is but one of many sites of resistance to imperial domination. As the camera lens is drenched with water, we understand its position to be not of an indifferent observer but of an active participant in the struggle against the airport.

Like in *Columbia Revolt*, in *Sanrizuka no natsu*, the camera becomes one of many objects ready at hand that are transformed into instruments of struggle. Highlighting the importance of everyday objects, a sequence

Figure 12. Film still, field in the rain, *Sanrizuka no natsu* (1968).

focuses on participants gathering rocks in in a field, placing them in a pile, tossing them in the air, catching them, and fondling them with their hands in anticipation of a confrontation with the surveyors. Soon after, a long take of the interior of a shed pans rudimentary farming tools hung on the walls, which, although not in use, seem pregnant with a potential that is fulfilled in a later scene in which farmers and students march in formation holding the tools as weapons. Referencing a long tradition of peasant struggle, such scenes highlight the ways that the implements of quotidian life are adapted, put to new use in the being-in-struggle at work behind the barricades. At the moments when it is jostled, drenched by water cannons, its operator beaten and arrested by the police, we come to understand that the apparatus for recording events has also become part of the arsenal of the Hantai Dōmei.

As with *Columbia Revolt,* a discussion of the role of *Sanrizuka no natsu* within New Left and student struggles is incomplete without attending to its circulation and exhibition. Building on the practices developed with earlier Jeiso films, the organization of screenings of the Sanrizu-ka series was as much a part of the political work of the collective as

Figure 13. Film still, protesters being sprayed with water cannons, *Sanrizuka no natsu* (1968).

producing the films, and members traveled across the countryside forging connections and exhibiting the films with whatever was at hand, often using bedsheets in the place of proper screens.[66] Resembling Solanas and Getino's "film-acts," screenings were what Nornes describes as scenes of "amazing participatory spectatorship" in which "audiences clapped, booed, chanted, and sang."[67] The collective went so far as to hand out surveys after screenings to measure the effectiveness of the film as a vehicle for political mobilization that asked audience members questions like the following:

> Have you participated in the struggle to stop the Sanrizuka airport?
> From now on do you want to participate in the obstruction struggle and farming support activities?
> Do you support independent screenings?
> Do you feel like joining the organizing committee?[68]

The positive responses to the surveys indicate the capacity of the film to incite audiences to participate not only in the struggle at Sanrizuka but also in the political work of disseminating the film. Nornes attributes the power of the screenings as "activist acts" to their "kinesthetic quality built out of a gestural 'language' that is aesthetic *and* participatory. Through their own form of sensuous lyricism, the films constituted their audiences through a complex of interaction: cat calls, booing, clapping, flinching, crying."[69] Produced with these screenings in mind, *Sanrizuka no natsu* engages its audience in the co-constitution of alternative ways of affectively experiencing an ongoing series of events in the struggle against the airport, inviting them to enter a space of antagonism as an already-politicized collectivity. These spaces are an extension of the communal life being produced behind barricades, forged through antagonistic knowledge that resists the imperial logic of enclosure.

COMMUNAL LUXURY AND UNPAYABLE DEBT

In their communiqué on the Columbia strike referenced earlier, SDS reflects on the social and political space opened up within the occupied buildings:

> Life within the communes, as the liberated buildings were called, was a totally liberating experience for those inside, the core of the strike. Politics and life were integrated as the communards spent hour after hour discussing.... For many, the communal life within the buildings represented a break with their individualistic, isolated, fragmented lives as Columbia students: many talked of this as the most important experience of their lives, a new, beautiful, high.
>
> The goal of the action was kept in mind at all times—students were not only fighting for significant social (non-student) issues, they were not only uniting with those in the buildings, but with the oppressed of the world.[70]

By choosing the language of the communes and identifying students as communards, the communiqué speaks to the ways that the immediate histories of struggles (civil rights, Black Power movements, the Vietnam War) were woven together with distant histories (in this case, the Paris Commune) to construct a political imaginary within which the students of the New Left located themselves. This association with the communards by a group of mostly middle-class students might appear to us as trite or even as a farce. But before denouncing, off hand, their elected affinities and self-identification with events that unfolded in Paris a century earlier,

I want to pause to consider how the occupations discussed in this chapter might resonate with the practices and aspirations of the communards as Kristen Ross describes them in *Communal Luxury*. While noting the significant differences in the historical context and scale, the occupations discussed in this chapter, along with many others undertaken by New Left social movements, are what Ross refers to as "communal laborator[ies]" in which new orientations toward the world and one's place within it are articulated through and enabled by communal life.[71] The first striking resemblance between life behind the barricades in the New Left context and the Paris Commune as Ross describes it is the internationalist inclinations of each movement that contain within them an implicit rejection of the nation-state as a frame of reference. The Paris Commune, according to Ross, was "at once smaller and more expansive" than the nation-state: "the Communal imagination operated on the preferred scale of the local autonomous unit within an internationalist horizon."[72] For the Columbia students and surrounding community, a fight against a gymnasium and the occupation of university building were struggles that united them "with the oppressed of the world," while urging others to "create two, three, many Columbias," in reference to Che Guevara's statements on Vietnam.[73] The enemy of Sanrizuka farmers was not simply an unwanted airport proposed by the Japanese state but a world historical process of displacement and dispossession imagined by drawing analogies between their own efforts and resistance to colonial and imperial rule elsewhere. In each case, these communes were formed through an epistemological framing in which the subjects involved become "possessed by the dispossessed," in Harney's words, linked in speculative practice to struggles elsewhere seen through the lens of a general antagonism.[74] At the same time, they become dispossessed anew, experiencing a sense of dependency and the deterioration of the liberal self that the commune affords. Furthermore, each case is constituted by political subjectivities beyond the figure of industrial worker, supporting Joshua Clover's claim that "the commune is unthinkable without the modulation from traditional working class to an expanded proletariat."[75] In the struggles of the New Left, the student is one among other figures who battle against dispossession outside of the wage relation.

Moreover, communal life in each instance afforded opportunities to erode entrenched barriers that organize the daily life of study—town–country, university–neighborhood, mental–manual, individual–society, student–nonstudent, and art–life. Echoing her discussion of May 1968 considered in the previous chapter, Ross understands the inversion of "entrenched hierarchies and divisions," particularly manual and intellectual labor, to be the starting point for communal luxury.[76] For Ross, the development of the logic of communal luxury by communard Eugène Pottier was enabled by an epistemological inclination in which, as mentioned earlier, "anything that can be laid hold of can become a starting point for emancipation. You can start anywhere—you do not have to start at the beginning."[77] As I have suggested, cinema is one of these starting points for *Columbia Revolt* and *Sanrizuka no natsu*. Like a piece of farm equipment, a chair, a mimeograph machine, a steel drum, a gallon of milk, or a rock, its meaning is transformed within the barricades. In its capacity to organize sounds and images into arguments that generate affects and amplify antagonisms, cinema extends the life of the commune. Moreover, in participating in these occupations, the cinema itself becomes an occupation for its New Left practitioners or, better, a *pre*-occupation. In its deprofessionalized form, the cinema is not a vocation but a preoccupation where art and life blur. As a preoccupation, the cinema is a starting point for a new form of study, employed to organize ways of knowing and feeling that are grounded in an essayistic politics of the common.

In the spring and summer following the strike, the Columbia Strike Coordinating Committee organized an entire countercurriculum to expand the new knowledges that were forged as part of the strike. Seminars included subjects such as "Cuba: Its History and its Revolution, Homosexuality, . . . Economic Aspects of US Imperialism, Background of the Present Crisis in France, . . . Socioeconomic Functions of the University, Tenant Organizing, Guerrilla Filmmaking, the Disintegration of Bourgeois Cultural Hegemony, Afro-American History, Woman in American Society."[78] These courses offer a glimpse of how the political exigencies confronting the New Left helped to formulate new areas of inquiry that had been excluded from the university, with radical cinematic practice understood as an essential part of this alternative curriculum. This list also portends the way that New Left inquiry would challenge knowledge production within the university, as each of the courses offered in the alternative university morphed into new disciplines, subdisciplines, and interdisciplines as they entered university curriculums: women's studies, African American studies, cultural studies, LGBTQ studies, and so on. However, as Ferguson and others have argued, the hard-fought integration of these new questions and epistemological paradigms into university spaces both challenged those spaces and at the same time instigated new methods for policing minority difference. As Ferguson puts it, "affirmation and regulation become bound up with one another like never before, producing minority difference as a site of a new contradiction that straddled valorization and devaluation, change and status quo."[79] The recuperative and neutralizing power of the institution composes a large part of the contradictory legacy of the student New Left, with the multicultural, neoliberal "university of excellence" taking shape as a counterformation to resistance.

While policing minority difference, universities have also taken on a new role in the financial exploitation of the student. The attacks against capitalist institutions, especially institutions of higher learning, by the student New Left were followed by insidious forms of financial control leveled against student populations; it is worth noting that the United States and Japan are now the countries with the highest per capita student debt in the world. The financialization of student life in these countries, as I have suggested elsewhere, is a counterrevolutionary technique deployed against populations that disciplinary measures could not contain (a theme that I discuss at length in the following chapter).[80] I opened with Moten and Harney's conversation on debt and black study to think about the ways that new modes of study within New Left social movements generated the inverse of financial debt, a mutual and unpayable debt that is bound up with the communal luxury of life behind the barricades—however fragile or short-lived. These spaces of mutual debt subvert historical experiences of dispossession by making possible the affirmative dispossession of the self within collective life and the new values that arise from it. In what Colver describes as "a tactic that is also a form of life," the commune generates ways of knowing that flow from subjectivities intertwined in struggle.[81] The highly situated and antagonistic knowledges produced by these cinematic collectives are artifacts of what Gigi Roggero calls "militant inquiry" or "co-research," in which "it is only by taking a partial position that it becomes possible to understand the whole and transform it—that is, to organize the common."[82] How might this imperfect, essayistic, collaborative, and antagonistic knowledge endure in recent struggles against student debt, understood as battles against enclosure and accumulation by dispossession today?

In their widely circulated "Communiqué from an Absent Future," put out in 2009, students occupying the University of California, Santa Cruz take the "bankruptcy" of the university that produces the indebted student with no future as a starting point for an analysis of contemporary capitalism, calling for political formations based on "new kinds of collective bonds" that arise through occupation.[83] Citing a recent student occupation at the New School, the collective stresses that "occupation will be a critical tactic in our struggle," anticipating calls to "occupy" that would galvanize international disruptions two years later.[84] Signed "Research and Destroy," the communiqué situates militant inquiry as its defining character. Against increasing calls to neutralize study, to make it "practical," this militant inquiry implies the generation of a new system of valuation—communal luxury—that supplants financial debt. Aligning with what Annie McClanahan calls "crisis subjectivity," a knowledge born from "what it means to grapple with history as it happens, to acquire politics as it slowly emerges from history's mist," the Research and Destroy collective takes the bankruptcy of the present as an occasion for building new political movements and subjectivities.[85] In doing so, it repeats the tactics of the student New Left, but within a distinct historical framework. Drawing out these red threads, we should emphasize that the student was never outside of capital relations but remains situated, though differently, as a potential force in the struggle against them.

3

Finally Got the News at the End of the Short American Century

Time does not pass, it accumulates.
— IAN BAUCOM, *Specters of the Atlantic*

Force is the midwife of every old society which is pregnant with a new one. It is itself an economic power.
— KARL MARX, *Capital, Volume One*

"I don't think there's any doubt about the fact that as the automotive industry goes, so goes the city of Detroit, so goes this country," states an African American Chrysler executive in a matter-of-fact manner as his white colleague smokes a cigar nonchalantly and gazes at him with cool disinterest. From the other end of a long boardroom table, the executive continues, "Naturally, we lose money when we're not working, so it's for the best to be getting along. It eliminates lost time that is not necessary as far as we are concerned." The "getting along" he refers to is the congenial relationship between the management of the automotive industry and the United Auto Workers union, a relationship that, in his mind, "eliminates some of the problems we faced in the early years of unionism, and when you have an elimination of those problems it means for regular working. You don't have the wildcat stoppages, the strikes, and what have you."

This interview occurs midway though *Finally Got the News* (1970); it crystallizes the ideological position that the film's theses actively work to disrupt. Visually, the shot implies racial reconciliation within the sterile administration of a smoothly functioning industrial machine. However, this image, along with the discourse of "getting along," is besieged by a series of counterimages and arguments that refuse it. The ideological

Figure 14. Film still, interview with auto executives, *Finally Got the News* (1970).

position of the industry is embodied in both the ordered system of production suggested by framing of the shot and the tempered relationship
between management and organized labor that the executive expounds.
This image also captures the ways that we might envisage the Fordist
system in our collective memory of it and sometimes nostalgia for it.
Finally Got the News is nothing if not a refutation of such nostalgia; it is
a film, I argue, that compels us to revisit accepted narratives about how
we arrived at the present state of affairs.

Exemplary of New Left cinema's attention to labor struggles, particularly those that took place outside of the traditional labor unions, *Finally
Got the News* captures how new alliances, discourses, and temporalities
were born from these struggles. By way of an analysis of *Finally Got
the News* and its historical context, this chapter revisits the crisis of the
American automotive industry and Fordist industrial labor in the late 1960s
and early 1970s through the lens of the radical African American labor
organization at the heart of that industry. It demonstrates the capacity of
the New Left's essay film to both critique and intervene in larger historical

and economic transformations taking place during this period, seeking to further understand how these images of struggle endure in our present. Examining the refusal of industrial labor and its temporality in *Finally Got the News*, this chapter interrogates the broader theme of temporality within New Left cinema.

The executive's statement, "as the automotive industry goes, so goes the city of Detroit, so goes this country," is one that haunts us in the aftermath of the collapse of the industrial system of production in the United States. It is a truism of an era of capitalist organization that sought to reconcile a series of contradictions, contradictions that eventually led to its demise. If anything haunts this interview, however, it is the specter of the wildcat strike. The "natural" functioning of the Fordist system of production demands that time *not be lost,* and the wildcat is nothing if not the entrance of lost time into production—the disruption of production by a time that is "not necessary" from the standpoint of the industrial capitalist.

When asked during the interview if he is aware of the activities of the Revolutionary Union Movements, the executive nervously concedes that he is, but quickly adds,

> Our contract is with the UAW/CIO; this is Mr. Walter Reuther's big union. As far as the Revolutionary Union Movement is concerned, we know that it exists but as far as knowing any of the details, how strong they are, how many members, what have you, we haven't bothered with that. We have a contract with the UAW/CIO and these are the people we deal with.

His equivocal discounting of the radical African American labor organization operating outside the recognized activities of the UAW elides the fact that during the years leading up to this interview, the Revolutionary Union Movement had initiated a series of wildcat strikes, reintroducing the very problem of "unnecessary, lost time" into the automotive industry that the executive wishes to relegate to a distant past.

Finally Got the News disallows this containment of struggle in the "early years" of unionism by forcing struggle back into the image of the Fordist system of production as a whole. As the executive sits smugly after dismissing the Revolutionary Union Movement, the boardroom is taken over by the sound of nondiegetic voices chanting, "Black workers power!" Disrupting the smooth temporality of the Fordist assembly line, the emergence of radical, anti-UAW labor organization registered the introduction of a new temporality onto the scene of the "American Century." While this temporality can be likened to the "unnecessary" time of the wildcat, *Finally Got the News* also reveals a deeper kind of "lost time" in the transition between industrial modernity and our present—a time that only appears to be "lost" when looked at from a limited historical perspective.

DETROIT, A CAPITAL OF THE SHORT AMERICAN CENTURY

Like the cinema of the Old Left, New Left cinema was deeply invested in the figure of the worker—the industrial worker in particular. Like other New Left cinematic movements, films shot within and alongside worker's movements aspired to facilitate political alliances and mobilization. Among the numerous examples of groups that endeavored to advance worker's struggles were Mexico's Coperativa de Cine Marginal, which produced Super 8mm films in the late 1960s that were vehicles for political communication among worker unions; the Les groupes Medvedkine and their participatory experiments with factory workers discussed in the first chapter; Italian Collettivo Cinema Militante di Torino's *La fabbrica aperta* (The open factory, 1971); and the British Berwick Street Collective's *Nightcleaners* (1975), in addition to familiar examples such as the Dziga Vertov group's *British Sounds* (1969).[1] The relationship between workers and New Left filmmakers, often representatives of the petite bourgeoisie, was tenuous at times, as we will see. Nevertheless, in the work of these collectives and others, one can draw out a set of themes taking shape in labor movements that reflect a broader tendency toward autonomy and horizontalization within worker's struggles; new alliances with groups outside of the workplace, such as students; and the foregrounding of figures, such as migrants and women, that challenged the hegemony of the white, male worker. In the case of *Finally Got the News,* the challenge to traditional forms of organized labor comes by way of the autonomous organization of black workers in the auto industry. As the epicenter of an entire system of industrial production that had ruled the postwar global economy, the confrontation with the auto industry in Detroit captured in *Finally Got the News* provides a lens into the ways that the New Left and its cinema engaged with the crisis of that system of production.

How can a place and time come to embody the contradictions of an era of capitalism, and how do these contradictions endure beyond that time and place? In *Specters of the Atlantic,* Ian Baucom grapples with these questions through his provocative thesis: "Liverpool, a Capital of the Long Twentieth Century."[2] With this statement, Baucom proposes a historical condensation that places the eighteenth-century slave trade within our present. More importantly, Baucom's thesis weds Walter Benjamin's historical materialism—contained in his statement "Paris, capital of the nineteenth century"—with Giovanni Arrighi's understanding of cycles of capital accumulation, the "Long Twentieth Century," oscillating periods of commodity production (MC) and financial expansion (CM) that move from the fifteenth century through the end of the twentieth. Significant for Baucom is the way that, in the *Arcades Project,* Benjamin locates the allegorical form of the nineteenth century associated with the burgeoning commodity culture in the seventeenth century and, thus, develops a materialist theory of repetition in the relationship between these two historical moments: "the nineteenth century does not repeat the seventeenth in some attenuated or residual form. Rather, the later moment repeats the earlier by intensifying it, expanding it."[3]

Together, both Benjamin's and Arrighi's theories of historical repetition within the cycles of capitalist expansion form the historical scaffolding Baucom uses to produce a theory about what lies between the seventeenth and nineteenth centuries: the eighteenth century, the transatlantic slave trade, and the inauguration of modern finance. Baucom argues that this period is both repeated and intensified today; it is the historical precursor that is imbedded and expanded in our present. In other words, our hyperfinancialized present amplifies the eighteenth century and the new "speculative discourses" of insurance and credit developed in places like Liverpool; it stands in "nonsynchronous contemporaneity" with that moment.[4] It is for this reason that Baucom declares Liverpool "a capital of the long twentieth century."

Keeping Baucom's notion of historical repetition and intensification in mind, I change the scale of historical analysis and look not at the deep cyclical time that finds the origin of our present in the eighteenth century but instead at what we might think of as our immediate prehistory. Using Baucom's nonlinear framework as a starting point, this chapter considers not the Long Twentieth Century but what we instead might call the short American Century, whose capital was, arguably, Detroit. Paramount to Fredric Jameson's periodization of postmodernism is the end of the American Century, which, he suggests, spanned the period from 1945 to 1973 and "constituted the hothouse, or forcing ground, of the new system."[5] Characterized much more by a logic of historicist periodization borrowed from Ernst Mandel than by a theory of cyclical accumulation and repetition as that which defines Arrighi's history of capital, Jameson locates the origins of postmodernism in the various crises that occurred in the early 1970s, including the end of the gold standard and the proliferation of international wars of liberation.[6] Of consequence is Jameson's understanding of the American Century as the "hothouse" that ushers the postmodern era into being; however, I take issue with how it functions as the "forcing ground" for our present.

Finally Got the News is a film that, as I argue, provides insight into temporalities of historical transformation and repetition. It offers its own historical and theoretical account of the period we might call the "American Century," its emergence, decline, and the implications of understanding it to be the "forcing ground" of contemporary capitalism. How might a periodization of the short American Century fit within, while further expanding and complicating, Baucom's and Jameson's historical narratives regarding the origins of our present? In answering this question, I argue that we must insert a theorization of historical *transition*—an adequate assessment of the rupture that lies between industrial capitalism and our financialized present. To do so, I retheorize the transition from the American Century through the crisis in its capital: Detroit. Specifically, through an account of *Finally Got the News* and its historical context, I reinsert an image of struggle into our understanding of this transition, exploring both the process and the temporality of historical transition from the standpoint of struggle. To do so, I analyze how *Finally Got the News* portends the breakdown of the Keynesian pact between capital and labor that defined the American Century, which entailed the dual stabilization of the global monetary order in the wake of the collapse of the 1930s and the brief stabilization of relations between capital and labor following an intensive period of labor militancy.[7] An artifact of this transitional period, *Finally Got the News* is a film through which to analyze the disintegration of both a monetary and a productive order. Moreover, this chapter explores the temporalities of struggle embedded within New Left cinema, asking how these temporalities endure, how they exist in a "nonsynchronous contemporaneity" with the present.

In defining the contours of this historical narrative, we will need to tell yet another story, or perhaps a story within a story, of the short American Century and the Keynesian pact between capital and labor. This account grounds itself in the history of the U.S. auto industry, which is, at the same time, the history of Detroit. The dates that bookend my story likewise frame Jameson's historical periodization. In a version of the narrative told from the perspective of labor struggles in Detroit, the American Century begins with Ford's recognition of the United Auto Workers union in 1941 and the subsequent election of Walter Reuther as president of the UAW in 1946, leading to the "golden age" of American unionism. The century ends with a series of events: the wildcat strikes of the late 1960s and early 1970s, the official split of the League of Revolutionary Black Workers from the UAW in 1971, and the subsequent crisis and reordering of the American auto industry around 1974. As *Finally Got the News* demonstrates, Detroit is the capital of the short American Century because of its intensive confrontation with and inability to resolve the contradictions of race and class in the industrial age.

To trace the history of African American workers within the U.S. auto industry is to trace a narrative that runs counter to the prevailing one often told of the Fordist era of production. Ford was the first auto manufacturer to systematically integrate his workforce, and Ford's method of hiring and maintaining control over black workers demonstrates the extent to which the paternalism ingrained into the southern plantation system was perpetuated within the industrial era.[8] Ford's paternalistic rule over the black community was only broken with the victory of the

UAW in 1941, after more than a decade of struggle. However, as David M. Lewis-Colman argues, the relationship between black workers and the union from its inception could be described, at best, as an "ambivalent solidarity."[9] The persistence of dynamics of segregation within the American Century that defined the early industrial period were compounded by the UAW's exploitation of racial hierarchies to contain radical politics among its ranks.[10] The systematic scapegoating of black radicals throughout the Cold War allowed for Walter Reuther to both consolidate his power over the more left-leaning sections of the union and at the same time exploit "the vacuum caused by the demise of independent black radicalism to implement a more moderate civil rights agenda for the union."[11] "Racial liberalism" is the name Lewis-Colman gives to the strategy by which the UAW simultaneously contained influence of the black leadership while exerting a liberal, anticommunist agenda. Over the late 1940s and early 1950s, this strategy ultimately produced what Lewis-Colman describes as the "triumph of racial liberalism."

This triumph became a defining characteristic of the Keynesian pact between capital and labor at the center of the auto industry, explaining how it is that the UAW became a lever for the liberal control of industrial labor in America. In his 1963 book *The American Revolution: Pages from a Negro Worker's Notebook,* James Boggs laments the deradicalization of the union movement in Detroit in the postwar era, in which, he argues, "the struggle was shifted from the plane of relations on the job to the economic plane," a phenomenon that I discuss in more detail later.[12] Nonetheless, the "triumph" of racial liberalism in Detroit was short-lived. A generation of young black workers and students began to organize in the early 1960s, forming groups such as UHURU, whose political rhetoric directly countered the platform of racial liberalism that the union advanced. While in the early 1940s the coalition between the UAW and black workers was formed through an "ambivalent solidarity," the new black radicalism emerging in the 1960s "expressed no ambivalence about their loyalty to race or union" and "had little attachment to their workplaces and a great deal of hostility toward the UAW."[13] Whereas the contradictions of race were exploited in the formation of the liberal organization of industrial labor, these same contradictions would soon prove to expedite its crisis.

Though we often attribute the birth of the postmodern—aesthetically, politically, and theoretically—to events of May 1968 in Paris, one could argue that the events that occurred simultaneously in Detroit equally signal the disintegration of industrial modernity. Following a series of wildcat strikes at Dodge Main in 1967 and the early part of 1968, the legacy of black radicalism that had been continually repressed by the UAW came to the forefront of activity within the plants. On May 2, 1968, a wildcat strike broke out that, over the course of several days, grew into the largest work stoppage the factory had seen in decades. While the wildcat was instigated by a group of white women, and the picket line was honored by the majority of workers at the plant, "when the strike ended several days later, the company discharged and suspended black workers disproportionately."[14] With little protection offered to blacks by the UAW, management reenacted the strategy of containment for radical activities within the plants by targeting and punishing black workers. This strategy only further catalyzed radical movements, both inside and outside of the plants. Immediately after the strike, the Dodge Revolutionary Union Movement (DRUM) was formed, the first of numerous Revolutionary Union Movements to spring up in Detroit that would eventually consolidate into the League of Revolutionary Black Workers.

The May 1968 strike and subsequent formation of DRUM indicates the beginning of the end of the racial liberalism that had been foundational to the liberal consolidation of power within the UAW and what had become of the Fordist mode of production. The formation of DRUM signaled the crisis of the strategy of both racial and radical containment pursued initially by Ford and later taken up—in a tempered and transmuted form—by the UAW. As Dan Georgakas and Marvin Surkin write in their seminal account of the rise and fall of the League of Black Revolutionary Workers, the May 1968 wildcat and the formation of DRUM caught the attention of global financial markets:

> No less an authority than the *Wall Street Journal* took them [DRUM] seriously from the day of the first wildcat, for the *Wall Street Journal* understood something most of the white student radicals did not yet understand: the black revolution of the 1960s had finally arrived at one of

the most vulnerable links in the American economic system—the point of mass production, the assembly line.[15]

Among the workers suspended after the wildcat was General Baker, a young black radical. In an open letter to the Chrysler Corporation to protest his dismissal in the aftermath of the May 1968 wildcat, Baker writes,

> Yes, the struggle between black workers and white racist Corporation owners and operators is the most vicious of all existing struggles in the world today. . . . Let it be further understood that by taking the course of disciplining the strikers you have opened that struggle to a new and higher level and for this I sincerely THANK YOU. You have made the decision to battle me and therefore to do battle with the entire black community in this city, this state, this country, and in this world of which I am a part.[16]

After signing the letter with both his name and his employee number, Baker adds the following postscript: "You have lit the unquenchable spark."[17]

The "unquenchable spark" lit by the events of Detroit's May 1968 was both a repetition and intensification of the struggles of the "early years" of the UAW, evident in the union's attempt to contain activity that was both radical and unsanctioned by UAW central authority through the isolation and punishment of black radicals. The formation of DRUM, at the same time, signals the escalation of resistance to liberalism as a strategy of containment. As Baker writes, Chrysler's reaction to the wildcat "opened that struggle to a new and higher level."

In this sense, the repetition and intensification of the beginning of the American Century as it comes to an end is not only the reiteration of forms of containment and discipline but also the escalation of resistance to them. Thus, on the eve of the new financial order in which we now find ourselves, an order that Baucom argues is a repetition and intensification of the eighteenth century, we find another repetition and intensification that bookend the short *durée* directly preceding it. To the extent that it exemplified the conclusion of a cycle of struggles, the end of the short American Century in its capital became, in Jameson's words, the "forcing ground of the new system."

"ENDURING IMAGES": FINALLY, BUT WITHOUT FINALITY

While Ian Baucom draws a great deal on Benjamin's *Arcades Project* to produce his notion of historical repetition in *Specters of the Atlantic,* he ultimately departs from Benjamin by rejecting his understanding of the historical image outlined in the "Theses on the Philosophy of History." Pulling from a number of writers whose work argues for the centrality of the the middle passage in the formation of modernity, such as Paul Gilroy and Édouard Glissant, Baucom elaborates on his thesis that time does not simply "pass" but instead "accumulates." In generating this theory of history, Ian Baucom leans on the work of Glissant to develop a concept of the "enduring image":

> Where Benjamin's flashing image thus brings to light something to know and something to dream (the total if impossible coming of an ethical and redemptive modernist knowledge of history), Glissant's images reveal something to endure, something which itself endures, or more resonantly, something which accumulates: time.[18]

For Baucom, Glissant offers a more thoroughly materialist understanding of a historical image, or better yet, an image of history. While both Benjamin and Glissant provide ways of thinking a historical image outside the logic of representation, Glissant's ultimately points to the possibility for an enduring, nonlinear notion of time contained within the image itself. Benjamin's image of history implies the redemption of the accumulated historical wreckage and violence. Glissant, on the other hand, understands the historical image not as the redemption of the past but as its persistence. These images endure in that they are inseparable from the birth of modernity, in the sense that "the slave trade refuses to detach itself from slavery, nor the slave ship from the plantation, nor the plantation from the ghetto and the shantytown."[19] The historical image that endures is also the historical image that repeats: "if it moves toward the future it does so by doubling back on what has been."[20] An image that endures can be neither a flash nor an instant but the "doubling back" on what is accumulated within it, that history which is inseparable from it. Baucom's conception of the enduring image complements the Deleuzian time-image discussed in the introduction by proposing a nonlinear and materialist conception of historical repetition, one that foregrounds the density of time that "accumulates" in the image.

An enduring image of the American Century is the image of Detroit, and more specifically, it is the image of struggle that repeats and intensifies at the end of the period. *Finally Got the News* captures this very image. An essay film on and by the League of Revolutionary Black Workers, *Finally Got the News* is composed of a series of interviews, found and filmed footage, which not only documents the activities of the League but also forwards a number of historical and political theses regarding the place of black labor in the history of modernity, as well as its central position in the struggle against exploitation under industrial capitalism. Produced within the first two years of the League's short history, the film's depiction of this history is, by constitution, open and unfinished. It comes into being, like the essay films discussed throughout this book, as an artifact of the movement, embodying the dynamics of the struggle from which it was born. It does so both in the open form of its composition and in the collective process of its production, the latter of which I discuss in the next section.

The opening montage of *Finally Got the News* is of particular interest here because it tells, in a more precise manner, the story of the status of African American labor in the short American Century and its place within the Long Twentieth Century. Unlike the remainder of the film, which uses voice-offs from interviews with prominent League figures to make its arguments, the opening sequence is composed of a montage of still images that tell the prehistory of the League. The film begins by panning an illustration of slave children and then an advertisement that reads "Negroes for Sale," followed by images of slave auctions and photographs of plantations and sharecroppers. A second series of images include a montage of photographs of factories in the 1930s and 1940s, strikes, and Walter Reuther speaking to a group of workers, before zooming in on a still image of a banner hung outside of the Dodge factory that reads "Victory is ours!" followed by a single "?" *Finally Got the News* begins by placing the idea of racial reconciliation within Fordism under question, bringing the weight of the history of what Cedric Robinson called "racial capitalism" to bear on its present.[21]

Figure 15. Film still, factory worker, *Finally Got the News* (1970).

Thus *Finally Got the News* outlines a historical narrative that frames its engagement with the League's activities. It refuses to allow the image of the factory to detach from the image of slavery. Without putting the two into equivalence, the film demonstrates that slavery's image endures within the factory, and it frames the struggles within it. The sequence highlights the contradictions inherent in labor struggles of the 1940s, disputing the pronouncement that "Victory is ours!"—which declares the triumph of the UAW—by casting uncertainty on the narrative of the alleged victory of the working class at the inception of the American Century. It throws into doubt not only what this victory claims but also who composes this "ours" to which it applies. Through this sequence, we come to understand that the "ours" to which the victory is attributed is only formed through a constituent exclusion.

The opening montage concludes with footage of the 1967 Detroit riots, otherwise known as the Great Rebellion. Through a graphic match, the sequence juxtaposes footage of a black worker shoveling coal into a furnace with footage of the city of Detroit in flames. The visual continuity

Figure 16. Film still, buildings burning during the Detroit Rebellion, *Finally Got the News* (1970).

of these images produces a rupture between the interior and the exterior of the factory, and Detroit becomes a site of conjoined urban and industrial crises. While the image of the factory constantly refers to that which is outside itself temporally, it is also related to that which is outside itself spatially, its own upheavals repeated in the urban center of Detroit. After footage of the riots, police brutality, and the city in a state of chaos and destruction, the title of the film appears over the last image in the montage, a still photograph of a black man pressed up against a tank with the letters "U.S.A." prominently displayed on its side while a white national guardsman points a gun at him: "Finally got the news..." The title of the film comes from a slogan used by the League of Revolutionary Black Workers, "Finally got the news, how your dues being used," referring to the League's outward hostility toward the UAW.[22] While the image documents an instance of state violence, urban crisis, and racial inequity, the text directly links these crises to the breakdown of "ambivalent solidarity" within the UAW. What "*finally*" happens is not a messianic revelation of

Figure 17. Film still, film title and man being held at gunpoint during the Detroit Rebellion, *Finally Got the News* (1970).

the news, a moment of totality or historical reconciliation; it is rather the intensive moment where the accumulation of images of historical violence is contained in a single image, an image that signals the beginning of the end of the American Century.

The photograph that concludes the film's opening montage was taken from an issue of *Life* magazine devoted to the Detroit riots that appeared on August 4, 1967, of which the cover read, "Negro Revolt: The Flames Spread." Appearing in an article titled "City at the Blazing Heart of a Nation in Disorder," the caption of the photograph claims that the man being held at gunpoint is an arson suspect. Placed within such an inflammatory context, the man in this image comes to stand for the hidden pyromania at the center of what appears to be the spontaneous combustion of the country. He is roving in the dark, alone, setting fires that defy rationality; he is the epitome of the uncontainable minority that threatens to ignite the American way of life, its "unquenchable spark."

Finally Got the News wrests the alleged arsonist from the image of arbitrary violence he had come to occupy in popular discourse and re-frames him within the nuanced political theses that the opening montage advances. For *Finally Got the News,* the Great Rebellion cannot be under-stood without taking into account the racialized violence of the industrial mode of production. By juxtaposing images of the Great Rebellion with footage from the factory, the film implies that the flames of the factory have engulfed the city and that the forty-three civilian deaths that occurred during the riots were an extension of the coercive violence occurring every day within the plants. In doing so, *Finally Got the News* insists on the intimate connection between struggles at the point of production, the strike, and struggles that take place within the spaces of reproduction, the "social factory," which is the city of Detroit.[23]

While hardly the first in the city, the 1967 riots came as a shock to the nation. With the liberal urban renewal policies pursued under the admin-istration of mayor Jerome Cavanaugh, Detroit was heralded as "a racial model," the "All American City," and was lauded by the popular press and academic circles alike.[24] However, strategies of urban renewal were merely an extension of the strategies of "racial liberalism" that were carried on within the factories.[25] The reorganization of the urban environment by the policies of "urban renewal" in Detroit only intensified an urbanism that continually reproduced a concentrated, segregated, and dependent labor pool from which the auto industry could draw. In addition to the growing outrage around police brutality and the increased militancy of the black community exhibited by groups like UHURU and the Revolutionary Ac-tion Movement, the riots also signaled a rejection of the practices of urban restructuring in the city around the compromise of racial liberalism that had been undertaken within the plants themselves. Though the rebellions in Watts and Newark had already shaken white America, images of the Great Rebellion that spread throughout the popular news media exposed the volatility of "racial liberalism" in the heart of urban industrialism. They obliterated Detroit's image as a model of racial reconciliation by delivering the news of its crisis.

In his reflection on the wave of riots that had swept the country in the late 1960s, H. Rap Brown makes a point that drives home the significance of these upheavals:

Take the Washington, D.C., rebellion, for instance. They arrested something like 3,000 people and when they booked 'em, they found out that the great majority of them worked for the government. Had jobs, making money, still these were dudes who were out on the street. In Detroit it was the same thing. It wasn't only the unemployed brother. It was the one who was bringing home $110 every Friday. It was the one who has a Thunderbird, and some clean vines. He was the one who had tried to enter white america [*sic*] and had found that no matter what he did, he was still a nigger to the white man.[26]

The riots, in other words, were a symptom of a broader recognition that hard work and the wage were utterly insufficient strategies to escape from racial caste. In the auto industry, being black did not only mean being excluded from union representation; it meant being exposed to daily violence. In *Detroit: I Do Mind Dying,* Georgakas and Surkin cite a report on death and injury within the plants that expresses, more than perhaps any other statistic, the quotidian violence of the lives of workers. The report, which came out in 1973, estimated that in America alone, there were at least "65 on-the-job deaths per day among auto workers, for a total of some 16,000 annually," and these figures do not even take into account illness and death caused by long-term exposure to chemicals and other hazardous conditions within the plants: "Even these limited figures made it clear that more auto workers were killed or injured each year on the job than soldiers were killed or injured during any year of the war in Vietnam."[27] Furthermore, as both *Finally Got the News* and *Detroit: I Do Mind Dying* emphasize, this workplace violence was most often visited on those sections of workers who were segregated to the most grueling and dangerous parts of the plant, such as the foundry—areas with the highest concentration of black workers.

These statistics, whether or not they accurately reflect the death toll within the factories, provide a possibility for reframing, or perhaps literalizing, the New Left demand, explored in previous chapters, to "bring the war home." Kristen Ross suggests that the Vietnam War provided the conditions for "the emergence of a new political subjectivity passed by way of the Other, and this figure of the other in '68 is first and foremost that of the Other who defines political modernity: the worker."[28] The Vietnam war against American imperialism, Ross argues, was an actuality through which the figure of the worker had to pass to occupy a new revolutionary subjectivity, as was evidenced by the slogan of Fiat workers in Turin in the late 1960s: "Vietnam is in our factories."[29] As we saw in the previous chapters, the production of a new political subjectivity demanded an identification with the figure of Third World revolution, and this identification was necessary to affirm a new militant position by the industrial worker of the First World because "it was the North Vietnamese peasant, and not the auto worker in Billancourt, who had become, for many French militants, the figure of the working class."[30] Undeniably, establishing a sense of political urgency and militancy around the violence of quotidian life under industrial capitalism often necessitated this type of political identification with Third World struggles. However, as the statistics regarding workplace deaths make clear, the autoworker in Detroit, while *loin de Vietnam,* did not need to imagine the direct violence of everyday life as existing elsewhere: for many black Americans, the Third World already existed within the First.

Drawing together the Great Rebellion and the factory, the image of the "arsonist" expresses the complicated temporal and spatial relations that the opening montage articulates. While the civilian appears to have "finally got the news," the news being delivered at gunpoint, the ellipses suggest a lack of finality, an indeterminacy. Accumulated within this image is a density of time, and the text "finally got the news . . ." opens up the image to all of the political, spatial, and temporal dimensions that unhinge it from linear temporality. This image of violence at the end of the American Century endures today, and the attempt to make this enduring quality of this racial violence *matter* is again at the center of a politics of cultural resistance. It endures, in particular, in places like Ferguson, Missouri, and across the country, where images of the highly militarized policing of minority populations repeat and intensify the image of a man against a tank with a gun at his back. As Jordan T. Camp correctly argues, the escalating discourse of "law and order" that followed moments like the Detroit Rebellion constructs "domestic enemies against which the neoliberal project of expanding police and prisons has defined itself."[31] In addition to its persistence in the growth of the neoliberal state that profits from police brutality and incarceration, I argue that this image also endures in the reconfiguration of capital itself as it tried to recover from the crisis of the American Century.

POWER, PRODUCTION, AND THE "PROCESS OF BECOMING AN IMAGE"

The Detroit riots of summer 1967 disrupted a liberal system that functioned through the normalization of quotidian, racial violence. In this section, I turn my attention to activity in the plants and the intensive period of struggle and transition in Detroit that began with the riots of 1967 and ended with the comprehensive crisis and restructuring of the American automotive industry in the mid-1970s. Produced in the center of this moment of transition, 1969–70, *Finally Got the News* provides a forceful analytic through which to approach labor militancy in the auto industry. While the opening montage emphasizes the multiple and overlapping temporalities of violence and struggle that have endured since slavery, in the scenes I discuss next, the film focuses on the temporal rhythms of daily labor. In doing so, it underscores a central political project of the League, which was to subvert what Boggs had previously identified as the union's shifting of the struggle "from the plane of relations on the job to the economic plane." Returning the struggle to "the plane of relations," *Finally Got the News* further highlights the ways difference is central to mapping out an essayistic politics of the common within New Left cinema.

Before turning to the film and political struggles in the plants, let me note that I am not the first to argue for the significance of *Finally Got the News* as a cinematic text that captures the political problematics crucial to understanding our present era. In *Postmodernism*, Fredric Jameson claims that the League's activity, while constituting "the single most important political experience of the American 1960s," came to a surprisingly "undramatic end."[32] Jameson reads the League's short history as symptomatic of the constitutive failure of postmodern political organization, too bound to the *particularity* of Detroit to bring together a complex set of global contingencies into a coherent and sustained political project. The League, in short, was incapable of "mapping a totality."

Finally Got the News, for Jameson, is indicative of an ambitious media strategy undertaken by the League that expedited its ultimate political failure. According to Jameson, when members of the League traveled to Europe to promote the film and connect with other militant groups, particularly in Italy, members were alienated from their constituencies in the process of becoming "media stars."[33] Though the narration of these events is debatable, Jameson concludes from them that, "in the process of becoming an image and a spectacle, the referent [the League] seems to have disappeared as so many people from Debord to Baudrillard have warned us."[34] That is, the image—dialectically opposed to the League— managed to consume its revolutionary fervor and, in its devious nature, lured the militants into a fantasy of power while undermining the actual movement. In this account, *Finally Got the News* is exemplary of the failure of New Left politics and aesthetics to produce a viable political project.

In his discussion of *Finally Got the News,* Fred Moten counters Jameson's reading of the film by arguing that it presents not an image of totality but rather a "tonality of totality."[35] Moten reads the use of sound in the film, particularly a voice-over by League member Kenneth Cockrel (which I discuss at length in the next section), as that which interrupts Jameson's "occularcentric" notion of totality, providing an important rejoinder to Jameson's account by placing the film firmly within the African American aesthetic tradition.[36] In addition to Jameson's "occularcentric" understanding of totality so deftly subverted in Moten's reading, I want to emphasize more fundamental problems in Jameson's reading of *Finally Got the News* and his argument that it embodies a kind of strategic aporia of politics in postmodernity. Jameson's recourse to Debord's theory of the spectacle as a way to read the "process of becoming an image" within New Left political movements presents us with a notion that, in the process of making a political movement visually legible in the form of a film, the League was itself degraded. This argument hinges on the implicit assumption that aesthetic artifacts stand outside of, and are ontologically separate from, the social movements from which they arise, an assumption, I would argue, that blinds us to the ways aspects of the struggle are woven into the very fabric of the film.

A recounting of the tumultuous production of *Finally Got the News* allows us to highlight the fact that the "process of becoming an image" was in no way uniform but rather was shot through with the material contradictions that make up the conditions of possibility for any particular enunciation, in this case, a cinematic image. Coming out of the Newsreel movement, the story of the production of *Finally Got the News,* like *Columbia Revolt* discussed in the previous chapter, reveals implicit contradictions that New Left cinema faced in the U.S. context. According to Georgakas and Surkin, members of the New York Newsreel collective initiated production of the film to be modeled on similar films about the Black Panthers made by the California contingent of the collective, namely, *Black Panther: Off the Pig!* A portion of the white, mostly student filmmakers were keenly interested in the vanguardism of Panther politics and openly criticized the autonomist worker organization of the League, taking it to be a less-advanced model of political action in black America.[37] Many members of the League resented the filmmakers' paternalistic intentions and did much to resist and subvert their efforts to document the League's activities. The League, itself a complex and heterogeneous political coalition, was never in full agreement as to the production of the film.[38] The film was, from the beginning, not a self-evident expression of the League's desire to "represent" itself as a unity but was always already fraught with internal race, class, and strategic discrepancies. These dynamics came into relief in 1970 when members of the League began to tire of the presence of the white filmmakers and their alliance with the Black Panthers: "the radical forces within the city became increasingly annoyed that a small group with no local membership base and no local work continued to advocate projects contrary to the wishes and detrimental to the safety of local activists."[39] As Chris Robé argues, these external pressures were combined with internal strife around sexism within the collective and led to the collapse of the Detroit Newsreel.[40] The League, in turn, seized the collective's equipment.[41] In an act that can only be described as an overthrowing of cinematic authorship, the League took control of the cinematic means of production and set the project again in motion, but in a direction befitting their vision, using the seized equipment and footage under a new organization, Black Star Productions. They enlisted a few of the remaining members of the Newsreel collective to help finish the film.[42]

Newsreel member Peter Gessner reflected on the film's production in 1972:

> I think *Finally Got the News* represents both a breaking of new ground and simultaneously an end post of some kind. At the same time it signals the end of white filmmakers making films about other people's struggles, it re-opens a whole area and direction long ignored by the New-Left—that of the lives and importance of working people in this country.[43]

Gessner's commentary on the turbulent inception of *Finally Got the News* rightly sees the film as a microcosm of various struggles happening within New Left cinema at the time.[44] While the film certainly did not indicate "the end of white filmmakers making films about other people's struggles," it did invert the power relations implicit within this statement. Born out of a rejection of political strategies imposed by primarily white institutions (be it the UAW or the Newsreel collective), *Finally Got the News* comes to typify the ways that the New Left cinema struggled with representational hierarchies. It did so by wresting the film from a mode of production that implicitly reproduced the racial hierarchies that the League sought to undermine. In contrast to Jameson's characterization of the relationship between the film and the League, I read *Finally Got the News* to be a productive failure of the *essai* (attempt) of the Newsreel Collective to negotiate difference within the crucible of Detroit at the end of the American Century. Out of this failure comes an essay, an open cinematic form that, at every moment, contends with the contradictions of cinematic representation, as they are witnessed by the audiovisual content of the film and as they are embedded in the material history of its production. In this sense, *Finally Got the News* exemplifies the New Left's essay film in that the process of its production was put on trial; it was interrupted by historical forces entrenched within the struggle it sought to engage.[45]

In both its political message and in the process of its production, *Finally Got the News* is a film that sought to return labor struggles to "the plane of relations," that is, to the political power of workers to struggle over production and to autonomously represent themselves in that struggle. As a part of this political project, the League's activities must be seen as integral to a much larger series of upheavals occurring within the Fordist system of production in the postwar era. As wages and benefits became the primary terms over which the UAW bargained by the early 1960s, Boggs argued that the UAW had betrayed the workers by giving "back to management every right over production won in the movement of the 1930s and the war years."[46] Making clear that "man does not live on bread alone," Boggs insists that "workers use the wildcat as a defensive weapon to fight off encroachment on their control at the point of production."[47] An affront to both management and the union, the wildcats of the late 1960s and early 1970s were an attack on an entire mode of production that had, while increasing wages, undermined the political power of workers. In their 1975 essay "Crisis in the Auto Sector," Peter Linebaugh and Bruno Ramirez demonstrate the principal role the auto industry played in American capitalism at the time, noting that as of 1974, the auto sector held one-sixth of all the jobs in the United States, one-sixth of the gross national product.[48] The fact that "a sixth of every retail dollar was locked into the auto industry" meant that the outbreak of the work stoppages that occurred in American auto plants spanning from 1967 to 1971—the highest cycle of stoppages in postwar history—had devastating effects for the U.S. economy.[49]

Linebaugh and Ramirez examine these stoppages in the context of the auto industry's strategy of "niggermation," or the intensive acceleration of productive outputs that resulted from compulsory overtime and speedups on the line. While the discourse within the industry attributed augmented outputs to innovations in the "automation" of the production process, the term *niggermation* was used by workers within the plants to ascribe increases in productive output due to the worsening of labor conditions. It was against these production speedups and horrific safety conditions that most of the autonomous organization within the industry was directed, and the term *niggermation* implies a deep sense of racial injustice contained within the workers' rejection of the industry's strategy for increasing profits. Out of the "violence of technology" came a new form of workplace violence: the "growing armament of both the working class and the union."[50]

The increasing militancy within the plants was, as Boggs suggested, a struggle not over the wage relation but over the question of work itself. This fact was echoed in the demands of workers on the third day of the 1974 wildcats that took place within the Dodge plants in Warren, Michigan: "They asked for 'everything'; one worker said 'I just don't want to *work.*' The separation between income and productivity, enforced by the struggle, could not have been clearer."[51] The increased militancy within the auto industry at the end of the American Century detached itself from the wage demands, and the rash of wildcats was exemplary of the general crisis of the UAW's control over labor organization within the plants. Moreover, these struggles expressed the rejection of a form of life defined by industrial production—they were an outright assault on a Fordism that compelled the sacrifice of life and limb. The wildcat strikes of the late 1960s and early 1970s were a refusal of the violence of work under the disciplinary regime of industrial capitalism, striking the industrial system, in America and elsewhere, at the point of production.

The 1967–73 strategy of speedup is a focal point of critique in *Finally Got the News.* The film depicts the factory as a site of violence and terror, one that demands the very life of the worker. After the opening montage discussed in the previous section, the film commences with the advent of the working day in Detroit with the stark silhouette of a man standing in the cold dawn, waiting to be picked up for work. As a car pulls up, and the worker gets in, Joe L. Carter's song "Detroit, I Do Mind Dying" begins to play nondiegetically. The lyrics reverberate through the drive to work, accompanied by a montage of images of an industrial landscape defined by the automobile. Over footage of factories and cars, Carter, a Ford employee, sings in a drawn-out, soulful Motown style, "Please mister foreman, slow down the assembly line, I don't mind workin', but I do mind dyin'." The footage of the ride to work functions as allegory of a quotidian existence defined by the automobile. The city is revealed from the interior of an automobile transporting the worker to and from the factory, and the automobile, which that worker must produce throughout the working day, is also the vehicle that confines him within the city, dominating its visual landscape.

Along the voyage to the working day, the car passes a billboard with a

Figure 18. Film still, ticker of cars produced in 1964 shown in the drive-to-work sequence, *Finally Got the News* (1970).

ticker measuring the number of cars produced in 1969 that turns in rapid succession like the odometer of a car. The measure of millions of cars in real time visualizes the ceaseless time of work, the relentless and repetitive nature of life on the line. This ticker neutralizes and naturalizes the violence of this rapid succession enabled by the process of niggermation. The sign functions as the odometer of quotidian life within the industrial city, the unending procession of cars down the line. It captures the temporality of existence within industrial capitalism—working to convey the mechanization of factory life within the vertically integrated system of production in which each waking moment is defined by the endless inputs of labor and outputs of commodities from the factory. *Finally Got the News* depicts the site of production as space that is indiscernible from the city itself—a kind of totalitarian nightmare in which rhythms of the factory have overtaken all other rhythms and the speed and tempo of life are set by the conveyer belt alone. Halting this time and the unceasing movement that accompanies it, the film seeks to disrupt quotidian life and insert a different temporality, one that valorizes the "lost time" of work stoppages.

Following the sequence depicting the drive to work, the film moves into the factory itself, commencing the working day. Composed of three minutes of multiple voice-offs of autoworkers speaking about overwork and the worsening of safety conditions in the plants over footage taken from the interior of factories, the sequence on the working day directly addresses the problem of speedup within the factories central to the niggermation thesis. The soundtrack from the original footage of the plant is not subtracted, which causes shrill, mechanic sounds to accompany the workers' voices. The first worker's voice-off articulates an intense aversion to life within the plants: "This motherfucker's got to go to that *goddamn* job every day of his *goddamn* life, and you go and ask him what he wants, and he's gonna say, 'Motherfucker, I want to get off that motherfuckin', no good, dirty-ass line.'" Subsequent voice-offs discuss abhorrent safety conditions in the plants resulting in workers losing limbs, stories of compulsive overtime, and the general hatred of both management and union. As Jonathan Kahana argues, Newsreel films made productive use of "voice, noise, and music to unsettle the social relations presumed by liberal documentary."[52] In this short sequence on the working day, the disquiet produced by the voice-offs coupled with the harsh and penetrating factory noises disrupt the space of the working day, opening up a new space for politics. Setting the stage for the exploration of labor militancy in the League, the sequence uses sound to underline both the violence of life within the plants and the growing rejection of work itself.

After a short interlude on finance capitalism, discussed at length in the next section, the film contrasts the oppressive regime of the working day with an interview with Chuck Wooten, a member of the League's executive committee. As he drives his car through the streets of Detroit, Wooten recounts a story of a confrontation with the mayor of Dearborn and the police after the League attempted to get Ron March elected to the UAW general committee. According to Wooten, after the election, the mayor showed up at their headquarters with a gun and fifty police officers who began attacking League members. This encounter and the disproportionate show of force by the city, he says, "tipped [the League] off to the power of black workers organizing an independent black workers movement." The story throws into relief the immediate and armed nature of the backlash of the industry and civic authorities against the League's activities and anticipates the broader and more systematic reaction that would follow.

Close-up shots in this sequence focus on Wooten shifting gears, adjusting the rearview mirror, and turning the wheel. Unlike the images taken in the interior of the vehicle in the sequence depicting the ride to work, Wooten seems to have control over the machine he is operating, and not the reverse. The subtle differences between this and the sequence on the drive to work communicate a relationship between worker and car that is not one of confinement but one of power. In contradistinction to the unilinear movement of the assembly line, Wooten moves through the streets of Detroit on a trajectory that is self-determined. The car's power as a symbol of self-determination is possible precisely because we have come to understand it, through the previous sequences, as a product of labor (rather than the symbol of individual freedom it has long represented in American culture). This sequence thus underscores Wooten's political power as the producer of the automobile. In claiming, affirming, and redirecting this power, Wooten's meander through the city in *his* car asserts the power of autonomous organization to intervene in and disrupt the perpetual motion and tempo of life under the disciplinary regime of Fordist production.

Autonomous organization on the shop floors of the late 1960s and early 1970s had transformative power, a point that is too often neglected as we interrogate the origins of today's post-Fordist regime of production. Analyzing the crisis of the auto industry from the standpoint of autonomous labor organization in the midst of the crisis of the 1970s, Linebaugh and Ramirez argue that responses to autonomous struggles within the plants provided the organizational logic for the restructuring of the entire industry in 1974: "Workers' informal organization became the basis of the capitalist re-organization of work to reproduce the value relation within the labor process. The counter-planning on the shop floor in the sixties becomes capitalist planning of exploitation in the seventies."[53]

Through an analysis of strategy reports from the industry in 1974 in the wake of massive lay-offs enacted to offset its crisis, Linebaugh and Ramirez identify the four main principles upon which the reorganization of the industry was based:

(a) reduction of the domestic production base
(b) the forcing of a major increase in the mobility of labor—inside the plants, within industry, and in the labor market generally
(c) increase of labor productivity, through the terror of "losing the job"
(d) undermining the practice of "paid absenteeism"[54]

In their early diagnosis of the consequences of autonomous organization, Linebaugh and Ramirez account for the ways that radical transformation of the Fordist system of production within the American auto industry laid the groundwork for the transformation of labor in post-Fordism generally. The strategies that composed the basis of the broad restructuring of the industry in reaction to increased labor militancy became fundamental to the reorganization of the labor force as a whole, forming a cornerstone of a counterrevolutionary logic with untold repercussions.

The image of the League's "undramatic end" that Jameson advances is thus directly countered by the reconfiguration of the auto industry in the late 1960s and early 1970s. Jameson's account fails to consider struggles to reclaim power over the production process occurring within the capital of the American Century and thus cannot account for the enduring quality of these struggles within the present.[55] It is ultimately colored by an understanding of capital that sees it, rather than struggle, to be the primary engine for transformation. If the League is met with failure, then it is imperative that we understand the *material effects* of this failure, an end without end.

TIME REGAINED: COUNTERREVOLUTION
AND THE FINANCIAL KATRINA

As we come to understand how the material effects of the crises of Fordism took form in the management of post-Fordist labor, we also need to account for the ramified force that was unleashed from these crises that transformed the other side of the "Keynesian pact" discussed earlier: global financial markets. How did the hothouse at the end of the American Century became an end without end for our financialized present? How does the "lost time" of which the executive speaks return? Capital's response to the disruptions at the end of the American Century were economic, but they were also political. As workers asserted their political power over the production process and over daily life, counterrevolutionary forces were realigning to retake "lost time." This realignment takes shape through what Marx called "primitive accumulation," a "power of relation" from which capitalism and the system of modern finance were born.[56] Primitive accumulation is a process that repeats throughout the history of capitalism, intensifying again in the neoliberal era.[57] What Jason Read characterizes as the "noneconomistic" theory of capital, Marx's understanding of primitive accumulation brings together as a network of financial, organizational, and "brute" forces that compel a process of historical transformation.[58] When Marx writes that "force is the midwife of every old society which is pregnant with a new one. It is itself an economic power," he is referring to a temporality that wrests the future from the womb of present, thus condensing different epochs within an intensive moment of rupture and reconfiguration.[59] The temporality of transition Marx suggested is one in which force, accompanied by the mechanisms of finance, radically reconstitutes social reality. *Finally Got the News,* I argue, captures precisely this temporality—a time that accumulates, which is also a time of primitive accumulation.

This time appears most starkly within an interlude in the film, about a minute and a half long, that offers a prescient glimpse of the forms that a financial counterrevolution was to take over the next decades. It contains a diatribe by Kenneth Cockrel, the League's primary lawyer, which acts as a voice-off for images of an auto showroom and Ford's corporate offices and occurs between the sequence on perilous working conditions and an interview with a League member that serves to introduce the League and its activities. Both visually and in its content, the voice-off appears as an aside to the theses the film presents regarding black labor in industrial America, conditions within the plants, and the activities of the League. The tone of Cockrel's voice-over is crass and humorous—departing from the mostly solemn and scholarly tenor that constitutes the rest of the film. Visually, the shots are clean and minimal, populated by one or two figures, who are all white. The sequence opens as the camera follows a solitary figure down an escalator and then spans what appears to be an auto showroom as Cockrel's lecture commences:

> They give you little bullshit amounts of money for working—wages and so forth—and then they steal all that shit back from you in terms of where they got this whole other thing set up, that old credit-stick-'em-up gimmick society, man—consumer credit—buy shit, buy shit—on credit. He gives you a little bit of shit to cool your ass off and then steals all that shit back with shit called interest, the price of money....
>
> The motherfuckers who deal with intangibles are the motherfuckers who are rewarded in this society. The more abstract and intangible your shit is...I mean stocks, what is stocks? A stock certificate is evidence of ownership of something that's real, *ownership*. He owns and controls, and, you know, therefore receives the benefit of. He fuckin' with shit in Bolivia. He's Anaconda. He's United Fruit. He's in mining. He's in what? He ain't ever in his life produced shit. Investment bankers, stockbrokers, insurance men—it's the motherfuckers who don't do nothin'.

Cockrel provides an astute and concise analysis of the mechanisms of exploitation that occur through the financialization of consumer life, those mechanisms that are in excess of the wage relation. The car in the showroom is not simply the product of labor, as we saw in the previous section, but an object that oppresses the worker through the operation of credit. An image that portends our current situation in which the Ford motor company now generates more profit through auto financing than manufacturing, the car signals the systemic shift in the structure of the U.S. economy from the extraction of surplus value through the wage relation to the generation of profits through financial rents.[60] The interlude also links the practices of consumer credit domestically to imperialism abroad, further complicating the connections between finance, imperialism, and the "colonization of daily life" we saw in *Hora de los hornos*. Cockrel's lecture indicates that in finance, money is a direct relationship of power.

This sequence does not merely confirm *Finally Got the News*'s ability to analyze the totality of capitalist exploitation within its contemporary

Figure 19. Film still, corporate office footage during Cockrel voice-off, *Finally Got the News* (1970).

moment. It stands apart from the film as evidence of its capacity to capture the intensive, transitional juncture it inhabits. The sequence is placed between two continuous moments in the overall argument of the film: a sequence on life within the plants, which explores the experience of niggermation, and the experience of both the resistance of the League and the direct force with which it was met. However, it refers directly to neither, aesthetically nor thematically. What comes through in this interlude, which first seems to be tangential to the subject at hand, is an interstice between the dynamic materiality of Cockrel's voice and the sterility of the architectural landscape and insipid figures that populate it. The interstice between sound and image is the chasm opened from which the violence of finance capital comes forward.

In other words, this audiovisual image of finance works as an enduring image that, in Baucom's words, "moves toward the future," operating as a kind of messenger of what is to come: the explosive financialization of capital markets. However, it does so only through "doubling back on what has been," the crisis of industrial modernity, the Fordist system, and Keynesian regulation instigated by a cycle of struggles against these very managerial strategies. The interlude is a fragment born from the forces that ushered in the new financial regime in which we presently live. It is the shock of the future nestled within the present of the crisis of 1970. Although in the film, this segment takes the form of an aside, this aside comes to constitute the aftermath of the crisis, an aftermath forged in the "hothouse" of the transitional moment in which the League operated. At the end of the American Century, the violence of industrial modernity is intensified; at the same time, financial violence (re)emerges.

Cockrel's sharp analysis of debt/credit culture foretells the financial strategy through which capital will enact a simultaneous restructuring and counterrevolution on postindustrial urban centers. In contrast to a strictly violent and suppressive movement, Paolo Virno defines counter-revolution as

> revolution in reverse, . . . an impetuous innovation of modes of production, forms of life, that, however, consolidate and again set in motion capitalist command. . . . The counterrevolution enjoys the very same presupposi-tions and the very same (economic, social, and cultural) tendencies that the revolution would have been able to engage.[61]

Like the reconfiguration of the time of labor within post-Fordism, so too is financialization born out of resistance. In contrast to theories of financialization that understand it to be a historical process driven by capital alone, *Finally Got the News* helps us to understand how finance, in its present historical instantiation, is a counterrevolutionary formation through which capitalism was forced to radically rearticulate itself on a formal level and to dispose of forms that were no longer adequate to the control of an increasingly global and heterogeneous network of resistance.

We can see this counterrevolution in expansion of consumer credit generally since the crises of the early 1970s, which has been a mode of circumventing the wage relation and deploying tools of financial control. Accordingly, the most insidious and predatory lending practices have been targeted at populations who defied the regime of discipline, such as students, as I discussed in the previous chapter. Intensifying with the lowering of interest rates in the mid-1980s, the augmentation of consumer credit has taken place within the broader context of the financialization of all levels of capitalist accumulation and has been characterized by many as the withering of the distinction between profit and rent.[62] As has been well documented, the real estate bubble was largely driven by the expansion of the mortgage industry into subprime markets and targeting of minority populations, particularly African Americans. Following in the footsteps of Ford himself, mortgage companies exploited existing social networks, such as churches, to expand subprime divisions and bring large numbers of African Americans into what would be only temporary homeownership, forcing many into subprime mortgages even when they qualified for prime loans. The desegregation of credit led to conditions that are as, if not more, unequal and exploitative as the desegregation of the Fordist system of production. In a lecture on the subprime mortgage crisis titled "A Financial Katrina," David Harvey demonstrates that this disproportionate targeting of this population has resulted in the greatest expropriation of wealth from the African American population in history, or at least since slavery.[63]

But how is it that the financial Katrina came to be born, in a counter-revolutionary formation, out of the crises of the Fordist mode of production? As discussed earlier, the enduring image of violence at the end of the American Century occurs not only in the factory but also in the image of the Detroit Rebellion, which signaled the crisis of the liberal organization of urban life that generated a poor, dependent minority population that fed the industrial labor pool. Segregation of urban life, as has been well documented, was produced through the systematic exclusion of minority populations from homeownership by way of discrimination and denial of mortgage credit, while homeownership among white Americans greatly expanded in the postwar period. As Gary Dymski argues, it was precisely *because of* the history of systematic racial exclusion in credit markets, and not in spite of it, that the exploitative system of subprime lending and the financial crisis it induced came to be.[64] Dymski demonstrates that with the end of the Bretton Woods agreement, the pressures of inflation destabilized the mortgage industry, a cornerstone of the American financial industry. This led to the subsequent deregulations of the early 1980s and "forced the rethinking of long-established banking processes: *how* housing is financed and *how* banks generate earnings."[65] In other words, the aftermath of the global crises of the 1960s forced the conditions of capital's reconfiguration and subsequent financialization.[66] In the decades leading up to the financial crisis, the extension of credit into areas that were both credit and income starved relied on predatory lending practices, generating profits through fees and high interest rates.[67] And thus areas and populations that had long been excluded from credit markets through redlining and discrimination became the epicenters for the largest financial crisis in decades.

If it is niggermation, rather than automation, that best characterizes the attempts of the automotive industry to regain lost profits during the intensification of the crisis of the Fordist mode of production, then might we understand the subprime mortgage crisis as the repetition and intensification of such a strategy? That is, as capital confronts the internal limitations of the post-Fordist mode of production, is something like the niggermation of credit capital's response to this crisis? This argument would have to be predicated on seeing urban minority populations not simply as helpless victims of opportunistic and predatory practices. A further analysis would need to examine why and how the mechanisms of financial control were formed in the collapse of the industrial system of production and how the dynamics of the cycles of struggle that hastened its destruction come to be embodied in its aftermath, if only obliquely.

In the aftermath of the subprime crisis, we find that Detroit remains a crucial bellwether for the ways that investments and disinvestments by capital markets transform urban life. As the city grapples with the largest civic bankruptcy in U.S. history, caused by the very forces of accumulation by dispossession wrought by the financial Katrina, it operates as a kind of testing ground for methods of neoliberal civic management and financial control. The image of the man being held at gunpoint at the end of the American Century endures in our present crisis as it returns to urban centers. The financial Katrina counters and corrects the disturbances caused by a population that disciplinary measures had failed to contain; it is the weapon that the financial industry has held to the backs of the urban poor. It is a power equal and opposite to the lost time of the wildcat itself; it recuperates this lost time and sets it again into circulation (and, as Marx reminds us, finance circulates nothing if not time). *Finally Got the News* stands as both a prescient glimpse of our present and an artifact of a different kind of time, a disruptive time that offers a counterimage to the time of primitive accumulation. It is a counterfactual to our present that simultaneously affirms the potential for resistance within it.

4

Italian Feminist Collectives and the "Unexpected Subject"

Attributing high value to "unproductive" moments is an extension of life proposed by women.

— RIVOLTA FEMMINILE, "Manifesto" (1970)

Capital rules by division. The key to capitalist accumulation is the constant creation and reproduction of the division between the waged and unwaged parts of the class.... Thus, it is the political recomposition of the waged and unwaged that imposes the crisis on capital.

— ZEROWORK COLLECTIVE, "Introduction," *Zerowork: Political Materials* 1 (1975)

Midway through *L'Aggettivo donna* (The adjective woman, Italy, 1971), the camera pans a desolate suburb on the outskirts of Rome. Reminiscent of the dusty landscapes populated by mid-century apartment complexes that frame characters in iconic scenes from Italian neorealism, the shot reveals the poverty of everyday life. The trope of the bleak suburb and modernist architecture had become common refrains in postwar political cinema, particularly New Left cinema, as films such as *Deux ou trois choses que je sais d'elle* (*Two or Three Things I Know about Her,* France, 1967) and *Hora de los hornos* used these landscapes as backdrops against which to explore themes of alienation. Set inside a sequence examining domestic labor, however, the panning shot in *L'Aggettivo donna* stands out among its analogs. The shot is not a detached meditation on suburban space but a point-of-view shot of a housewife looking out of her apartment window. The emptiness of the immense middle ground that separates the foreground and background impresses upon the viewer a powerful sense of isolation. It is the only glimpse of the outside world we are given

Figure 20. Film still, panning shot from interior of apartment, *L'Aggettivo donna* (1971). Courtesy of Centro Sperimentale di Cinematografia.

in a sequence that otherwise takes place entirely within the interior of an apartment, as we witness a housewife going through the motions of her daily routine: making the bed, washing dishes and clothes, sweeping and mopping, cooking, setting the table, feeding her children, and generally carrying out the affective labor of mothering. In long takes that anticipate later feminist films on domestic labor, such as Chantal Akerman's *Jeanne Dielman 23, quai du Commerce 1080 Bruxelles* (Belgium, 1975), this segment of *L'Aggettivo donna* focuses on the seemingly endless and repetitive nature of housework. Functioning as a moment of reflection, the exterior shot is accompanied by a voice-over that states, "When women labor in the house, it is considered private; public labor is reserved for men." The pan of the stark exterior, then, interrogates the abyss that divides public and private, interior and exterior, productive and unproductive labor. A voice-over at the end of the shot rejects the separation of public and private spheres in postwar industrial society, insisting that women's

Figure 21. Film still, housewife at work, *L'Aggettivo donna* (1971). Courtesy of Centro Sperimentale di Cinematografia.

liberation needs to refuse the "false hierarchy" created by patriarchy that imposes this separation.

In his discussion of political cinema in *Cinema 2,* Gilles Deleuze returns to his writings on Kafka and minor literature, arguing that, while major literature maintains the division between the "political and the private," in minor literature, "the private affair was immediately political and 'entailed a verdict of life and death.'"[1] Classical political cinema, for Deleuze, functions much like major literature: the boundary between the private and the political is preserved. However, in postwar political cinema, and particularly third cinema, the division is eroded and the film pushes "everything into a state of aberration, in order to communicate violences as well as to make private business pass into the political, and political affairs into the private."[2]

The immediately political nature of the private sphere and the violences conducted within it are perhaps nowhere of more concern than in the feminist cinema that flourished in the 1970s, a phenomenon that Deleuze neglects to discuss. Feminist collectives in Italy and elsewhere produced films and videos that interrogated sexuality, rape, abortion, domestic labor, and identity, while drawing on the insights of the feminist movement to generate formal techniques based on nascent feminist epistemologies and organizational strategies. In addition to demonstrating the political nature of the private sphere, feminist cinema questioned the logic of separation that constituted the divide between public and private, working to undermine the boundary itself. An exemplary instance of feminist cinema of this era, *L'Aggettivo donna* rejects the material basis upon which, it argues, the division between public and private was derived: the separation of productive (waged) and reproductive (unwaged) labor.

The political cinema of the minority, Deleuze claims, creates "not the myth of a past people, but the story-telling of the people to come."[3] I argue that films coming out of the Italian feminist movement of the 1970s, however, are less interested in the "people to come" than in what Carla Lonzi calls the "unexpected subject" in her seminal manifesto, "Let's Spit on Hegel" (1970).[4] Far from the essentialism often associated with second-wave feminism, the "unexpected subject" is the product of the transvaluation of norms and values conducted by the feminist movement that challenged the boundaries delimiting the properly political. Lonzi's ambiguous figure suggests a new and unforeseen political subject that materializes only when political movements begin to undermine the gendered division of labor and the separation of public and private domains. The unexpected subject, or *soggetto imprevisto,* implies a subject that is not only unforeseen but an extempore subject that comes into being through a process akin to improvisation, and it is notable that Lonzi uses *imprevisto* and not the visually oriented synonym *inaspattato.* When Lonzi writes "we are the Unexpected Subject" at the end of her manifesto, she is announcing a new collective subject whose constitution is a political project. As I argue in this chapter, the antiauthoritarian, improvisational, and experimental nature of Italian feminist cinema of the 1970s was such a political project, one which opened creative spaces through which to engender unexpected subjects.

Through the cinematic experiments of the Collettivo Femminista di Cinema-Roma (Feminist Cinema Collective-Rome) and the Gruppo Femminista Milanese per il Salario al Lavoro Domestico (Milanese

Feminist Group for Wages for Domestic Labor), this chapter examines how feminist cinema challenged even the most radical approaches to cinematic solidarity by developing rhetorics and tactics through which to constitute new political subjectivities. Accordingly, I argue that the cinema of the Italian feminist movement is a crucial archive through which to develop the implications of Lonzi's "unexpected subject," taken as an experimental form through which an essayistic politics of the common was elaborated by the feminist movement. I begin with a discussion of gender and reproductive labor in the Italian context, considering how, by moving class struggles into the "social factory," Italian feminists challenged ideas of class solidarity and the definitions of labor and revolutionary subjectivity. I then turn to a discussion of how the unexpected subject is constituted through the transvaluation of norms and values undertaken in the antiauthoritarianism of the Collettivo Femminista di Cinema-Roma and its first film, *L'Aggettivo donna*. After examining the importance of antiauthoritarianism, I consider how openings for the unexpected subject take shape when insisting that "the personal is political" in the collective's second film, *Lotta non è finita!* (The struggle is not over, 1973). I argue that through the feminist practice of *autocoscienza* (autoconsciousness), *Lotta non è finita!* creates a reflective cinema that makes tactical contributions by building layers of cinematic meaning that foreground a transindividual political framework. Finally, I consider how unexpected political subjects are called into being through cinematic provocation by examining the Gruppo Femminista Milanese per il Salario al Lavoro Domestico's paracinematic performance *Siamo Stufe!* (We are fed up!, 1975). This section explores how the Wages for Housework campaign used cinematic performance to articulate demands centered around reproductive labor and constitute political subjectivities through those demands. In each of these cases, I am interested in how openings for an unexpected cinematic subject are produced through collaborative feminist approaches to the essay film that foreground the reproductive sphere and all that it implies. I conclude by contemplating what the unexpected subject might mean in a world where labor has been "feminized" and the divide between productive and reproductive spheres has been eroded and reconfigured. Moreover, I argue, creating the conditions for the production of unexpected subjects is essential to the project of left politics today, which too often veers toward ossified positions and forms.

FROM PRODUCTION TO REPRODUCTION: MOVING STRUGGLE INTO THE "SOCIAL FACTORY"

"We spit on Hegel."[5] An antagonistic line from Rivolta Femminile's manifesto plastered around the walls of Rome in July 1970, these words offered a trenchant rebuke not only to patriarchal society but also to the orthodox communist Left in Italy. The manifesto went on to claim that the "servant-master dialectic is a settling of account between groups of men" and that the concept of "class struggle," an extension of this Hegelian logic, had excluded women and was inadequate to the task of women's liberation.[6] On the heels of the previous years of unrest—the student and workers' movements of the late 1960s—the feminist movement in Italy, as in many places, posed one of the most significant challenges to New Left social movements, expanding both the domain of politics and the composition of revolutionary subjectivity. It did so, in large part, by developing new organizational forms and shedding light on a sphere largely excluded from leftist inquiry: reproduction.

Arguably, Italy's 1968 extended well into the late 1970s (often referred to as the "creeping May"), and the narrative of autonomous labor organization, particularly within Italy's auto sector, has been the subject of much political and historical examination and debate. Exploding in the "Hot Autumn" of 1969, new alliances between workers and students and autonomous forms of organization—outside of traditional unions and the Italian Communist Party (PCI)—led to massive work stoppages within northern factories spurred by a great influx of southern Italian migrants into those factories. Long marginalized within union activity in the plants, these southern migrants came to the forefront of organizational activity in the 1960s and 1970s. Along with new alliances and modes of organization, the Autonomists put forward an alternative theory of the relationship between resistance and capitalist development (to which this book is clearly indebted) that, in the words of Kathi Weeks, "concentrates on class struggle as the primary engine of change."[7]

The manifestation of autonomous organization within Italian factories bore striking resemblances to workers' demands in the U.S. auto industry discussed in the previous chapter; in both cases, workers asserted their political power over the process of production, using wildcats, in the words of James Boggs, "as a defensive weapon to fight off encroachment on their control at the point of production." As Georgy Katsiaficas recounts,

> their [Italian workers'] demands and aspirations fell outside the purview of traditional labor unions. While unions negotiated wage increases, the workers fought speed-ups, piecework, merit pay, production bonuses, and salary differentials; they wanted the elimination of poisonous fumes, unhealthy working conditions, and much more: "We Want Everything!" is what they screamed in the huge Mirafiori Fiat plant in Turin, where over sixty thousand workers were concentrated.[8]

The demand for "everything," like in the case of autonomous struggles within the U.S. auto industry, signaled a refusal of a life organized by industrial labor and a rejection of the limited terms, primarily the wage, through which traditional unions negotiated on behalf of the workers. The expanded nature of the struggle was captured in militant films like *All'alfa* (Italy, 1969), which documents the experience of migrants and the new political organization within the Alfa Romeo factories in Milan and is perhaps the closest Italian analog to *Finally Got the News*.

Associations between autonomous labor organization in Italy and Detroit were more than coincidental; they registered international circuits of New Left exchange of which cinema was an integral part. The activities of the League of Revolutionary Black Workers—along with the broader Black Power movement—provided examples of class recomposition for *operaismo,* and extraparliamentary groups made active political connections with autoworkers in Detroit. Steve Wright documents how, as early as 1967, groups like Potere Operaio were arguing that "American Blacks do not simply represent, but rather *are,* the proletariat of the Third World within the very heart of the capitalist system. . . . *Black Power means therefore the autonomous revolutionary organization of Blacks.*"[9] While the League and the Black Power movement functioned as models outside of traditional unions and leftist groups, *operaismo* was far more hostile to organization around gender difference within its own ranks.[10] Insisting that women "stop shedding tears about women's 'equality,'" Potere Operaio saw women's issues as subordinate to broader strategies of class unification. For the workerist movement at the time, "the real problem was how women workers might be organized in an anti-capitalist manner."[11]

Finally Got the News, which found its widest European distribution and popularity in Italy among the extraparliamentary Left, seems to share Potere Operaio's thesis that women's place in the struggle was primarily to be found in their role as waged workers.[12] In a short section on black women's labor toward the end of the film, a voice-off gives an overview of the predicament that black women face: the majority are forced to work outside of the home to make ends meet, relegated to low-paying service sector positions, and are among the most precarious of workers within the labor force. Differentiating them from their white counterparts, the voice-off asserts that black women have a great potential for militancy, as the harsh conditions to which they are subjected in the labor market make them understand their antagonistic relationship to capitalism better than any other population of workers.[13] In this assertion, the voice-off makes clear that black women's potential for revolutionary activity begins with their status as waged workers. Nevertheless, the sequence seems to complicate this thesis by juxtaposing this voice-off with footage of black women not performing waged labor but rather shopping at a grocery store. It is unclear what this footage is intended to communicate. On one hand, perhaps it is offered to illustrate the difficult position women are put in, having to perform waged labor to provide basic sustenance for their families. On the other hand, it might also be read as complicating its own definition of work. Maybe these women—at the point of consumption rather than the point of production—are working nevertheless. The film stops short of offering this thesis, preferring instead to legitimate black women as part of the struggle insofar as their status as waged workers makes them allies.[14] While recognizing the ways that struggles within the factory are connected to those outside of it, *Finally Got the News,* like many films of the New Left, delimits the definition of work and workers and therefore affords a revolutionary class position to those who perform productive (waged) labor.

The ambiguity that *Finally Got the News* implies, however, registers the ways that strict divisions between productive and reproductive spheres within Marxist theory came under question during this period, as many argued that an analysis of capitalism must extend beyond the walls of the factory.[15] In the Italian context, Mario Tronti's publication of the seminal *Oparai e capitale* in 1966 had a profound impact on the Italian Left. In a 1971 article taken from the book titled "La fabbrica e la società" (The factory and society) in the workerist journal *Quaderni Rossi,* Tronti argued, "The whole of society exists as a function of the factory and the factory extends its exclusive domination over the whole of society."[16] The "social factory," for Tronti and a generation of autonomist Marxists, indicated the expansion of capitalist relations beyond the sphere of production. Tronti's analysis, as has been noted, bears similarities to and certainly influenced the analysis of capital coming out of the feminist movement at the time.[17] Throughout the 1970s, struggles within the "social factory" became increasingly important to the development of autonomous consciousness and practice within Italy. For example, the tactic of *autoriduzione* (auto-reduction), which started as a technique of labor refusal in the factories, soon became a widespread form of dissent in which people would collectively set their own prices for electrical bills, rent, and transportation.[18] Often led by women, *autoriduzione* movements, rent strikes, and neighborhood committees brought struggles over reproduction to the fore in Italian politics. The 150 Hours Courses were another consequential achievement of autonomous movements within the sphere of education and everyday life, institutionalizing a militant form of study in line with that discussed in chapter 2. First pursued by factory workers, the majority of the courses were neither technical training nor career development but covered a broad range of topics directed by worker interest: "the aim was to retrieve what they had been deprived of at the proper time, to work less and think about their own conditions of life and work."[19] The program quickly expanded to include the unemployed and housewives and facilitated connections between factory workers, feminists, and student movements.[20] In Milan, in particular, the 150 Hours Courses became a locus of feminist activity, where courses allowed women to explore themes of sexuality, domestic labor, and identity through creative writing, performance, the visual arts, and cinema.

As is evident in these few examples, the feminist movement in Italy and elsewhere was instrumental in expanding militant struggles into the domain of social reproduction. These struggles demonstrated, contra the dismissive tone Potere Operaio took toward them, that groups like Rivolta Femminile and Lotta Femminista were after far more than "equality." In fact, the Italian feminist movement largely rejected the discourse of equality, a point that is made explicit in a number of early feminist texts, including Lonzi's "Let's Spit on Hegel," which asserts, "Equality is what is offered as legal rights to colonized people.... The world of equality is the world of legalized oppression and one-dimensionality."[21] Rather, the feminist movement that came out of New Left struggles of the late 1960s also wanted "everything." In moving struggles into the sphere of reproduction, feminists in turn challenged the definition of "everything," reformulating the demand to include a whole sphere of social reproduction neglected by the traditional labor movement. Lonzi insists that Marxism's relative historical disinterest in the question of reproduction was due to the fact that it was "developed within the framework of a patriarchal culture."[22] For Marxist feminists, unpaid reproductive labor, hidden by its designation as "natural," was not newly relevant to capitalism, as Tronti and others intimated, but a constitutive aspect of capitalist accumulation from its inception. As Lopoldina Fortunati would later frame the problem, "it is only by positing the process of reproduction as 'natural' and reproduction work as a 'natural force of social labor' that costs nothing to capital, that capital can valorize itself."[23] In other words, capitalism cannot function without the systematic relegation of reproductive labor to a "hidden abode," an insight that became a requisite starting point for any anticapitalist politics.

The critique of reproductive labor and class solidarity developed within the feminist movement in Italy was foundational to the political perspective of the cinematic collectives discussed in this chapter. For example, in language reminiscent of the feminist group with which they were most closely associated, Lotta Femminista, the Collettivo Femminista di Cinema-Roma argued in 1971,

> The family is the pillar of this society, in which we experience our specific exploitation by performing free labor for the reproduction of the working

class. . . . But when opposing the system, we realized that our fight goes much further than that of our male "comrades." We realized that it is not possible to fight the capitalist mode of production without calling into question "private" life as well, because that would ignore the fact that our own characters and structures are formed by economic necessities.[24]

Rendering this political stance cinematically, the collective furthered the critique of reproductive labor proposed by the feminist movement. In doing so, Italian feminist cinema complicated the ways that the essayistic politics of the New Left worked to unravel the distinction between private and public, discussed in the first chapter, while simultaneously expanding the formal and theoretical possibilities for militant cinema by placing an emphasis on the reproductive sphere and its political potentials.

ANTIAUTHORITARIANISM IN *L'AGGETTIVO DONNA*

As I have suggested, when Lonzi identified the unexpected subject, one might argue that she was less interested in defining that subject than she, along with the broader feminist movement, was concerned with creating the conditions for such unexpected subjects to appear.[25] First and foremost, laying the groundwork for these conditions entailed confronting a pervasive culture of patriarchal authoritarianism that dominated Italian social life, including the Left. In addition to its rejection of the discourses of equality and emancipation and its insistence on autonomy, the feminist movement in Italy made the repudiation of all forms of authority and authoritarianism a basic tenet of its writings and organizational strategies. This repudiation is nowhere more clear than in one of the earliest articulations of the feminist movement, the 1966 manifesto of the Demau (Demystification of Authority) group based in Milan. Advancing a set of political and theoretical positions that would remain more or less consistent throughout the Italian feminist movement of the 1970s, the manifesto calls for the

demystifications of authoritarianism as a theory and as a mystique of the moral, cultural and ideological values on which the current division of labor and society as a whole are based; as a coercive element on individual values;

and the restraint upon the rights, the needs and the potentialities of all humankind in favor or privileged groups.

Demystification of values, therefore:

(a) in the area of rights
(b) in the area of sexual relations and its related ethics
(c) in the area of conflicts of roles in family and social relations in general
(d) in the area of education, instruction and culture
(e) in the area of work and intellectual and scientific production
(f) in the area of scientific types of theorizing

The search, therefore, for new values concerning the whole system of relationships.[26]

In short, the manifesto calls for the transvaluation of all norms and values founded on authoritarianism that ruled, for Demau, the "whole system of relationships" and upon which the "division of labor and society as a whole is based." The extensive scope of the manifesto's approach to the problem of authority recognized the co-constitution of its macro- and micropolitical dimensions. Furthermore, the emphasis on antiauthoritarian politics in a country that had experienced fascist rule in its recent past signals the degree to which the cultural memory of World War II weighed heavily on Italian feminism.[27] Demau's manifesto thus echoed the broader antiauthoritarian tendencies of the New Left as both a political and philosophical project, recalling Foucault's introduction to Deleuze and Guattari's *Anti-Oedipus,* in which he identifies its central project to be "tracking down all varieties of fascism, from the most enormous ones that surround and crush us to the petty ones that constitute the tyrannical bitterness of our everyday lives."[28]

Its resonance with a pervading antiauthoritarianism in New Left culture notwithstanding, Demau's manifesto brings the insights of a nascent feminism to bear on the question of authority. Specifically, it calls attention to the ways authoritarianism upholds the "division of labor" in society and the cascading cultural and social effects of this primary problem of authoritarian domination. By critiquing authority from a feminist perspective, the manifesto registers an essential point about authoritarianism Hannah Arendt made a decade earlier. In her 1954 essay

"What Is Authority?," Arendt argued that the conception and practice of authority in Western culture was derived not from the political sphere but from the realm of the household in ancient Greece, a space in which the focus centered on "keeping alive as such and coping with the physical necessities involved in maintaining individual life and guaranteeing the survival of the species."[29] In the space of the household, a free man could exert his domination over others, coerce them and behave in ways otherwise unacceptable in the political, or what we might refer to as the "public," sphere. It is from this "prepolitical" realm that Arendt contends Plato and Aristotle, albeit differently, sought to "find a concept of authority which would prevent the deterioration of the polis and safeguard the life of the philosopher."[30] Accordingly, Arendt writes of authoritarian forms of government that "the course of their authority, which legitimates the exercise of power, must be beyond the sphere of power and, like the law of nature or the commands of God, must not be man-made."[31] Claiming that ancient Greek conceptions of authority were perfected in Roman political culture, Arendt explores the ways that the figures of the expert and the author become representative of an authority that augments the foundations of political power without being properly political themselves.[32] In its desire to demystify authoritarianism, the Demau manifesto recognizes the ways that the authority that underpins the reproductive sphere as a "prepolitical" space of domination connected to forms of authority that cut across social and cultural life.

Italian feminist cinematic collectives, in particular the Collettivo Femminista di Cinema-Roma, took this insight about the nature of authoritarian power and worked to create new collective forms of cinematic production and sense making to subvert it. Formed in 1971 with the production of *L'Aggettivo donna,* the collective was made up of members who were already active in Rivolta Femminile and Lotta Femminista.[33] The collective's organizational model shared the features of the broader feminist movement in Italy that, as elsewhere, was based on small affinity groups of women that emphasized horizontal relationships and dialog.[34] The antiauthoritarian principles of the movement translated into the collective's rejection of film authorship, intersecting with and complicating New Left cinema's critique of the auteur. In a manifesto titled "Per un cinema clitorideo vaginale" (For a clitoral vaginal cinema) published with the release of *L'Aggettivo donna,* the group critiques auteur cinema's approach to feminism, claiming it both commercializes it and reduces it to a "socio-psychological problem."[35] The manifesto goes on to link commercial and auteur cinema with an "authoritarian mode" of communication: "instead of speaking 'with,' it speaks 'at.'"[36] As Annamaria Licciardello argues, in its identification of the authoritarian monologue in dominant cinema and its demand that the spectator no longer remain passive, the manifesto certainly has "situationist echoes."[37] Similarly, these sentiments resonate with the anti-auteurism of other cinematic manifestos of the New Left, particularly Solanas and Getino's "Towards a Third Cinema."

While rejecting passive spectatorship and calling for a cinema that promotes dialogue and critical reflection, "Per un cinema clitorideo vaginale" does not simply inherit the politics of New Left cinema and its rejection of authorship. Rather, the collective comes at the problem of authorship from a different angle, linking the idea of spectatorial passivity to the imposed passivity of women by patriarchal culture and foregrounding the arena of personal relationships and private life:

> IT IS IN THIS WAY THAT WE ARE INTERESTED IN THE AUDIO-VISUAL MEDIUM: in order to talk with other women, to express a new way of being a woman without wanting to impose new models. Until now, women have been expressed by men or have expressed themselves through men that capitalize on their creativity, their ideas, their work and their vital energy. We want to speak in the first person about our experiences, about our alienation, about our hardships, in an aggressive and alienated society that is based on exploitation and division of labor and tasks according to sex.[38]

The gendered division of labor, then, becomes the analytical framework through which to explore "cinema of the first person," which should not be confused with the cinema of the individual or the auteur. As the manifesto emphasizes, its feminist approach to cinema proposes a mode of collaborative research initiated by the feminist movement that is precipitated by "the open discussion of experience and personal problems."[39] In doing so, it argues that cinematic research is capable of producing forms of knowledge that have been marginalized within political inquiry, including "subjective, intuitive, dialogical, [and] emotional" ways of knowing and understanding, a point I explore at length in the next section.[40] Drawing on the antiauthoritarian and incipient feminist epistemology articulated in Demau's manifesto, Collettivo Femminista di Cinema-Roma expands New Left cinema's critique of auteurism to include its gendered dimensions while elevating affective and collective forms of cinematic research and knowledge production within a feminist epistemological framework. Advocating for a antihierarchical documentary ethics involved "in the creation of 'life itself,'" the collective takes on new political and strategic forms that become evident in its two essay films: *L'Aggittivo donna* (1971) and *Lotta non è finita!* (1973).[41]

Before turning to these films, we should note that sentiments put forward in "Per un cinema clitorideo vaginale" resonate with a critique of classic Hollywood and auteur cinema that was simultaneously developing in an emergent feminist film studies in the United States, the United Kingdom, and elsewhere, as seen in publications like *Women and Film* magazine (1972–73) and the writings of figures like Claire Johnson. In her seminal essay "Women's Cinema as Counter Cinema" (1973), Johnson draws on Barthes and Freud to offer a critique of myth making and phallocentrism in classic Hollywood (to be popularized by Laura Mulvey later in the decade), arguing that collective filmmaking within the feminist movement was "an expression of sisterhood, it suggests a viable alternative to the rigid hierarchical structures of male-dominated cinema and offers real opportunities for a dialogue about the nature of women's cinema within it."[42] For Johnson, collective filmmaking practices provide a space to "interrogate and demystify the workings of ideology" and ultimately lead to a "genuinely revolutionary conception of counter-cinema."[43] The promise of collective filmmaking projects within the feminist movement in the United States inspired projects like Newsreel's *Up against the Wall Miss America* (1968), *She's Beautiful When She's Angry* (1969), *Jainie's Jainie* (1971), *The Woman's Film* (1971), and New Day Film's *Growing Up Female* (1971), addressing issues central to the feminist movement, such as domestic labor, domestic violence, abortion, and identity.[44] In the United Kingdom, the London Women's Film Group produced and distributed films that dealt with women's place within the labor movement, namely,

Women of Rhondda (1973) and *The Amazing Equal Pay Show* (1974).[45] In France, taking up the new technology of video, the Mouvement de libération des femmes advanced a feminist labor agenda through videos like *Grève de femmes à Troyes* (Women's strike in Troyes, 1971). Feminist collectives like Les Muses s'amusent and Vidéo Out also explored what Ros Murray describes as a "protoqueer politics," examining the intersections between the feminist movement and the early gay liberation movement in videos like *Le désir homosexuel* (Homosexual desire, France, 1972).[46] Among the first feminist film collectives established in Latin America, Colectivo Cine Mujer, started in Mexico City in 1975, produced films that took up issues like abortion and rape, mixing conventional documentary style with fictional narrative.[47] In each of these instances, collective feminist filmmaking practices maintained close ties to the social movements from which they arose, using cinema as a tool for debate and mobilization. Furthermore, while taking up diverse formal approaches, these movements integrated aspects of feminist thought and organizational politics into the composition of their films.

A part of this larger conversation on the role of cinema in feminist movements, the essay films of Collettivo Femminista di Cinema-Roma stand out as some of the best early examples of feminist cinema that directly address the problem of reproductive labor. While attending to issues critical to the broader feminist movement—women's labor, abortion, identity, and so on—the collective took up and elaborated on Marxist–feminist critiques of reproduction and authoritarianism being developed in the Italian context. Intertwining this critique with dialogic exploration, *L'Aggettivo donna* begins with a seemingly simple question: how does one make a feminist film? This topic is discussed by a group of female voices offscreen while the opening credits roll. The conversation continues over an opening sequence of canonical images from Western art as a voice-over argues that from the perspective of patriarchal culture, "women are painted, but do not paint, are written about, but do not write, do not have their own language." Their discussion resonates with Linda Nochlin's essay "Why Have There Been No Great Women Artists?," published the same year as *L'Aggettivo donna*'s release, which argues not only that women have historically lacked the resources to become "great artists" but that the concept of the "great artist" itself is largely rooted in a sexist understanding of artistic production that values qualities historically associated with men, such as genius and individual authorship.[48] *L'Aggettivo donna* drives home the point that Western culture is patriarchal to its core in the next sequence, in which street shots of women are overlaid with text featuring misogynist quotations from a canon of great thinkers: Nietzsche, Baudelaire, Kierkegaard, and so on. As two well-dressed young women walk by, a quote from Schopenhauer reads, "Women have great talent, but no genius, for they always remain subjective." The opening of *L'Aggettivo donna* intimates, however, that it is precisely the subjective quality of inquiry that the film celebrates. The film thus embraces is own positionality, performing the demystification of values of authority and objectivity called for in Demau's manifesto.

L'Aggettivo donna's formal and thematic innovations are striking when compared to previous films on women's labor coming out of the Italian Left, such as Cecilia Mangini's *Essere donne* (Being women, 1965). Produced by Unitelefilm, a company associated with the PCI, *Essere donna* addresses issues of women's labor, but primarily as they relate to women's role as waged laborers and therefore members of the proletarian class. Though containing Eisenstein-inspired montages of women's labor and images from pop culture, the audio track maintains the classic "voice of God" cadence, as a male voice explains the oppression of women in society, peppered with interviews with proletarian women. *L'Aggettivo donna* instead uses a combination of voice-offs taken from interviews with women and subjective voice-over commentary. It is unclear whether the Collettivo Femminista di Cinema-Roma had seen *Essere donne,* but the titles of each of the films reveal their markedly different approaches to feminist questions. While *Essere donne* considers the problem of *being* women within capitalism, *L'Aggettivo donna* contemplates the manner in which the term *woman* modifies not only half the population but also their labor, affects, political concerns, and so on. Rather than an ontological identity, the adjective *woman* describes a social position. In their assessment of gender, the collective alludes to Simone de Beauvoir's well-known statement, "one is not born, but rather becomes, woman."[49]

How is the adjective woman imposed on half the population? A sequence near the end of *L'Aggettivo donna* analyzes a classroom scene where young girls are taught to play with toy irons, brooms, and ovens

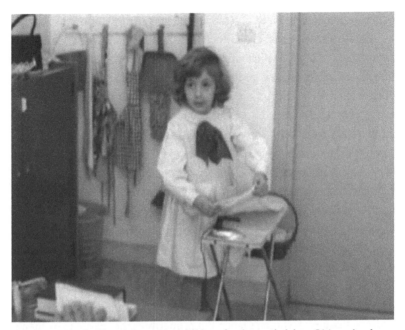

Figure 22. Film still, training schoolchildren for domestic labor, *L'Aggettivo donna* (1971). Courtesy of Centro Sperimentale di Cinematografia.

and are instructed to demurely pretend to serve tea to their male class-mates with child-sized teapots and cups. A voice-over argues that the educational system teaches authoritarianism and the need to be good workers but also implies that a key function of education in reproducing the workforce is the reproduction of the gendered division of labor. As the children leave the classroom in two orderly, gendered lines, a shot of a female teacher is framed with a cross hanging over her head on the wall behind her, a reminder of the patriarchal authority that enforces the natural, hierarchical order of things. In this sequence and elsewhere, the film demonstrates that gender is something that is learned, performed, and reinforced through authoritarian regimes. In analyzing how the adjective *woman* comes to modify a whole sphere of subjects and activities, the film denaturalizes gender, framing its argument in terms similar to Maya Gonzalez and Jeanne Neton, who assert gender is the "*anchoring* of a certain group of individuals in a specific sphere of social activities. The result of this anchoring process is at the same time the continuous reproduction of two separate genders."[50]

In exploring this anchoring process, the structure of *L'Aggettivo donna* performs the political evolution of the larger feminist movement. The film is divided into two sections: it starts with a discussion of struggles over women's exploitation in the sphere of waged labor, only to expand to a general discussion of reproductive labor. The first section starts with an exterior shot of an older woman in a food market struggling to lift a heavy basket of vegetables as a number of men pass by, seeming not to notice, until finally another woman arrives and helps her lift the basket to her head. Similar shots highlight the division of labor in the market, women always being paid less for more strenuous labor, as voice-offs of female workers describe the hardships they faced in the decades that they toiled. The next sequence features an occupied textile factory. Exterior shots of women workers sitting outside, talking and knitting, are juxtaposed with empty shots of the interior of the factory whose machines sit unused. Close-ups of the women engaged in conversation, listening and reacting to one another, underline the autonomous organizational strategies of the feminist movement. Through voice-overs and voice-offs of interviews with the striking workers, the sequence analyzes the problem of the "double shift": taking on waged work outside of the home does not exempt them from domestic labor but only lengthens the working day. While the women on strike at the factory are waged, proletariat workers, the film begins to dissect the ways that their issues differ from those of their male counterparts. At the end of the sequence, a voice-over concludes that the liberation of women cannot be achieved by further integrating them into the sphere of production; instead, the movement must recognize the role of women's labor within the capitalist system and work to overturn capitalism itself. A sound bridge provides a link to the next sequence on domestic labor discussed earlier, which opens with a shot of an unmade bed.

The remainder of the film addresses the private sphere: domestic labor, women's health, abortion, child-rearing, and education. Interspersed with footage from feminist protests, each of these segments contends with the immediately political nature of these areas and the need for women to organize autonomously to take control of their bodies and lives and reject the reproductive function to which they have been assigned. Focusing special attention on those processes that perform an essential function for capital—the reproduction of labor power itself—the film challenges and expands a Marxist understanding of the "social factory." According to Gonzalez and Neton, the attention to the reproduction of *labor power*, rather than reproduction *in general*, distinguishes Marxist feminists' analyses of reproductive functions within capitalism from a more general Marxist understanding of processes of reproduction.[51] A close-up of a poster at a feminist rally sums up the tone of indignation that the film takes toward the role women play in reproducing labor power; the poster depicts a pregnant woman standing in front of a house, a school, and a factory and reads "UN FIGLIO PER I PADRONI" (a child for the bosses). Refusing to have one's body, labor, and life used up in the reproduction of labor power, the poster identifies the multiple "bosses" whose authoritarian power controls life both within and outside the factory. The concluding voice-over of *L'Aggettivo donna* insists that "the liberation of women necessitates a cultural revolution" and that women should "reject the identification with masculinity or femininity" and "refute the definition of woman." In conducting a transvaluation of norms and values that attacks authoritarian regimes that fix certain individuals and practices to a set definition of "woman," *L'Aggettivo donna* prepares for an undefined and unexpected subject whose future is a political project.

L'Aggettivo donna's ending is itself anything but expected, a final and curious antiauthoritarian gesture. The intertitle for the final chapter reads "In Memoriam" and is followed with a montage of genitals of nude, male marble statues that concludes with a static, extreme close-up of a flaccid penis. Well lit, the penis shot lingers on the screen for an unsettling duration, and one cannot help but notice its corporeality, the small pulsations and beads of sweat that accumulate in parts of the image. A memorial (perhaps premature) for phallocentrism, the close-up endeavors to further demystify patriarchal authoritarianism by exposing the fleshy material associated with it for our contemplation, subjecting it to the scrutiny of both the camera and the feminist viewers who are invited to detect not its power but its vulnerability. Whatever visual pleasure the viewer might derive from this curious image—a true anomaly in the history of cinema—it is interrupted by an animated fist (the Lotta Femminista emblem) that takes over the screen, signaling the end of the film. Like Che Guevara's dead face at the end of *Hora de los hornos,* this long take is presented in a confrontational manner, forcing the viewer to consider its meaning within the context of the film's arguments while being overtaken by its imposing visual presence. It similarly attempts to elicit a reaction, one that might be transposed to political action. However, the underlying playfulness of *L'Aggettivo donna*'s conclusion departs from the militant tone of New Left essay films discussed in previous chapters, using humor as a subversive technique. The levity of the concluding sequence is produced through an intimacy with corporal existence. Consistent with the film's overall strategy, it suggests that patriarchal authority can only be undermined by bringing that which is deemed private into view, an approach that would be developed into a coherent formal strategy in the collective's next film.

AUTOCOSCIENZA IN *LOTTA NON È FINITA*

"The personal is political." This statement, which became an anthem of the international feminist movement, is attributed to Carol Hanisch's essay with the same title that appeared in 1970.[52] Though the author disputes having coined the phrase, her essay was a significant intervention into feminist politics in the United States and elsewhere, offering a defense of consciousness-raising groups as a model for political organization. Refuting the idea that these groups were simply "therapy," Hanisch maintains that they provided a space of dialogue through which "personal" problems came to be understood as shared. Moreover, this collective recognition could be transformed into political action around issues previously relegated to the private domain. According to Victoria Hesford, Hanisch's essay shows the influence of the New Left and the civil rights movement on early feminism in the United States but draws a contrast between the meaning of Hanisch's use of the "personal" as a site of politics and earlier New Left expressions that sought to produce "authentic, autonomous, free-thinking selves."[53] Instead, in the context of the women's movement, "the personal becomes a site of interrogation and the focus of political action rather than its beneficiary."[54]

Early feminist films took these group discussions, understood as a mode of organizing that foregrounds affective relationships and "gut understanding" of political life, as their subjects.[55] In the United States, films such as San Francisco Newsreel's *The Women's Film* and Kate Millett's *Three Lives* (1971) sought to capture the practice of consciousness raising, filming conversations among women as they develop a political consciousness. Collettivo Femminista di Cinema-Roma's second film, *Lotta non è finita,* further refines this cinematic approach by developing formal methods that make film itself an interrogation of layers of feminist political strategy. It does so by framing *autocoscienza,* or "autoconsciousness"— the gathering of small groups of women to discuss political matters by drawing on personal experience—within a broader reflection on feminist tactics. According to Paola Bono and Sandra Kemp, the term *autocoscienza* differed slightly from its English counterpart, "consciousness raising," by stressing "the self-determining and self-directed quality of the process of achieving new consciousness/awareness. It is a process of the discovery and (re-) construction of the self, both the self of the individual woman and a collective sense of self."[56] Although it is unclear how much *autocoscienza* departed from consciousness raising in practice, it was inflected with an autonomous ethos that defined Italian radical politics. The prefix *auto-* foregrounds both the sense of the automatic, unmediated nature of these political conversations and the autonomous disposition of this mode of political organization, which relies on the experience, creativity, and insights of the participants to build new subjectivities and collectivities.

Lotta non è finita is composed of three types of footage: theatrical performance, the documentation of the practice of *autocoscienza,* and b-roll of feminist protests. As I will discuss, this layered composition performs the tactical invention of *autocoscienza,* allowing the film to both reflect and build on militant cinematic style. The body of the film opens with a group of women of various ages discussing *autocoscienza* and the ways that it inaugurates a new form of politics that distinguishes the feminist movement from other radical movements because of its expansive politics that includes home life, labor, culture, and so on.[57] Similar to the cinematic rendering of the striking workers in *L'Aggettivo donna,* the sequence focuses on reaction shots rather than the speaking participants and cuts between pans of the group, close-ups of women's faces as they listen, and small gestures that communicate the casual and intimate nature of the setting, such as the lighting of a cigarette or a pair of hands knitting. The expressions on the faces of the participants also convey a sense of affinity, as the listening appears to be thoughtful and active. As a viewer, one is invited to listen in to the conversation from the perspective of a participant.

This sequence demonstrates that the rapport and intimacy developed within these groups allow for reflection on both personal experience and political strategy. At the same time, *autocoscienza* is achieved through a mode of realization that blurs the boundaries between individual and collective. The unexpected subject, in this instance, is a collective one—the collective political subject that arises from this process of dialogue and exchange. Better yet, the unexpected subject is transindividual—neither individual nor collective but existing in the mutual composition of both individual and collective.[58] Considering feminist politics from the 1970s in Italy, Étienne Balibar insists that this focus on transindividual politics reconstituted the domain of the political: "second-wave feminism, rather than affirming the 'private is political' in a simplistic fashion, focuses on the transformation of transindividual relations, and the way in which they affect individuality itself."[59] Organized around not only the collective production of knowledge but also the collective production of self, *autocoscienza* recognizes the processes of transindividuation necessary for the production of new political subjects. Departing from a politics that seeks to do away with the individual in favor of the collective, *autocoscienza* takes individual experience and understanding—already assumed to be social—as its starting point through which to arrive at a new collective figure. Moreover, in its cinematic rendering of this process of transindividuation, *Lotta non è finita* brings out the improvisational dimension of the collective, feminist subjectivity suggested in Lonzi's *soggetto imprevisto,* understood as a figure that comes into being through creative dialogue that exists in the combined affective and intellectual capacities of that collective.

Lotta non è finita builds on these insights to demonstrate the ways that *autocoscienza* became a crucial tool for the feminist movement to both craft and reflect on political strategy. It does so by having the group discuss the tactics used in two consecutive International Women's Days,

March 8, 1972, and March 8, 1973, which are shown through footage of the events. The footage from the 1972 demonstration documents a gathering of demonstrators holding signs and listening to a woman give a speech through a megaphone about the role that women play in capitalist society sustaining and maintaining families and workers, arguing that the only true revolution would be one that abolishes these gender roles. The protesters then march and chant, "In our families, the men are the bourgeoisie and the women are proletarians!" Chaotic shots, reminiscent of myriad protest scenes in New Left cinema, capture protesters arguing with onlookers, conducting a sit-it, clashing with police, and ultimately being arrested. Striking a different tone, the footage of the 1973 day of action opens with a woman beating a drum and reciting the history of International Women's Day, remembering first-wave feminist struggles as a group breaks into song with the chorus, "The fight is not over, we are still fighting for liberation." Conducting interviews, the filmmakers gather together groups of women to converse about feminist issues. One group discusses the unpaid status of women's labor, arguing that women need to talk about the need to be compensated for their work (a demand of the movement that is addressed at length in the following section). Further interviews that discuss abortion, education, and child-rearing are accompanied by footage of street theater that employs performance, humor, and drag as forms of political engagement.

After reviewing the footage from these protests, *Lotta non è finita* returns to the group of women, who then use the technique of *autocoscienza* to contemplate the differences between 1972 and 1973. They conclude that the 1972 protests were taken from the script of other social movements and remained "static" because their style was too "masculine," in comparison with the protest of 1973, which endeavored to create the space for dialogue. Two of the participants emphasize the role of creativity and performance in making the protests more dynamic and argue that these techniques are indispensable to newly forming political consciousness. Taking the insights of this conversation to heart, *Lotta non è finita* underscores the need for new political forms and tactics in its introduction and conclusion. In these segments, women from the collective, adorned with theatrical dress and makeup, perform cliché feminine gestures and behaviors: glancing over

Figure 23. Film still, *autocoscienza* group discussing feminist politics, *Lotta non è finita* (1973). Courtesy of Archivio Audiovisivo del Movimento Operaio e Democratico.

one's shoulder, gazing seductively into the camera, and dancing. At one point, members of the collective speak directly into the camera about the benefits of feminism as if in a television advertisement. Opening and closing with these performances, the film models feminist reflection on militant filmmaking on multiple levels: it documents the protests, conducts collective reflection on political tactics based on those documents, and integrates insights gained from those reflections into its own formal composition. Through these episodes of performance, *Lotta non è finita* breaks from the often sober tone of *L'Aggettivo donna,* interjecting more humor and mixing genres, accentuating play and solidarity among women rather than an oppositional stance. With the layering of formal strategies, the collective members themselves take on the process of testing possibilities for feminist cinematic expression and engagement, re-forming and reinventing themselves and inviting the viewer to join them as a participant in the ongoing process of *autocoscienza*. In doing so, *Lotta non è finita* is

Figure 24. Film still, theatrical performance, *Lotta non è finita* (1973). Courtesy of Archivio Audiovisivo del Movimento Operaio e Democratico.

exemplary of the ways feminist cinema expanded not only the purview of New Left discourse but also the formal strategies employed in the New Left's essay film, augmenting the tried and true arsenal of techniques.[60] Bringing new meaning to Solanas's idea that the New Left's essay film must remain "unfinished," *Lotta non è finita* similarly takes the position that "the struggle is not over." However, in the case of *Lotta non è finita,* the idea that the struggle is not over suggests less of a temporal connotation. Instead, for feminists, the struggle cannot be finished because it has not yet encompassed all domains of life in the here and now, especially those that are gendered and therefore deemed to be private. Articulated in a feminist register, this political stance insists that new revolutionary cinematic forms must be adequate to the new revolutionary subjectivities that come into being through the recognition that the personal is, indeed, political.

In its efforts to enlarge the definition of the political and complicate approaches to it, *Lotta non è finita* is indicative of the often experimental and open nature of the feminist movement in Italy and elsewhere. Their radical approach was, unsurprisingly, often met with hostility, and the alliance between women's autonomous organization and the remainder of the extraparliamentary Left in Italy remained tenuous. Like innumerable New Left social movements of the late 1960s, the status of women within radical political organizations often duplicated the division of labor of the industrial era, marginalizing women and assigning them supporting roles. The fact that women's reproductive labor was hidden not only in capitalism but also in the reproduction of revolution was reflected in the sardonic slogan "from the angel of the hearth to the angel of the copying machine."[61] The early feminist movement also had to contend with the explicit expression of misogyny within much of the counterculture and the Left, as *L'Aggettivo donna* indicates in its opening sequence with a quotation from Abbie Hoffman: "the only alliance I would make with the women's liberation movement is in bed." Nevertheless, throughout the 1970s, the practice of "double militancy," the concurrent participation in leftist political struggles and *autocoscienza* groups, was an essential aspect of the feminist movement in Italy. This practice persisted despite hostility and, at times, outright violence against autonomous feminist groups by men within the Italian Left.[62] The pejorative and even violent attitude taken toward the feminist movement was not unlike the attitudes taken by much of the Left toward the gay liberation movement. As Mario Mieli would go on to argue in *Towards a Gay Communism: Elements of a Gay Critique* (1977), attacks against both women's and gay liberation movements were made from a Left that was "phallocentric and heterosexual," and their inability and unwillingness to work with women's and gay liberation movements exposed them to be "male supremacist," giving support to "the public and private capitalist Norm, and hence the system itself."[63] While advocating for a revolutionary politics against the heterosexual "Norm," Mieli acknowledges the crucial role feminism played in challenging that norm: "the movement of revolutionary women has shaken the entire society, putting in crisis even those groups who call themselves revolutionary and yet have so far been ramparts of male supremacist bigotry."[64] Despite being marginalized within both the Italian Left and its historical legacy, Katsiaficas argues that the feminist movement had a profound role in shaping autonomous movements within Italy, laying the groundwork for later struggles, particularly the disruptions of 1977.[65] The feminist movement's capacity to unsettle established divisions and hierarchies and widen the horizon of possibility for politics is perhaps nowhere more evident than in the Wages for Housework campaign.

CINEMATIC PERSPECTIVES AND PROVOCATIONS IN THE WAGES FOR HOUSEWORK CAMPAIGN

"If having to do domestic labor determines our basic weakness and all the other aspects of our life, our liberation must start from here: the generalized demand for a salary for domestic labor paid directly from the State. In fact, domestic labor is productive labor."[66] So reads the preface to *Siamo tante, siamo donne, siamo stufe!* (We are many, we are women, we are fed up!, 1975) created by members of the Gruppo Femminista Milanese per il Salario al Lavoro Domestico. The documentation of a series of performances called "Audiovisuals," made up of projected photographs accompanied by an audio track that included speech and song, *Siamo stufe* offers a glimpse into the ways in which aesthetic experimentation within the Wages for Housework campaign expanded both cinematic form and revolutionary subjectivity. Arising from the confluence of the emergent feminist movement with struggles within the "social factory," Wages for Housework was one of the most radical and controversial feminist campaigns of the era. Launched in Padua in 1972 by the International Feminist collective with women from Italy, England, France, and the United States, the Wages for Housework campaign was unique within second-wave feminism because, according to Silvia Federici, the women who formed it came from "a history of militancy in Marxist-identified organizations, filtered through the experiences of the anti-colonial movement, the Civil Rights Movement, the Student Movement, and the 'Operaist' movement."[67] The campaign was popularized by Mariarosa Dalla Costa and Selma James's *The Power of Women and the Subversion of the Community,* published simultaneously in English and Italian, which contended that the position of woman within capitalism was that of "the slave of the wage slave . . . [whose] slavery insures the slavery of the man."[68] Echoing earlier Marxist feminists, Dalla Costa and James insist that the unpaid status of domestic labor allows it to be understood as natural, solidifying capitalist oppression through the nuclear family. Its renumeration, then, would undermine the naturalization of domestic labor and therefore gender hierarchies. Furthermore, the demand for wages for house*work* rather than house*wives* was a strategic move, according to Federici, that was part of a political project aimed at ultimately "degenderizing work."[69]

The development of the Wages for Housework campaign demonstrates how a radical political position can be built from a seemingly impossible demand. Making a critical distinction, Federici argued in her 1975 essay "Wages against Housework," the movement saw wages for housework not as a "thing" but as a "political perspective."[70]As a political perspective, the demand for wages for housework is a first step in a politics of refusal:

> *It is the demand by which our nature ends and our struggle begins because just to want wages for housework means to refuse that work as the expression of our nature,* and therefore to refuse precisely the female role that capital has invented for us.[71]

A political perspective aligned with the kinds of arguments we saw developed in *L'Aggittivo donna,* the Wages for Housework campaign focused attention on the gendering of whole spheres of human activity by attaching to them the modifying term "woman's" work. For Kathi Weeks, asserting that the demand for wages for housework is a political perspective is crucial to its power, allowing it to operate as "a force of demystification, an instrument for denaturalization, and a tool for cognitive mapping."[72] As a tool for cognitive mapping, the political perspective of Wages for Housework also provided a framework from which to align itself with other New Left social movements, challenging and widening the basis of revolutionary subjectivity.

This effort to remap revolutionary alliances and subjectivities can be seen in the 1975 defense of Wages for Housework offered by Federici and Nicole Kox, "Counterplanning from the Kitchen":

> We refuse to accept that while a male autoworker in Detroit can struggle against the assembly line, starting from our kitchens in the metropolis or from the kitchens and fields of the "Third World," our goal must be

the factory work that workers all over the world are increasingly refus-ing. . . . Inherent in this rejection is a redefinition of what capitalism is and who the working class is—that is, a new evaluation of class forces and class needs.[73]

Part of decentering and relocating who constitutes the protagonist of revolutionary struggle, the Wages for Housework campaign was intent on expanding the definition of the working class while at the same time redefining what counted as valid laboring activity. In other words, by demanding a wage, the movement ultimately endeavored to displace the wage as that which defines one's class position. For example, Federici and Kox single out struggles over social welfare, led primarily by black women, in the United States that came out of the civil rights movement as a principal site of influence:

> In the United States the struggles of blacks and welfare mothers—the "Third World" of the metropolis—expressed the revolt of the wageless and their refusal of the only alternative that capital offers: more work. These struggles, which had their center of power in the community, were not for development, but for the reappropriation of the social wealth that capital has accumulated from the waged as well as the wageless.[74]

"The revolt of the wageless" and the refusal of more work that Federici and Kox find in the struggles of women receiving AID for Dependent Children use the "imaginative geography" characteristic of the New Left to reframe class struggle.[75]

It is from this enlarged class perspective that *Siamo stufe* starts, re-counting the history of the feminist movement from the Suffragettes and early socialist feminists to the present, while underscoring alliances with "the young, the unemployed, the Black Panthers and blacks in general, so-called 'ethnic minorities,'" and struggles against imperial domination in Latin America, Africa, Asia, and elsewhere.[76] Grounding resistance to the gendered division of labor within the global New Left imaginary, *Siamo stufe* draws out points of connection, rather than divisions, between First World and Third World feminist positions. Before exploring further the arguments of *Siamo stufe* within the context of the larger Wages for Housework campaign, I want to discuss first how its experimental formal approach complemented the expanded political position it aimed to incite. Like the collective filmmaking experiments tied to the feminist movement in Rome, *Siamo Stufe* was part of an ongoing feminist exchange in northern Italy that sought to build a social movement out of the critique of the gendered division of labor.[77] Combining sound and images projected on a screen, *Siamo stufe*'s paracinematic performances, which the group called "screenings," relied on conventions of cinematic experience. At the same time, they took advantage of an "expanded" cinematic form that enhanced the possibility for audience engagement and participation. These types of paracinematic events certainly had antecedents within the world of avant-garde and documentary cinema, a notable precursor being the slide show presentations that were put on in France in the early 1960s by members of the Centre culturel populaire de Palente-les-Orchamps (Popular Cultural Center of Palente-les-Orchamps), who would go on to form Le groupe Medvedkine, Besançon.[78] The Gruppo Femminista named these paracinematic events "Audiovisuals" (recalling the use of this term in Collettivo Femminista di Cinema-Roma's manifesto), arguing that an audiovisual format had the capacity to reach more women and act as an "instrument of intervention" capable of "arousing debate."[79] In addition to the financial and logistical reasons for not using film, the group's choice of the "audiovisual" format is an example of the creative extension of cinematic experience beyond the medium of film within New Left social movements. Blurring the distinction between performance, cinema, and education, the "audiovisual" in this context is at the same time a vehicle for information and a catalyst for struggle.

Accounting for the ways that the gendered division of labor is enforced by the state and capital, the first section of *Siamo stufe* resonates with *L'Aggettivo donna*'s critique of authoritarian patriarchy as it narrates the everyday violence through which young girls are coerced into proper modes of female behavior. These passages are reinforced by images of children adorned in feminine attire and playing with toy ovens and dolls. Later, the script locates the control of women's reproductive capacities in the demands for labor and soldiers by capital and the state that were intensified under fascism. Juxtaposed with an advertisement for Singer sewing machines from World War II that depicts two women sewing a fascist uniform for a little boy who wears it proudly, holding up a pistol in one hand and a book in the other, the voice-over narrates,

> In 1929 Mussolini introduces the Rocco code that outlaws any contraceptive measure and persecutes abortion as a crime against birth. In 1930 the Casti Connubi of Pope Pio XI on Christian marriage excludes abortion even in the case of a pregnancy or birth that endangers the woman.... After the war ended and soldiers were no longer necessary, the problem of controlling births was re-raised. The same system that was used to incentivize reproduction is now used to limit it, also because a future mass of unemployed is a hypothetical mass of disruptive revolutionaries. It is no coincidence in fact that the pill and sterilization were first experimented with and then encouraged in black ghettos and Third World countries.

Identifying the state's management of the population through birthrates, *Siamo stufe* anticipates arguments about "biopower" Michel Foucault would make at the Collège de France in the subsequent year.[80] Unlike Foucault, however, the feminist critique presented in *Siamo stufe* demonstrates the degree to which these politics are directly played out through the reproductive capacities of women's bodies and labors, intimating how these very bodies might become sites of resistance. Like the poster from *L'Aggettivo donna* that reads "UN FIGLIO PER I PADRONI," *Siamo stufe*'s examination of the various figures of patriarchal authority—the church, the state, the medical establishment—who rule over reproductive capacities simultaneously calls on its participants to refuse this authority.

Concurring with Federici's insistence that the demand for wages for housework opened onto a political perspective of refusal, the performance transitions to the topic of domestic labor with the song "Siamo stufe!" by the Gruppo Musicale del Comitato per il Salario al Lavoro Domestico di Padova. Encapsulating the antiproductivist stance that pervades the performance, the song lists the things with which women are fed up:

We are fed up with making babies
Washing dishes and ironing diapers
A man who is a boss/master and forbids contraception[81]

At the conclusion of this song, *Siamo stufe* sets forth the demand for wages from the state, accusing it of "wage theft" by continuing to keep domestic labor unpaid.[82] A photograph of a woman gazing at a mountain of unwashed dishes is accompanied by the following voice-over:

> One of the most obvious exploitations that the Feminist Movement has identified is the situation of women's domestic labor.
>
> This massive amount of unpaid labor that women are forced to do sustains our capitalist society. According to our society, domestic labor is something that enriches the mind and character of those that perform it. However, reality is very different as we very well know that domestic labor is very hard work that is often monotonous and keeps women busy at every minute of the day.
>
> It is no coincidence that this labor has always been made personal: a woman is a mother, a wife and a dedicated daughter only if she is willing to perform hard labor for free for her whole life. . . .
>
> The man in the office and the women in kitchen: making family bonds sacred, exploiting family affections, and making women accept that domestic labor is not productive, while still societally indispensable, all serve to stabilize the power of the capitalist State.
>
> We know that there are approximately 15 million housewives and that the value of their labor is estimated at 400,000 lire per month by calculating the salary of a maid, a babysitter, a cook, a launderer and a teacher.[83]

Using what Miranda Joseph would call "counter-accounting," *Siamo stufe* calculates the wages owed to women by the state, paired with an illustration that breaks down the sum of 400,000 lire into various activities a typical housewife would perform in her daily routine.[84] This calculation functions as evidence of the value-producing labor of the housewife that supports the demand for remuneration. At the same time, this illustration represents an effort to destabilize "the power of the capitalist State" by profaning the sacred family bonds that uphold it, attributing monetary value to the supposedly immeasurable love of the wife/mother.

Beyond its ability to disrupt the natural order of industrial capitalism, *Siamo stufe* makes clear that the politicization of housework is a strategic necessity. By isolating and naturalizing domestic labor, the Left undermines its own capacity to fight capitalism:

Another thing that causes housewives to live as inferior and impotent is social isolation. Because housewives have not been recognized as a "worker of the house," they have also been excluded from leftist organizations of the working class and therefore have no choice but to find individual solutions.

On an individual level, for example, housewives have had to confront continuous rising prices....

In fact, while men are expected to take to the streets against the crisis of the cost of living, women are expected to make a stipend sufficient as this stipend becomes smaller.

In the face of inflation, the housewife is asked to do more with less—making ends meet and thus ameliorating what would otherwise be an occasion for protest. The unrecognized status of domestic labor *as labor* by the Left weakens its position against capital by forcing women to maintain the reproductive sphere, therefore propping up both capital and the state.[85] Left uninterrogated, housework remains the lynchpin of capitalism and the undoing of struggles against it. To reiterate an oft-cited passage from Dalla Costa, "we've never seen a general strike."[86]

Through *Siamo Stufe*'s expanded "audiovisual" essay, viewers are confronted by a series of arguments that, at the same time, interpellate them as political agents. By performing the demand as a political perspective, the demand for wages in *Siamo stufe* quickly morphs into what Kathi Weeks calls "a demand as provocation."[87] For Weeks, the demand as provocation implicit within the Wages for Housework campaign "served also to elicit the subversive commitments, collective formations, and political hopes it only appears to reflect."[88] The same could be said of the *Siamo stufe* "screenings," which staged this logic of the demand as provocation by creating situations that gathered together new collectivities, using the demand for wages—calculated in a seemingly logical fashion—as a pretext for engaging groups of women in the project of subverting capitalism by refusing to perform the labors that sustain it. By calling out the ways that division of labor is maintained by seemingly leftist political movements, *Siamo stufe* immediately addresses viewers as agents of revolutionary transformation. Expanding the frame of cinematic experience, the screenings enact an essayistic politics of the common through a demand that serves as a provocation to confront not only the divisions that structure capitalist society but also the ways that these divisions have excluded participants from claiming a position within leftist movements. *Siamo stufe* thus creates a space that summons the subject thought to have the least involvement in political life—the housewife—into an unexpected revolutionary position.

CODA: THE FEMINIZATION OF LABOR AND THE "UNEXPECTED SUBJECT"

Siamo stufe's illustration, which breaks down the hours and wages of discrete activities that make up the working day of a domestic laborer, is prescient in its depiction of an economy based on immaterial services that are remunerated by capital. The illustration considers these activities, naturalized within the domain of women's work by industrial economies, as distinct professions—teacher, babysitter, cook—each of which renders services that must be compensated by a wage. Highlighting the rationale for the demand for housework wages, this illustration might also be read as implicitly registering a shift that was already under way in the 1970s. The shift I am referring to is what economists, labor historians, and cultural theorists alike call the "feminization of labor," which signals not only the marked intensification of the influx of women into the labor market that had been gradually occurring in the postwar era but also the transformation to a service-based economy propelled by "feminized" forms of labor. Reflecting on the signs of this transformation, Silvia Federici locates the impetus for women to move into the workforce in "women's refusal to function as unwaged workers in the home, catering to the reproduction of the national workforce."[89] Though the movement of women into the workforce—often into service industry positions that offered lower pay than positions occupied by their male counterparts—had baffled economists at the time, Federici, grounding her analysis in the experience of feminist struggle, finds the explanation to be simple: "women have traded off unpaid housework for their families for paid housework in the marketplace."[90] She rejects the theory that mechanization was somehow responsible for women moving out of the home by locating the reorganization of labor in the politics of refusal cultivated by the feminist movement. A familiar version of this argument is put forward by Michael Hardt and Antonio Negri, who argue that by highlighting and contesting the social value of reproductive labor, the movements of the New Left, and the feminist movement in particular, put the industrial mode of production that had come into being around these divisions and hierarchies into crisis, precipitating new forms of labor and subjectivity in the post-Fordist era.[91] Following this thread, one can begin to see how each expression of the "unexpected subject" cultivated in the cinematic experiments of the 1970s becomes essential to the post-Fordist, feminized labor force. In post-Fordism, we witness the the breakdown of hierarchies and the division between production and reproduction, with reproductive activities becoming increasingly commodified. Moreover, in post-Fordist labor, collective, communicative, and affective capacities are called upon, precisely those that drove feminist political practices like *autocoscienza*.

The "feminization of labor," accordingly, transfigures not only women's work but also the entire organization of the economy and the subjects who populate it. Federici observes already in 1980 the growth of new industries that commodify reproductive capacities, and accordingly, "the productivity of reproductive work is no longer measured (as it used to be) by the productivity of the male worker on the job, but directly at the point where the services are delivered."[92] The transformation of reproductive labor and its sites of valorization foresee the broader restructuring of capitalism in the post-Fordist era. As Christina Morini argues, the feminization of labor implies not only the entrance of women into the workforce but the entire spatial and temporal reorganization of daily life: "'work which becomes a woman,' is tantamount to saying that the fragmentation of the services provided and the complexity of the dependence/absorption which women have experienced at various times in the labor market, ends up becoming a general paradigm, irrespective of gender."[93] Thus, as Morini and others have claimed, the recomposition of the working class in contemporary capitalism relies on the success of capital to transform labor into a precarious, flexible, fragmented form that draws on the cognitive and affective skills traditionally associated with reproductive labor.

We might argue that the "unexpected subject" that survives from the 1970s feminist movement is precisely the post-Fordist worker that Morini describes: flexible, fluctuating between spheres, and, to a certain extent, degendered. At the same time, we are acutely aware that the project of feminist liberation set out by the political movements discussed in this chapter is far from being achieved; the contradiction between production and reproduction has been transfigured, not effaced. It remains, according to Nancy Fraser, the "'social contradiction' inherent in the deep structure of capitalist society," one that "grounds a crisis tendency" within capitalism:[94]

> on the one hand, social reproduction is a condition of possibility for sustained capital accumulation; on the other, capitalism's orientation to unlimited accumulation tends to destabilize the very processes of social reproduction on which it relies. This social-reproductive contradiction of capitalism lies at the root of the so-called crisis of care.[95]

In every capitalist era—and always in relation to colonial and imperial conquest—capital's vampiric relationship to social reproduction also imposes a crisis upon it.[96] In the financialized, neoliberal era that has followed the crises of Keynesianism, Fraser recounts a familiar narrative with regard to the crisis or reproduction we currently face: while so-called gender equality is outwardly achieved in the sphere of production, reproduction within neoliberalism appears as "a backward residue" that must be overcome.[97] Even as the relationship between production and reproduction is transformed in different capitalist eras, the devaluation of reproductive labor is a constant that occurs alongside the production of gender, which is "reimposed and re-naturalized," according to Gonzalez and Neton.[98]

Rather than the epitome of the flexible post-Fordist laborer, we should consider another possible narrative about the "unexpected subject" called for by Lonzi and the way that this figure might endure in our present, reframed through the lens of contemporary struggles. For the autonomist feminists in Italy and elsewhere, the project of abolishing gendered spheres of labor that "anchor" subjects to particular gendered identities was necessary to any anticapitalist politics. As Gonzalez and Neton put it, the abolition of gender entails the "reproduction of life in which all separate spheres of activity have been abolished."[99] On the other hand, the contemporary "unexpected subject" might also be found in the anti-productivism of the demand for basic income, which Kathi Weeks deems a "worthy successor" to the demand for Wages for Housework.[100] The demand for basic income, for Weeks, is a crucial step toward imagining a life beyond work and calling such a future into being. As both a political perspective and a provocation, Weeks argues that the demand for basic income is part of what she calls a "post-work imaginary" that has its strength not only in the fact that it separates income from laboring activities but also because it is gender neutral and therefore its "benefits are not exclusive to any particular group."[101] There remain many unresolved questions regarding how a basic income would be organized and fairly distributed, as Weeks acknowledges. Nevertheless, as a demand, it holds within it the utopian potential of a life whose livelihood is not immediately tied to its productive capacities.

We might read the unexpected subject, then, as that subject that holds the radical potential that comes forward through the nexus of intertwined political projects: abolition of work and abolition of gender. When speaking of the possibility of a gender strike, Madaline Lane-McKinley reminds us that the abolition of gender is "not doing away with the question of gender but much the opposite."[102] For Lane-McKinley, the abolition of gender cannot be found in the calls for "unity" and "solidarity" on the Left by diminishing difference but by continuing to foreground gender, always insisting "that culture and politics cannot be separated."[103] In *L'Aggittivo donna*, the vast field, discussed at the beginning of the chapter, that both literally and symbolically divides the spheres of production and reproduction designates an abyss that only reinforces isolation. In a postwork and postgender world, however, this space could come to be understood as an opening through and against which a new figure or set of figures might appear, the shape of whose lives we cannot yet anticipate. In other words, the unexpected subject's future remains a political project, one that demands a new transvaluation of norms and values accompanied by a rigorous antiauthoritarianism that refuses to allow matters of reproductive labor, and the "private" sphere in general, to be relegated to "identity politics." Creating the conditions for new, unexpected subjects to emerge means continually expanding the domain of the political, while attending to the transindividual nature of political life by creating new forms of collaboration and collectivity.

5

Cybernetic Guerrilla Warfare

EARLY VIDEO AND THE AMBIVALENCE
OF INFORMATION

> You are information.
> —*Radical Software* Editorial Collective

> We do no lack communication. On the contrary, we have too
> much of it. We lack creation. *We lack resistance to the present.*
> —GILLES DELEUZE AND FÉLIX GUATTARI,
> *What Is Philosophy?*

"It's not an indigenous data bank. It's a control system. This is Big Broth-er." So remarks an off-camera voice over grainy, handheld video footage of an early closed-circuit surveillance system in a Los Angeles grocery store. "They got cats coming in here to buy this shit, and work their ass off so they can buy this shit. . . . They sell it to them over television, right? And they have this thing set up so you don't steal what they make you want to buy because they hype you up as a consumer." A store manager in a sterile white jacket appears and insists that they turn the camera off, to which the videographers protest: you're taking our picture, why can't we take yours? Once outside, they start conducting an impromptu interview with the manager, pressing him to reveal his own fatigue and alienation working for the grocery store. He concedes his job makes him tired. Occurring at the end of the Raindance Corporation's video essay *Proto Media Primer* (1970), the video has an amateurish quality, as the camera continually zooms in and out on objects and people and maintains only a loose connection with the footage that preceded it: person-on-the-street interviews and an extended conversation with Abbie Hoffman as he awaits the verdict of the Chicago 8 trail. One of three Media Primers produced by the Raindance Corporation, the video essay has a fluid and

Figure 25. Video still, surveillance monitor, *Proto Media Primer* (1970).

open form, testing the limits and possibilities of the medium as a mode of engagement and a tool for analyzing the media itself. The confrontation with the grocery store surveillance system accentuates a distinction between the use of television as a means of control and its potential use as a tool for subversion capable of producing new forms of participatory knowledge and affects, which constitute, in the parlance of the guerrilla television movement, "information."

The skirmish between members of the Raindance Corporation and the grocery store surveillance network illuminates the way that the videographers understood television to be wrapped up in a set of power dynamics mediated by the commodity: television sells commodities and is, in turn, used as a means to protect them. For scholars like David Joselit, mid-century artists took aim against broadcast television because it had become "a point of contact between networks and commodities,"[1] effectively privatizing public communication to the extent that the "drama of television is the birth and rebirth of the commodity."[2] If television had effectively produced a "closed circuit" of networked, commodity culture, then video activists sought to replace this unidirectional, commodified televisual image with a multidirectional, participatory image. These activists, to whom I refer as the guerrilla television (GTV) movement, took the release of the Sony Porta-Pak in 1967 as an opportunity to imagine a politics of the moving image in which everyday people could disrupt circuits of power by making their own television. Claiming "you are information," the GTV movement went beyond a critique of commodity culture by insisting that televisual networks could be radically horizontalized, affording each individual the capacity to assert her own value as information within the network.

Through the early alternative television movement in the United States, this chapter examines how the introduction of consumer-grade video in the late 1960s and early 1970s intersected with New Left imaginaries and cinematic practices, opening up new domains of critical inquiry and experimentation. Though typically understood as part of the legacy of "video art," I argue that the early alternative television movement—and particularly its most radical contingent, GTV—was inspired by concerns similar to those that animated New Left cinema more generally: participation; antiauthoritarianism and disinterest in authorship; decentralized models of communication; and a desire to create alternative messages, analyses, and networks of production and distribution. The latter interest in organizing networks of production and distribution of audiovisual information became the primary site of intervention for the movement. As Michael Shamberg of the Raindance Corporation put it, "we don't want to put alternate programming on the existing structure. We want an alternate structure."[3] Breaking with modernist ideas of medium specificity, the GTV movement proposed that *we do not yet know what a medium can do.*[4] In other words, we do not yet know how an audiovisual medium might become the occasion for reorganizing society in a more equitable fashion or how we might use a new medium to replace an old one. Less interested in the relatively modest goal of replacing film or television with video, the movement wanted to use video to circulate alternative information that, they believed, could generate a more just society and even come to supplant capitalist means of exchange. Forwarding a vision of techno-utopianism, the GTV movement extended the ambitions of

New Left cinema by placing its emphasis on the capacity of the moving image and its circulation to transform social life.

To understand these ambitions, I examine the ways that the GTV movement appropriated concepts from the field of cybernetics, or the science of control and communication, in ways that complicated the belief in the power of alternative information that motivated New Left cinematic practice generally. By the 1960s, cybernetics discourses and systems thinking originally developed in the context of the U.S. military-industrial complex had been taken up in diverse areas of both mainstream and counterculture. Examining this phenomenon in the GTV movement, I assert that the adaptation of cybernetic ideas was distinct from other areas of the U.S. counterculture and did not simply replicate the cybernetic language of information, difference, and feedback popularized by figures like Norbert Wiener, Marshall McLuhan, Gregory Bateson, and Buckminster Fuller. Instead, it used the language of cybernetics to advance visions of moving image culture that provided a secondary translation, a mutation, of cybernetic thinking that framed it within New Left principles and tactics, such as guerrilla warfare and participatory democracy.

Focusing on the influential journal *Radical Software* (1970–74) and Michael Shamberg's compendium to it, *Guerrilla Television* (1971), this chapter reexamines early video culture as a site of encounter between New Left cinema and the field of cybernetics to contemplate the ways in which the aims and aspirations of New Left cinema intersected with the emergent information economy. By examining how cybernetic concepts were adapted, developed, and circulated within the GTV movement, I argue that the movement, more than any other example of New Left cinema, worked to theorize the political and economic "value" of alternative information and its networks of production and distribution. Before turning to these questions, I give a brief overview of early GTV movements and the journal that connected them, *Radical Software,* placing them within the legacy of New Left cinema rather than the distinct, but sometimes overlapping, category of "video art." I then underscore the connections between New Left cinema and GTV through a discussion of Paul Ryan's concept of *cybernetic guerrilla warfare,* which imagines video to be a weapon against what he calls "perceptual imperialism." Using Ryan's cybernetic guerrilla warfare thesis as an entry point into a broader discussion of the adaptation of cybernetic concepts within the movement allows me to draw out how GTV practitioners imagined the political stakes of their intervention into communication systems.

I then turn to a more detailed discussion of the movement's use of the term *information,* examining how, in repurposing cybernetic theories in a New Left context, the GTV practitioners imagined a utopian direction for the emergent information economy. In contrast to existing accounts of the adaptation of cybernetic thought by the 1960s counterculture presented by scholars like Fred Turner, I understand GTV's relationship to the emergent information economy to be one of ambivalence rather than co-optation or collaboration.[5] In particular, I explore how we can read from the encounter between GTV and cybernetics an ambivalent account of the purported power of information and its capacity to renew social life. If previous chapters examined the ways that New Left cinema anticipated and engaged in larger reorganizations of the economy around financialization and feminization, in this chapter, I am interested in how New Left cinema registered and attempted to intercede in the increasing informatization of the economy in the late 1960s and early 1970s. In doing so, I interrogate how these movements employed video as part of the political strategy of producing and distributing ever more and different information—in the form of moving images—as a way to reinvent economic and political structures, testing both the potentials and the limits of what the medium could do. Ultimately, I argue that the GTV movement expanded New Left cinema while simultaneously exposing some limitations in its underlying assumptions regarding the power of the moving image as a tool for political transformation. In doing so, I am interested in how the translation of cybernetic theories in the GTV movement reveals a set of paradoxes in the New Left's approach to problems of information and communication in a capitalist system that increasingly relied on both.

EARLY GUERRILLA TELEVISION AS NEW LEFT CINEMA

Video was a novel technology, but many early experiments with the medium dovetailed with existing circuits and practices of New Left cinema as outlined in this book. In the few short years following the release of the Sony Portapak in 1967, video collectives sprung up in locations where New Left cinematic practices were already established, such as TVX in the United Kingdom, Vidéo Out in France (discussed in the previous chapter), Videobase in Italy, and Video Hiroba in Japan, in addition to numerous early collectives in the United States. These groups often congealed around political movements and projects of the New Left and developed formal strategies, such as the essay form, that drew from existing cinematic idioms. For example, in Italy, Videobase made struggles within the "social factory" their focus, producing a series of video essays in the early 1970s on topics such as *autoriduzione* rent strikes, struggles within prisons, and health care.[6] In Japan, Video Hiroba used video as a vehicle to engage social movements and regular citizens in an effort to generate a participatory alternative to mainstream media.[7] Conversations about the political potentials of video, like film, also traveled along international New Left channels. To trace these conversations, one might look at, for example, Roberto Faenza's book *Senza chiedere permesso: Come rivoluzionare l'informazione* (Without asking permission: How to revolutionize information, Italy, 1973). This manifesto on radical video and television production draws on cybernetic theories of communication outlined in Shamberg's *Guerrilla Television* and Latin American media theorists engaging with McLuhan to argue for an autonomous video culture in Italy, while at the same time providing a practical how-to guide.[8]

In early video culture, there was also a significant amount of cross-pollination with filmmakers already working in the New Left cinema, and many moved between media. However, video had a democratizing effect on New Left cinematic production. As many early practitioners have noted, video offered a newfound possibility for gender equality. Nancy Cain, member of the Videofreex, contends, "If there had not been portable video I don't think that it would have been possible for women to be equals in the new media. If it had been film, well, film was owned and run by men.... But it wasn't film. It was video. And no one knew how to do it. We were all beginners."[9] Appearing around the time of the women's and gay liberation movements, video did more than offer new technical capacities. Its relative affordability and the fact that it had not been colonized by patriarchal film culture broadened the field of moving image production in the 1970s, as has been well documented.[10]

The connections between the New Left and early video in the United States were exemplified in video collaborations such as the Mayday Collective, formed in 1971 with the explicit intent to use video as a political tool in the antiwar protests in Washington, D.C., honoring the first anniversary of the Kent State shootings. The resulting video, distributed widely throughout alternative video networks, features the kind of raw energy that New Left collectives brought to video, including chaotic footage of confrontations between video camerapersons and police.[11] It also captures how early video movements emphasized the need to engage with multiple perspectives, taking accounts and reactions from everyday people as its primary source material. In person-on-the-street interviews with participants and onlookers, the resulting video shows divergent political viewpoints and reactions, from a transgender woman who links sexual liberation to political freedom to a group of workers who express their displeasure with the protests and claim to represent the "silent majority."

In the United States, as elsewhere, New Left movements and the broader counterculture were the subjects of numerous early "tapes," as they were called, that demonstrated the ways that some early video makers sought to embed themselves within existing New Left political and cultural networks. In addition to the Raindance Corporation, notable among the first video groups coming out of New York were People's Video Theater and Videofreex. Throughout the early 1970s, People's Video Theater took their video cameras onto the streets to conduct interviews at women's and gay liberation marches, with the Young Lords while they occupied a Harlem church, and at an action by the American Indian Movement at Plymouth Rock. The People's Video Theater approached these events by conducting intimate person-on-the-street interviews with participants and bystanders, often revealing both tensions and surprising affinities across various sectors of the population, which they screened weekly in their "video theater." The group also set up interview stations in various parts of the city and surrounding areas where they would connect the video camera to a live monitor, creating "feedback" for participants, who could see themselves on television while being interviewed, as I discuss later.

Figure 26. Video still, subjects being interviewed at gay liberation rally by People's Video Theater, 1970.

People's Video Theater worked to build a process that the group called "video mediation" among different sectors of the population by "creating lines of communication between antagonistic groups whereby each can experience the information of the other without direct confrontation."[12] The Videofreex, on the other hand, traveled the country in 1969 taping countercultural events and New Left movements with initial funds from CBS to turn the footage into a series titled *Subject to Change*. Though the series was never aired, the group managed to attain both technical capacity and remarkable footage, including an interview with Fred Hampton, Chicago Black Panther, months before his murder by the police. In 1972, the Videofreex moved to Lanesville, New York, and established the first pirated television station, living and working collectively and developing networks of education and outreach until 1978. Though these collectives projected an image of equality, their relationships with diverse social movements were far from immune to the representational politics that plagued other New Left cinema movements discussed in previous chapters. Chris

Robé argues in his history of early video movements in the United States that collectives like Videofreex and People's Video Theater were made up of mostly white, middle-class members who were, like the broader New Left and counterculture, often tone-deaf to issues of race and gender, particularly within their own ranks.[13]

Though differing in tactics and style, all of these early collectives were tied together through *Radical Software,* the iconic journal of the alternative television movement, which functioned as a central node through which projects and ideas circulated in the United States and beyond. A publication of the Raindance Corporation, *Radical Software* put out issues from 1970 to 1974. Formed in New York by a group of video activists and artists after the influential Television as a Creative Medium exhibition in 1969, Raindance Corporation was conceived as, in Michael Shamberg's words, "the counter-culture's analogue to the RAND Corporation, a think-tank that would use videotape instead of print."[14] The RAND Corporation was founded by the War Department after World War II to connect the military with private industry and was, at the time, deeply embroiled in the Vietnam War. It had also become the center of systems thinking for both military and civilian applications, especially early experimentation with computer networking. Shamberg's reflection on the initiation of the Raindance Corporation seems to contradict its otherwise leftist and countercultural pursuits. As Shamberg reminisces in his account of the short history of the GTV movement, "in those days everyone was very taken with the fact that for a few hundred dollars you could form your own corporation and become an officer."[15] Aside from the sheer novelty and perhaps somewhat ironic and even cynical adaptation of the corporate form, Raindance's incorporation is symptomatic of a more complicated blurring of industry and counterculture embodied in the figure of the "network entrepreneur."[16] As I discuss later, the tension between network entrepreneurship and the countercultural, even revolutionary, aspirations of the GTV movement is indicative of the ways that the movement registered and participated in shifts toward a networked, information-based economy.

Radical Software was at the center of alternative media culture in the United States, and the first issues featured the ideas of key figures for

Figure 27. *Radical Software* journal cover. Courtesy of Ira Schneider.

the movement, such as Fuller, Bateson, and Gene Youngblood, whose cybernetic thinking framed much of the conversation. *Radical Software* also promoted the use of new media technologies, namely, video and cable television, to undermine the hegemony of broadcast television, which they saw as a unidirectional, centralized form of communication that needed to be replaced by decentralized, multidirectional, participatory communication channels. Cable television was understood as a means to break up the hegemony of the broadcast networks and democratize information. The utopian visions of cable television's potential for interactive communication intuited internet technologies that would realize these visions in the coming decades.

The magazine's form was modeled on the process-oriented ethos of the movement and included how-to guides for using video technology, "Cultural Databases" of various early groups across the country working with video in a variety of capacities, and a "Feedback" section that served as a forum for dialogue between early video groups. Directly inspired by *The Whole Earth Catalog,* the journal was conceived as an open text. In an editorial statement reflecting on the first issue of *Radical Software,* Beryl Korot and Ira Schneider write,

> In issue one, volume one of *Radical Software* (Summer 1970) we introduced the hypothesis that people must assert control over the information tools and processes that shape their lives in order to free themselves from the mass manipulation perpetrated by commercial media in this country and state controlled television abroad. By accessing low cost 1/2" portable video tape equipment to produce or create or partake in the information gathering process, we suggested that people would contribute greatly to resurrecting their own information environments: YOU ARE THE INFORMATION. . . . In particular we focused on the increasing number of experiments conducted by people using this 1/2" video tool: experiments in producing locally originated programming for closed-circuit and cable tv and for public access cablevision; construction of video information environments/structures/assemblages as related to information presentation and audience involvement.[17]

Promoting video as a technology that affords the possibility of "resurrecting" one's own information environment, the journal saw its role as one of empowering people to intervene in existing communication systems while inventing new ones. The hypothesis that "you are the information" advanced by *Radical Software* was not only the underlying philosophy of the journal but also integral to its composition and organization.

Contrary to its characterization in recent scholarship, *Radical Software* did not exclusively cater to early video artists but operated as a forum for many groups working to develop alternative media structures. For example, in March 1971, Eldridge Cleaver, minister of information for the Black Panther Party International Section, and living in exile in Algeria, wrote letters imploring the help of the GTV movement. In a letter to the editors of *Radical Software* reprinted in the journal, Cleaver briefly describes a "video tape program" that the party had initiated "directed to the United States and Europe on a regular basis to cover the spectrum of the international anti-imperialist revolutionary movement."[18] Proposing a tape exchange, Cleaver requested that a number of tapes mentioned in earlier issues of *Radical Software* be added to a "tape library" the party was in the process of building for the purposes of "information, research, and distribution." The tapes Cleaver requested included *Post Kent State— Washington D.C. Peace Demonstration, New York State CATV Operators Convention,* and *Glen Falls N.Y. Profile on a Town About to Install CATV.*[19] Cleaver's request demonstrates the impact *Radical Software* had in shaping the alternative television movement within its first year of publication and that its proposals regarding the political possibilities of new distribution networks, particularly cable television, had appeal across diverse social movements, as was later demonstrated in the publication *The Black Panther,* which featured an article titled "Cable Television: A Signal for Change" on its cover in 1972.[20] The same spring that Cleaver wrote to *Radical Software,* the Black Panther Party International Section sent a delegation to the People's Republic of the Congo with video equipment obtained by William Stephens, an American photographer living in Paris, from an unnamed French video collective.[21] The footage shot during the expedition by Williams and Cleaver was brought back to Paris and edited, remarkably, with the assistance of Chris Marker, and the final result was a forty-minute documentary *Congo oye (We Have Come Back)* (1971).[22] The tape was apparently never released, but its production, along with Cleaver's suggestion of a tape exchange to *Radical Software*'s readers, testifies to the ways that video, like film, followed and facilitated international circuits of political organization.

Video offered new promise to organizations like the Black Panthers, who immediately saw its political potential. Further evidence of this can be found in a letter Cleaver wrote to People's Video Theater asking for help from the collective in the Black Panthers' efforts to secure more video equipment for a delegation the party was planning to send to China: "having begun to use video for communication and information purposes, we have discovered the fantastic effectiveness of this medium as a political weapon and want to develop its potential to a much higher level."[23] In the letter, Cleaver hopes that what he calls "the video network" would also help to distribute the tapes after the trip and might also be enlisted in the project of developing a "Revolutionary People's Communication Network throughout Babylon for distributing and reproducing video."[24] Cleaver's letter to People's Video Theater was reprinted in *Guerrilla Television* and, commenting on the letter, Michael Shamberg insists on the importance of video for the "survival" of radical movements like the Panthers. Though Shamberg is hesitant to endorse the Panthers' vanguard style, he insists that the media ultimately played a central role in subverting the Panthers *"because they couldn't control their own image."*[25] As Cleaver's letters attest, the need to control one's own image—and therefore assert one's own vision of reality as information—was a pressing matter for social movements at the time. Video invigorated New Left political imaginaries by offering the potential for claiming the power of the moving image to mold social reality.

Histories of video like the one documented in Cleaver's letters complicate the institutionally received memory of early video as reducible to an art practice. Raindance member Paul Ryan later railed against the characterization of early video as art, arguing that with its institutionalization in the 1980s, "video itself mutated from a countercultural gesture to an art genre."[26] For Ryan, as a "countercultural gesture," early video "held promise of social change unmediated by the art world," a promise that was distorted as "video art" became the lens through which earlier collective experiments were viewed.[27] As I have argued to this point, video's early promise as a countercultural gesture aligns it with the essayistic politics of New Left cinema. Furthermore, its legacy cannot be confined to the art world. Instead, as scholars like Stephanie Tripp have argued, the early GTV movement prefigures contemporary digital activist culture. Tripp convincingly draws a genealogical thread between the early video movement's practices and the contemporary circulation of activist video through digital platforms such as YouTube, which, she contends, "may be reviving the promise" that early practitioners saw in video.[28] This promise, however, was found in the capacity not only to produce and disseminate moving images along alternate channels but to reimagine communication systems as a whole. As I discuss next, cybernetic and systems thinking offered a way for the early GTV movement to theorize communication systems and devise ways to disrupt and steer them in new directions. For some at the time, like Ryan, this project was tantamount to an all-out war against broadcast television.

"CYBERNETIC GUERRILLA WARFARE"

In 1971, Paul Ryan published a manifesto in *Radical Software* titled "Cybernetic Guerrilla Warfare." In it, he argued that experimentation with video opened up the terrain for a new form of warfare, which would combine cybernetic theories of communication with the principles and tactics of guerrilla warfare to transform the production and distribution of information in society. For Ryan and his early video activist contemporaries, experimentation with video was crucial to social transformation, "because having total control over the processing of video puts you in direct conflict with that system of perceptual imperialism called broadcast television that puts a terminal in your home and thereby controls your access to information."[29] If Hollywood and auteur cinema were the principal representatives of imperialist culture in Solanas and Getino's "Towards a Third Cinema," within the GTV movement, broadcast television epitomized the regime of "perceptual imperialism" that maintained control over one's senses and capacity to apprehend the world. Like third cinema, the GTV movement was aimed at conducting a war against perceptual imperialism by generating alternative messages by way of the moving image and, moreover, networks of production and distribution outside of existing channels. Adopting the language of cybernetics and its emphasis on communication systems, the GTV movement focused on the importance of seizing the means of the production and distribution of information throughout society.

The term *cybernetics*—derived from the Greek word for "steersman"—was coined by Norbert Wiener as the synthesis of interdisciplinary conversations taking place in the late 1940s and early 1950s and is, as Andrew Pickering describes it, the "science of steersmanship."[30] Within the past decade, there has been a resurgence of interest in the ways that cybernetics influenced postwar fields of computing, art, literature, poetry, design, psychology, management science, and government, among others.[31] Since the publication of Wiener's *Cybernetics; or, Control and Communication in the Animal and the Machine* (1948), there has also been a great deal of debate about the nature of cybernetic thought and its effects, with some scholars understanding cybernetics to be a discourse/science intrinsically focused on control *as* domination, while others, like Pickering, assert that cybernetic theories of control are, instead, more open ended and creative—"in line with its ontology of unknowability and becoming."[32] For the GTV movement, I believe that the adaptation of cybernetic thought lies somewhere between these two poles, but my primary aim is not necessarily to engage in these larger debates. Instead, my focus is on how the cybernetic vocabulary through which the GTV movement framed their undertakings intersects with broader questions and problems within New Left cinema. Caroline Kane rightly argues that cybernetic theories taken up by the video counterculture were "appropriated *not literally, but as a metaphor.*"[33] Ryan's theory of cybernetic guerrilla warfare represents precisely this kind of metaphorical adaptation of cybernetic language, which offered strategic ways to think about communication and information in the war against "perceptual imperialism."

Ryan is a principal figure through which to track the transmission of cybernetic thinking into video culture, as he was introduced to video in 1968 while working under Marshall McLuhan at Fordham University during his term as a conscientious objector to the Vietnam War. Through Ryan, we can trace the direct influence of McLuhan and his media-oriented understanding of cybernetic and systems theory on GTV. In particular,

McLuhan's notion that media are extensions of the human nervous system informed the GTV movement's belief that the transformation of the media environment was necessary for any social change. As McLuhan argued in 1968, by expanding consciousness to include the entire "global village," electronic media brought the general population in closer proximity to distant events, particularly war:

> We are now in the midst of our first television war. Television began to be experienced in the ordinary home after 1946. Typically, the FBI and the CIA were looking into the rearview mirror for the revolutionary agents who were shaping the country. The television environment is total, therefore invisible. Along with the computer, it has altered every phase of the American vision and identity. The television war has ended the dichotomy between civilian and military. The public is now a participant in every phase of the war, and the main actions of the war are now being fought in the American home itself.[34]

Resonating with the New Left demand to bring the war home, McLuhan collapses the distinction between civilian and military, supporting the conviction that every subject is complicit with, and perhaps constituted by, imperialist warfare. He also confirms that television is itself a "revolutionary agent" and that the "total" environment it produces is akin to a battleground. Ryan and the GTV movement expanded McLuhan's understanding of the television war, however, by proposing that the Left must conduct guerrilla warfare through the medium of television. Moving beyond the idea that television is an extension of our central nervous system that brings us in closer proximity to distant wars, Ryan contends that the televisual image is waging war against the population by way of "perceptual imperialism." When arguing for cybernetic guerrilla warfare, Ryan thus amplifies the meaning of McLuhan's statement that "the main actions of the war are now being fought in the American home."

Inspired by Third World struggles for liberation, Ryan pulls from the theory and tactics of guerrilla warfare to adapt McLuhan's systems thinking to the alternative television movement, pointing out what he sees as the salient aspects of guerrilla warfare: "the guerrilla tradition is highly relevant in the current information environment. Guerrilla warfare is by nature irregular and non-repetitive."[35] These qualities of guerrilla warfare, for Ryan, are the inverse of the cultural homogeneity represented by broadcast television, understood to be a closed system of regular, repetitive patterns. To subvert "perceptual imperialism," the movement must disrupt these closed systems by interjecting new and different information into them. Only difference, or "the difference that makes a difference"— an often repeated phrase borrowed from Gregory Bateson, the cultural anthropologist who helped extend cybernetic theory to the social sciences in the 1940s and 1950s—can break with a monolithic culture whose only expression is empty repetition.[36] Ryan sees encouraging difference as a tactical necessity: "in order to 'win' in cybernetic guerrilla warfare, differences must be cherished, not temporarily suppressed for the sake of 'victory.' A la McLuhan, war is education. Conflict defines differences."[37] Eschewing the violence of groups like the Weathermen, and implicitly any sort of vanguardism, Ryan argues for a guerrilla warfare that engages with the "information environment":

> The traditional tricks of guerrilla warfare are remarkably suited for cybernetic action in an information environment. To scan briefly.
>
> - Mixing "straight" moves with "freak" moves. Using straight moves to engage the enemy, freak moves to beat him and not letting the enemy know which is which.
> - Running away when it's just too heavy. Leaving the enemy's strong places and seeking the weak. Go where you can make a difference.
> - Shaping the enemy's forces and keeping our own unshaped, thereby beating the many with the few.
> - Faking the enemy out. Surprise attacks.[38]

For Ryan, cybernetic theory adds to traditional guerrilla warfare the insight that "power is distributed throughout the system."[39] The inscription of differences entails the accentuation of difference between the guerrilla forces and the enemy: "understanding the significant difference between us and them in such a way as to avoid processing what is dangerous and death producing. Learn what you can from the Egyptians, the exodus is cybernetic."[40] The enigmatic statement "exodus is cybernetic," to which I return later, reflects a set of assumptions in the theory and practice of the guerrilla television movement about the revolutionary potential of the application of cybernetic theory to social movements. Ryan's concept of cybernetic guerrilla warfare was a permutation of the cybernetic influences of McLuhan and others, placing concepts like "difference" within a new context that stressed the importance of nonhierarchical, decentralized tactics in the war against "perceptual imperialism."

Ryan's manifesto, from which the GTV movement allegedly got its name, synthesizes the ways that popular ideas about cybernetic communication systems were taken up within the context of New Left cinema.[41] The imperfect application of these ideas offered a way for video practitioners to situate their activities in terms of a larger "information environment" that, for them, needed to be disrupted and reinvented. Despite articulating a new, cybernetic framework, in practice, figures like Ryan embodied much of the ethos of New Left cinema. For example, while working in McLuhan's media lab in summer 1968, Ryan borrowed video equipment and began several collaborations, including a "documentary made by kids of their experience" in Resurrection City in Washington, D.C., part of Martin Luther King's Poor People's Campaign, and a project with high school students in Newburgh, New York, in which Ryan helped to "turn local high school kids on to portable video and let them transmit their programs over the town CATV [cable television] system."[42] Much like Chris Marker's contemporaneous experiments with factory workers in the context of the Medvedkin group, the horizontalization and deprofessionalization of the production of cinematic utterances were intrinsic to the GTV movement.

Given these similarities, why did figures like Ryan see the necessity of articulating leftist video practices within the language of cybernetics? The answer, I contest, lies in the way the GTV movement came to see their activities, sometimes unwittingly, in light of the shifting terrain capitalist culture at the time in which terms like information had been gaining new significance. Take, for example, Gene Youngblood's statement on cybernetic cinema in *Expanded Cinema,* his book-length exploration of the cinematic possibilities of new moving image technologies like video that appeared in 1968 (with an introduction by Buckminster Fuller).[43] Youngblood was interested in the idea of the "videosphere," a cybernetic system in which global consciousness was in a constant state of becoming in and through the moving image:

We're in a transition from the Industrial Age to the Cybernetic Age. When we say expanded cinema, we mean expanded consciousness. Expanded cinema does not mean computer films, video phosphors, atomic light, or spherical projections. Expanded cinema isn't a movie at all: like life it's a process of becoming, man's ongoing historical drive to manifest his consciousness outside of his mind, in front of his eyes . . . the intermedia network of cinema and television now functions as nothing less than the nervous system of mankind.[44]

While clearly appropriating McLuhan's vocabulary and prosaic style, Youngblood also situates the cybernetic cinema within what he, and other members of the movement, identify as a move away from industrial modernity. What is the form of social life that will succeed industrial modernity, and how will it be shaped by the moving image, the "expanded consciousness" of the species? These questions recall, though differently, the words of Solanas when he advocated for "a cinema fit for a new kind of human being" (discussed in chapter 1). In the cybernetic imagination of the GTV movement, this new kind of human being is one who is fully integrated within, and empowered by, networks of communication. The GTV movement endeavored to both intervene in and accelerate the shift to a "cybernetic age," whose currency would be information. It is this conviction—that moving image technologies could be used to produce more, better, and different information and that such a project was indubitably revolutionary—that I interrogate next.

THE UTOPIA OF INFORMATION AND RADICAL FEEDBACK

In a statement that introduces the first issue of the journal, the editors of *Radical Software* make a bold pronouncement on the need for "alternative information structures":

Power is no longer measured in land, labor, or capital, but by access to information and the means to disseminate it. As long as the powerful tools (not weapons) are in the hands of those who hoard them, no alternative cultural vision can succeed. Unless we design and implement alternate information structures which transcend and reconfigure existing ones, other alternate systems will be no more than products of the existing process.[45]

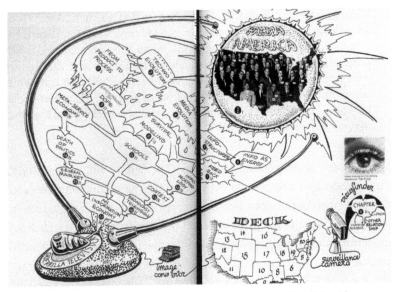

Figure 28. *Guerrilla Television* table of contents. Courtesy of Ira Schneider.

The belief that information was newly relevant to power structures and the capacity to change them made it a focal point for the GTV movement, a term around which all others revolved. Take Michael Shamberg's *Guerrilla Television* (1971), a synthesis of the first issues of *Radical Software*, and its preoccupation with information.[46] The first section of the book is composed of what Shamberg describes as a "Meta-Manual," which contains a kind of glossary of terms and principles deemed necessary to provide a context for the reader. The table of contents is itself designed as a kind of cybernetic system, a nonlinear hypertext that draws connections among the chapters in a cybernetic circuit that produces a signal of what it calls "Media America," positing the "information environment as an inexorable part of our ecology."[47] The concept of "media ecology," introduced by Neil Postman (heavily influenced by McLuhan), informs the group's attitude toward media that places information at the center of individual and societal evolution.[48] In a system of chapters, each of the relationships flows into a network that converges on the concluding chapter, "An Information Economy."

The Raindance Collective adopted the idea of an "information economy" from Peter Drucker, a key thinker in management science who had been working with cybernetic theory throughout the 1960s. Drucker's *The Age of Discontinuity* (1966) introduced the idea of a "knowledge economy" into popular discourse, emphasizing the production and circulation of information as its central feature.[49] However, unlike conceptions of the information economy popularized by Drucker—an economy based on the circulation of proprietary information conceived of as a commodity, and even embodied knowledge in the form of human capital—Raindance Corporation's utopian vision of the information economy involved the gradual displacement of money by information as the primary medium of exchange in society, ultimately supplanting the profit motive with the free flow of information. As Paul Ryan puts it, the information economy is a "non-money economy based on knowledge as value."[50] Though there seemed to be slightly variant opinions within the group about how an information economy would actually function, what is clear is that Raindance was insistent on the idea that the information economy implied both creating equality and expanding diversity within society.[51] As Ryan wrote, "our capitalist economy renders life uni-dimensional—more and more the same: uniformity via homogenous quantification. By contrast an information economy thrives on variety and diversity, quality not quantity, differences that make differences."[52] For the GTV movement, the idea of an "information economy" was a utopian vision that placed the highest value on the circulation of new, better, and different information, in the form of moving images, as a way to break up the homogeny of life under industrial capitalism.

To understand how information itself was thought to have such power and potential, one must look at how the group filtered the concept through a specific reading of cybernetics derived from Wiener. In *Cybernetics*, Wiener, drawing from communication engineering, identified information with difference: "the transmission of information is impossible save as a transmission of alternatives. If only one contingency is to be transmitted, then it may be sent most efficiently and with the least trouble by sending no message at all."[53] Information, for Raindance, is precisely this "transmission of alternatives," a definition of Bateson's characterization of information as "the difference that makes a difference." Reading

Wiener's *Cybernetics* further, we see that he equates the amount of information within a system with the circulation of energy in the second law of thermodynamics:

> The notion of the amount of information attaches itself very naturally to a classical notion of statistical mechanics: that of *entropy*. Just as the amount of information in a system is a measure of its degree of organization, so the entropy of a system is a measure of its degree of disorganization; and the one is simply the negative of the other.[54]

Wiener's thermodynamic-inspired theory of information gets special attention in the "Info as Energy" section of the "Meta-Manual," of *Guerrilla Television,* in which Shamberg argues that "information is the energy of control systems. Just as electricity magnifies physical action, information amplifies and controls processes."[55] And the essential nature of difference within cybernetics, for Shamberg, "means that unlike other forms of energy, which can ultimately be neither created or lost, only redistributed, information is inherently regenerative, or negentropic."[56] In their desire to generate a new information economy, the GTV movement was at war with what it saw as an entropic society. The endless production of the same by broadcast television needed to be countered by genuine information, conceived of as a diversity of images that presented real differences and alternatives to the status quo. They extrapolated from cybernetics the idea that information is a form of energy, which allowed them to make broad claims about information's value as a transformative tool within larger social systems.

In conceiving of the televisual image as information through the lens of cybernetics, the movement wanted to overthrow the society of the spectacle and its homogenization of culture, though not in the manner that Debord had in mind. Information is a form of energy but also a form of value that can circulate in excess of the capitalist economy through the proliferation of difference. As a generative force, information could be conceived of as the circulation of the creative potential of human labor and collaboration through new networks not determined by the homogenizing forces of the commodity form within the industrial era. When *Radical Software* posits that "you are information," they have in mind a world in which each person or group could create its own information through video and that this information would have inherent value when entering into a new, utopian "information economy."

For the GTV movement, this new information would serve as "feedback"—that is, information that allows a system to correct, or "steer," itself toward (or away) from equilibrium and, in turn, desired (or undesired) outcomes. As has been widely discussed, feedback was a cybernetic term that became a formal principal for many early video experiments. For example, cybernetic theories were often the inspiration for closed-circuit video feedback loops, such as Frank Gillette and Ira Schneider's *Wipe Cycle*, featured at the groundbreaking 1969 Television as a Creative Medium show, and used broadcast television, live feeds, and a series of delays and switches to produce an enclosed cybernetic video system that sought to empower viewers to understand their own images as information. As David Joselit puts it, the use of closed-circuit video loops in *Wipe Cycle*, like numerous gallery projects taking place in the late 1960s, "was meant to both represent and to pluralize the monolithic 'information' of networked TV through a spectator's unexpected encounter with her or his own act of viewing."[57] The interest in recursivity within these experiments led art historian Rosalind Krauss to characterize early video as an "aesthetic of narcissism."[58] In a more affirmative reading, Caroline Kane argues that video feedback mechanisms, such as those that appeared in the Television as a Creative Medium show, create a "post-Occidental," radical subjectivity: "through video access and video feedback, the doors could open to increased self-reflection and therapeutic self-awareness, thus radically redefining what it means to be human and to live in human community (or the 'earthship')."[59] These art historical readings of feedback share an emphasis on subjectivity of the artist and the viewer, as that subjectivity is produced through video as a discrete aesthetic object.

What these readings of subjectivity in early video miss, however, is the ways that the movement understood feedback as a process that shaped broader social systems and could be used to transform them.[60] GTV ultimately imagined video as a means to generate new inputs and feedback loops for the society as a whole by intervening in and developing new communication networks. If new subjectivities were produced, they were only legible insofar as they were tied into larger information networks. As Shamberg writes in the "Feedback" chapter of *Guerrilla Television,* "only through a radical re-design of its information structures to incorporate two-way, decentralized inputs can Media-American optimize the feedback it needs to come back to its senses."[61] Feedback, in this instance, is a principal steering mechanism in the "videosphere," the shared media environment that shaped the contours of society. Inspired by Wiener's expansion of the use of cybernetic theory to shape and govern societies in *The Human Use of Human Beings: Cybernetics and Society,* the GTV movement applied cybernetics beyond the terrain of the individual subject and its relation to the machine, understanding the entire media environment to be a cybernetic system.[62] Wiener's broader application of cybernetics to the media, and the image in particular, breaks with the Platonic figuration of the image as a degraded copy and instead sees it as a material force—in the form of cybernetic information—that has effects on the social world. For example, a flyer for People's Video Theater celebrates the opportunities for feedback afforded by video that are impossible with broadcast television: "see mini documentaries, speak back to the news, become a part of the news, see yourself, all on two-way television."[63] Through feedback, one was transformed from a passive consumer of information to a producer of information, creating new inputs into the system. This rendering of the televisual image, and the power of feedback, underpins the GTV movement's confidence that the televisual image could become an instrument of warfare against perceptual imperialism.

This expanded notion of feedback informed the design and implementation of numerous applications of video within the GTV movement that occurred outside the gallery context. In a series of collaborations with Survival Arts Media, People's Video Theater recorded what was called "street television," in which they set up television monitors linked to video cameras and interviewed people passing by, allowing them to see their own image on the monitor. In *Crime in South Orange, New Jersey* (1971), the street television produced a situation that gathered together adolescents complaining of poor education and lack of opportunities for recreation and older men passing by who vehemently spewed the rhetoric of "law and order" that had been popularized during the Nixon era. As an older man complains that things are not what they used to be, while occasionally casting a nervous glance to his own image in the monitor, a young woman jumps up and down behind him, also trying to appear on television. Video feedback, seeing and hearing oneself as information, seeing others as information, and being able to respond to them, creates the process of what Ryan refers to as "infolding," integrating information from a cybernetic feedback loop. In the case of *Crime in South Orange*, street television tries to instigate this process of infolding for the community as a whole, mediating between different populations and allowing them to understand themselves and each other differently. This experiment produces a microcosm of the feedback mechanisms that the GTV movement hoped to realize across the social field. As the Videofreex put it in a contribution to Radical Software, "we propose an immediate video feedback, an immediate honesty between people allowing all sides to feely express themselves. An interface of ideas and emotions that can open all forces to an understanding of different approaches and outlooks forward."[64] Feedback, for the movement, enabled an "interface of ideas and emotions" that generated an essayistic politics of the common, the attempt to relate and live together differently, creating the conditions for an alternative future. This future was dependent on the capacity for everyday subjects to produce more, better, and different information and to circulate that information as a means to supplant hierarchal information channels and means of exchange.

THE AMBIVALENCE OF INFORMATION AND
THE CYBERNETIC SERVICE ECONOMY

The impetus for social change that animated early video practice and its visions of the world to come were at the same time prescient and naive. By offering a model of a networked society organized around the equitable distribution of resources and information, the GTV movement anticipated the digital utopianism of the early internet. Moreover, the writings and practices of the GTV movement offer insight into how New Left and countercultural networks sought to intervene in the coming of a new "information economy." However, as might be evident already, there arises a friction between the GTV movement's desire to wage war against a society that produces perceptual imperialism and cybernetic theory, which was developed within the center of the U.S. military-industrial complex and had already come to dominate a new capitalist discursive formation, as is evident in Drucker's management science. In *From Counterculture to Cyberculture,* Fred Turner takes up a similar problem, focusing on Stewart Brand, founder of *The Whole Earth Catalog.* Turner argues, through Brand's example, that the counterculture's adaptation of cybernetic theory was essential for the eventual normalization of computing technologies within society, allowing them to move from being seen as tools for dehumanization and bureaucracy to implements of decentralization and individual expression. Turner paints Brand as the epitome of the counterculture's version of a "network entrepreneur," examining how he "began to migrate from one intellectual community to another and, in the process, to knit together formerly separate intellectual and social networks."[65] He accordingly describes *The Whole Earth Catalog* as a "network forum" that brought together these disparate groups: techoscientific capitalists, on one hand, and countercultural hippies, on the other. Essential to Turner's argument about the Whole Earth Network and the manner in which it paved the way for the New Economy is a refutation of the idea that the counterculture was simply co-opted by capital. Relying on Brand as the figure of the quintessential network entrepreneur, Turner argues that Brand's network brought together worlds of military–industrial technology with the counterculture in a context that allowed for them "to legitimate one another's projects."[66]

Turner makes a clear distinction between the counterculture, whose members "turned away from agonistic politics and toward technology, consciousness, and entrepreneurship as the principles of a new society,"[67] and the New Left, for whom "true community and the end of alienation were usually thought to be the result of political activity rather than a form of politics in their own right."[68] Drawing a sharp line between the New Left and the counterculture, the latter associated principally (according to Turner) with the New Communalist "back to the land" movement, allows him to argue that the counterculture was ultimately complicit with the New Right of the 1980s and 1990s and facilitated the rise of the New

Economy by creating the cultural conditions for its ascent.[69] By breaking with the New Left politics and simultaneously adopting cybernetic theories in their vision of new global consciousness and a harmonious universe, the counterculture, for Turner, paved the way for technocratic, neoliberal governance. Fantasizing that we might live in a utopian world "all watched over by machines of loving grace," in the words of poet Richard Brautigan, the counterculture fostered new regimes of mechanized control closely tied to the neoliberal economy, an argument Adam Curtis made in his 2011 film that borrows its title from Brautigan's poem.[70] Modeled on *The Whole Earth Catalog* as what Turner would describe as a "network forum," and sharing many of the catalog's attitudes toward technology and its gurus—Wiener, Fuller, Bateman, McLuhan—*Radical Software* and the GTV movement in general could be clustered with the counterculture as Turner describes it. With regard to early video culture, Chris Robé seems to concur with Turner's thesis, aligning groups like the Videofreex with the New Communalist movement and arguing for the movement's anarchist tendencies that eventually morphed into "the hacker ethic that predominates throughout the 1990s."[71]

However, the line between counterculture and New Left that Turner and others draw is perhaps too rigid, given the centrality of culture in New Left politics as I have described it in this book, and when speaking of the GTV movement, we cannot so easily separate cultural rebellion from politics. If anything, the movement complicates the division between the counterculture and the New Left. In straddling both worlds, the GTV movement had a much more ambivalent relationship to the normalization of technology that informed both the New Economy and the digital uto-pianism that Turner describes. Similarities to Brand and the Whole Earth Network notwithstanding, the GTV movement did not abandon New Left politics but rather represents a fusion of countercultural concerns, such as consciousness, networked entrepreneurship, and cybernetics, with the New Left's emphasis on participatory democracy, difference, and justice. Their rendering of concepts like the "information economy" and "cybernetic guerrilla warfare" is a prime example of this fusion. In practice, while *The Whole Earth Catalog* may have excluded racial justice, feminism, and critiques of imperialism in favor of the figure of a white masculinity embodied in the "cowboy nomad," the GTV movement, though composed of a vast majority of white members, often favored subject matter that reflected a strong connection with New Left social movements, albeit in a complicated and imperfect way.[72] By bridging countercultural and New Left movements, GTV practitioners expanded on the networks of the moving image already at work within New Left social movements through their embrace of new technology and cybernetics. At the same time, they infused these networks of the moving image with the entrepreneurial ethos that pervaded the turn toward a postindustrial, service- and information-driven economy. The movement's relationship to this new economy, thus, must ultimately be understood as one of ambivalence rather than one of simple collaboration or co-optation. Figuring the movement's relationship to an emergent, postindustrial society as one of ambivalence allows us to affirm its utopian impulses, its desire to transform communication systems and proliferate more, better, and different information. At the same time, we come to see how these impulses inadvertently coincided with and furthered the transition to a world where these horizontalized networks became the basis of new forms of exploitation.

This ambivalence comes across most clearly when looking at how alternative television groups tried to generate viable "economic support systems" outside of existing funding structures.[73] In its entrepreneurial spirit, *Guerrilla Television* demonstrates the movement's desire to identify and attune their actions and theories to the changing economic landscape, particularly the transformation from an industrial economy to a postindustrial, service economy. In the section of *Guerrilla Television* titled "From Product to Process," Shamberg ruminates on this transition:

> The death of hardware is the ultimate transformation of America to Media-America. It embodies our total shift from a product- to process-based culture. It's much like the difference between renting a car and owning one: you pay for the service of using it (process), not for the value of ownership (product).[74]

In its percipient discernment of the rise of the service economy in 1971, *Guerrilla Television* identifies those who are "hung up on products" and, by proxy, private property as the most "reactionary" forces in society.[75] Furthermore, Shamberg discusses the "ascendance of a super-psychological marketplace where psychic benefits replace physical ones as we're exhorted to buy moods and services, or processes instead of objects."[76] While it is popularly believed that Daniel Bell was the first to make such predictions in *The Coming of Post-industrial Society* in 1973, it is clear that these prognoses regarding the transformation to a service economy were already circulating within the counterculture.[77] Furthermore, groups like the Raindance Corporation were attempting to diagnose and intervene in these transformations in such a way as to steer new information networks and economies toward greater equality and democracy.[78]

Guerrilla Television's section on "Cybernetic Strategies and Services" identifies a "media bus" as an

> ideal cybernetic service. You go out to communities and do videotaping; they pay you to come. Ideally, you plug-in to existing hardware and show people how to use what they already have ... and then turn them on enough for them to want to set up their own media system after you've left.[79]

Videofreex and Ant Farm's media buses were vans outfitted with video equipment that traveled to various communities. In the case of Videofreex, the media bus became an instrument for outreach and education, stopping at "universities, museums, churches, and community organizations" to conduct training and research sessions.[80] For Shamberg, these types of cybernetic services bring together a decentralized ethos that combines the service economy—selling processes, not products—with the cybernetic, information-based economy. The "cybernetic service economy" epitomizes the DIY, entrepreneurial model that the early GTV movement wanted to foster. The slippage between cybernetic guerrilla warfare and cybernetic service economies became evident as early video groups sought to support their activities, aspiring to replace circuits of capitalist exchange with a new information economy.

This attention to process-based culture also informs *Guerrilla Television*'s rejection of some aspects of radical culture; in the "Death of Politics" section of the "Meta-Manual," Shamberg writes, "Most politicians don't understand information systems. Radicals are hardware freaks who

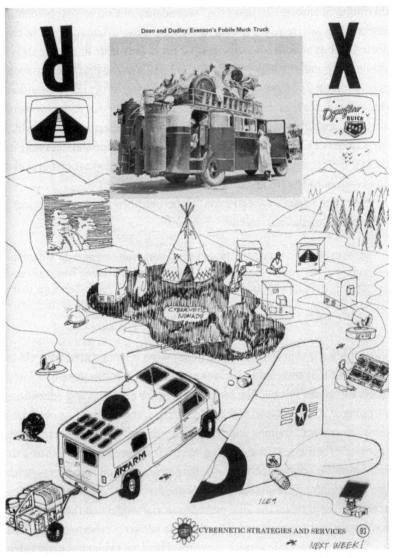

Figure 29. Illustration of Ant Farm media bus from *Guerrilla Television*. Courtesy of Ira Schneider.

think the computer is just another thing to blow up."[81] In their embrace of technology and the move away from traditional politics as well as tactics associated with more militant segments of the New Left, the Raindance Corporation and the GTV movement undoubtedly exhibited countercultural tendencies. Furthermore, the *Radical Software* journal and *Guerrilla Television* manual became models for early publications on computers that popularized ideas of DIY and digital utopianism, such as Ted Nelson's *Computer Lib/Dream Machines* (1974). Nevertheless, the GTV movement, at the same time, attempted to harness the power of information and its circulation, using it to create new communication systems in order to undermine perceptual imperialism. In testing ideas like the "cybernetic service economy," the GTV movement put its hypotheses about the information economy into practice, while simultaneously producing models of engagement that embodied a new, entrepreneurial ethos.

In the changing landscape of capitalism, the influence of cybernetics on the process- and serviced-based practices of the GTV movement are tied to forms of labor on the ascent across the economy in the 1970s. Jasper Bernes makes a similar point in his reading of the adaptation of cybernetic theory in the poetry and artwork of Hannah Weiner and Dan Graham, suggesting that their engagements with process-based cybernetic theories "prefigure and contribute to the actual restructuring of the labor process that begins in the 1970s and intensifies during the 1980s."[82] For Bernes, postwar artists' use of information theory is a crucial site of investigation because information and its processing become central in the reconfiguration of work in the transition to postindustrial capitalism. On the other hand, as Bernes rightly notes, information-as-value presents a number of dilemmas for a postindustrial capitalism, chief among them its "tendency . . . to devalue as it becomes generalized."[83]

The writings and practices of GTV are certainly among the influential "counter-laboratories," as Bernes refers to them, in which cybernetic theories were challenged and transmuted against the backdrop of the larger restructuring of work in the 1960s and 1970s.[84] The movement's guiding principles, like the "information economy," may be read as misapplications or distortions of cybernetic theories, but these poor translations are, at the same time, subversions. Implicitly exploiting information's slippery character as a commodity, the utopian information economy that the group conjures imagines information, and value, beyond equivalence. In foregrounding the power of difference—conceived as that which cannot be reduced to exchange value—the information economy, as proposed by the GTV movement, glimpses a world in which human activity is not reducible to the commodity form and where creativity and collaboration might be imagined outside of work. Recall Ryan's statement: "exodus is cybernetic." While it may seem odd to position cybernetics, the science of warfare, mechanization, and control as a form of exodus, within the context of Raindance's discussions of the "information economy," this association becomes clearer. The information economy as proposed by GTV is not an exodus to another special location but an exodus that takes place within already-existing forms of social life, reappropriating social "hardware," turning it to new use, and affirming creative activities and collective knowledge. In this sense, Ryan's politics of cybernetic exodus are not far from political theories of exodus coming out of the autonomous tradition, such as those of Paulo Virno, for whom exodus is the project of creating an autonomous "sphere" in which to affirm intellectual life, knowledge, affects, and so on, that have already been activated within post-Fordist economies.[85] Similarly, Michael Hardt and Antonio Negri write that exodus is a "process of *subtraction* from the relationship with capital by means of actualizing the potential autonomy of labor-power."[86] In some ways, it is in the spirit of this "process of subtraction" that GTV offers an alternative sphere—a "videosphere"—within which to produce and circulate information, conceived of as the creative potential of human knowledge and collaboration outside of capitalist command.

Complicating this narrative, however, the GTV movement's participation in new forms of creative labor, such as the "cybernetic service economy," suggests precisely the opposite. Robé argues that the early GTV movements were involved in a form of exodus but that "the guerrilla's exodus away from Fordist capitalism and suburbia also provided an entrance into a newly emerging postindustrial, commercial media system taking shape around them, one which they in part helped shape."[87] Furthermore, in proposing a flexible cybernetic service economy, the movement anticipates the precarious worker within the "creative economy," whose versatile skills and personality are transformed into a personal brand. The cybernetic service economy becomes an ideal template for "start-up" culture, facilitating the commodification and capture of creative potential rather than resisting it. In fact, is not the ethos of cybernetic guerrilla warfare epitomized in the contemporary culture of digital disruption? Indeed, seeking out homogeneity in systems and interjecting difference into them by creating new networks for the exchange of information has become a key feature of contemporary corporate strategy. In the space between the utopian information economy that the GTV movement envisioned and the new forms of entrepreneurial capitalism they anticipated, we find not the resolution of politics but a profound ambivalence that might serve as an opening, rather than a closure, for a discussion about the meaning and value of information in New Left cinema and beyond.

"YOU ARE INFORMATION": THE VALUE OF COUNTERINFORMATION AND THE "VICTORY OF THE VCR"

The promise that video held for controlling one's own image within the context of New Left social movements was never fully realized, nor did the radical alternative network that would enable the free flow of information, the "information economy," materialize on a large scale. Issues around funding that led to dependence on granting institutions and collaborations with major broadcast outlets also complicated the movement's autonomous ethos. Videofreex's aborted *Subject to Change* series for CBS highlights these tensions. The collaboration provided the group with ample equipment and travel expenses that enabled them to acquire remarkable footage, such as the interview with Fred Hampton weeks before his death that conveys an intimacy in its handheld approach that is unlike any other footage that exists of the Chicago Panther. After the series was cancelled, however, the group, fearing that the network would hand this footage over to the FBI, smuggled the Hampton tape along with others out of CBS headquarters in an empty guitar case.[88] The contradictions between complicity and innovation, appropriation and autonomy, remained acute within the movement as groups like Top Value Television (TVTV)—composed of members from Raindance, Videofreex, and Ant Farm—went on to make feature documentaries, such as *Four More Years* (1972) and *Lord of the Universe* (1974), that had wide influence

Figure 30. Video still, Videofreex interview with Fred Hampton, 1968.

and circulation, redefining documentary and journalistic styles.[89] Despite their eventual integration into the mainstream, the GTV movement also laid the groundwork for the rise of independent programming and public access television stations that flourished throughout the late 1970s and 1980s, inspiring the democratizing, participatory, and decentralized ethos of the "alternative media" movement to this day.[90]

Moving beyond the issue of independence versus co-optation, I conclude by reflecting on the assertion by the editors of *Radical Software* that "you are information." This direct address and interpellation is intended as an empowering statement, calling on its readers to participate in what Shamberg calls a "cybernetics of the self" in which video becomes a tool to "externalize and enhance" the subject's ability to see itself, through feedback, as part of an information system.[91] Videotape, according to Shamberg, provides a vehicle for a subject to "assert [their] own value as information."[92] To assert one's own value as information relies on a belief in the value of information as a material force in the world and the conviction that more and different information—in the form of moving images—is necessary to subvert the powers that be. This sentiment reflects broader assumptions about the value of moving images held by New Left cinema practitioners who saw the proliferation of more, better, and different images as a revolutionary act (a sentiment that is troubled in the next chapter).

The statement "you are information," full of revolutionary promise for the GTV movement, is further complicated when understood within the larger context of what Nick Dyer-Witheford calls the "doctrine of the information revolution" that cohered in the late 1970s and early 1980s. According to Dyer-Witheford, starting in the late 1970s, concepts like the "information economy" and the "information revolution" became prominent features of popular discussions of the economy as figures like Yoneji Masuda, Marc Porat, and Alvin Toffler argued that the exchange of information would be central in the world to come.[93] This discourse on the "information revolution" had immense cultural power, becoming an

> indispensable ingredient in a massive reorganization of advanced capitalist societies, centered on the introduction of new technologies.... The theory of an inevitable information revolution provides the rationale for this restructuring, legitimization for social dislocation, and exhortation toward a radiant future.[94]

In other words, a discourse that propounds the transformative value of information was as important to capitalist restructuring as were information technologies themselves. Some of these figures, like Toffler, timidly express an optimism about the ways that an "information economy" might eventually produce a more "egalitarian society" through the "gentle auto-dissolution of ownership."[95] These utopian imaginaries of the "information economy" expressed by mainstream thinkers like Toffler maintained some of the utopianism of the "information economy" coming from the GTV movement several years earlier. Nevertheless, as Dyer-Witheford points out, the "doctrine of the information revolution" was also quite compatible with Thatcherism and Reaganism, perpetuating the belief that social contradictions could be overcome and that the New Economy would engender a friction-free capitalism with limitless potential for profit—a fantasy in which information and technology, not labor, drive productivity. In adopting ideas like the information economy, the GTV movement inadvertently participated in the propagation and normalization of terms that would be indispensable in shaping the neoliberal counterrevolution.

In Francis Fukuyama's infamous *The End of History and the Last Man,* he describes the lack of alternatives and the inevitability of global capitalism as "the victory of the VCR," a statement that would have surely horrified members of the GTV movement.[96] Twenty years after the publication of the first issue of *Radical Software,* video's potential to decentralize and circulate more and different information promised not the liberation of society from capitalist homogenization but its opposite. Today, the statement "you are information" could not be more true, as the era of big data has transformed the individual subject into a series of endless pieces of information, data points that circulate independently of her. Rather than empowering us, our continuous capacity to generate information is most often used as means for control. However, one must hesitate before making this story of control and containment total. We may have too much information and too much communication, as Deleuze and Guattari argue, but creative resistance is an altogether different matter. As recent struggles against police brutality, among others, have demonstrated, video in the hands of everyday subjects still has the power to galvanize social movements.

The tension between the utopian visions for the equitable exchange of information and the realities of the New Economy that came to pass might prompt us to dismiss the GTV movement as too complicit with capitalist innovation. With nearly fifty years separating us from the GTV movement, it is easy to identify its failures and blind spots, but does this require us to read it as bankrupt from the outset? What I have suggested throughout this book, and what I will discuss at length in the next chapter, is that insights about radical movements gained with the benefit of hindsight are partial. The ambivalence of the GTV movement that I have underscored tries to hold this tension in balance. Despite their eventual complicity, we can still affirm a radical vision that endures, one that points to a world that could have been, or could still become, otherwise. In other words, the political possibilities of cybernetic guerrilla warfare are indeed ambivalent, but their potential has yet to be exhausted.

6

Inflation of the Image; or, The Image of Revolution in the 1970s

As we saw in the last chapter, practitioners of New Left cinema were often driven by the conviction that the production and distribution of more, better, and different images was tantamount to revolutionary insurgency. At times, this belief carried with it political assumptions that are best described as ambivalent in their approach to social transformation, dovetailing with the realities of an insipient networked capitalism. This chapter, which serves as a conclusion to the book, further contemplates the fate of these revolutionary images and aspirations in the face of the counterrevolution that was beginning to consolidate in the 1970s. The two films I address, Jean-Luc Godard, Jean-Pierre Gorin, and Anne-Marie Miéville's *Ici et ailleurs* (*Here and Elsewhere*, France, 1976) and Chris Marker's *Le Fond de l'air est rouge* (*Grin without a Cat*, France, 1977), are reflections on both the New Left and its cinema, taking raw footage shot in the midst of revolutionary fervor as a starting point for essayistic contemplation. Both of these films come at time that might be regarded as the closure of many of the radical potentials opened up by the long 1960s, especially in France, and grapple, albeit differently, with political economic formations taking shape with the onset of a new era. Evaluating two themes of the 1970s that run through the films—inflation and the rise of the New Right—this chapter analyzes counterrevolution at the level of the cinematic image. It does so by interrogating how the image of revolution comes to be seen differently in its aftermath.

ICI ET AILLEURS'S "POOR REVOLUTIONARY FOOL"

In 1970, during the intensive Dziga Vertov period in which Godard and his frequent collaborator Jean-Pierre Gorin, among others, were working out the contours of a revolutionary cinematic practice, the group embarked on what would become their most difficult project: to make a film about the Palestinian conflict. Like Vietnam, Palestine had come to occupy a central place in the New Left's imaginary as a site of resistance and potential revolution in the Third World context, and the Dziga Vertov group's engagement with the crisis was among several attempts to analyze and further the Palestinian cause among New Left cinema groups both within and outside of Palestine. In addition to the Palestinian Liberation Organization's (PLO) Palestine Film Unit, which made a number of documentaries, San Francisco Newsreel's *Revolution until Victory, A.K.A. We Are the Palestinian People* (United States, 1973) linked the Palestinian struggle to struggles against U.S. imperialism globally. Moreover, Masao Adachi and Koji Wakamatsu's *The Red Army/PFLP: Declaration of War* (Japan, 1971), made in collaboration with the Japanese Red Army and the leaders from the Popular Front for the Liberation of Palestine, used Adachi's "landscape theory" of reading power relations in built environments to create an agit-prop call for solidarity with the Palestinian people.[1] In their project, to be similarly titled *Jusqu'à la victoire* (Until victory), the Dziga Vertov group worked to "build" a revolutionary image through the production of a film that was to be the center of their contribution to a militant cinema.[2] After considerable effort in filming and fund-raising, however, the project collapsed in the most devastating and bloodiest of ways, as discussed later. The footage shot in Jordan remained untouched until 1974, when, following the disintegration of the Dziga Vertov project, Godard and his collaborator Anne-Marie Miéville gave it new life in *Ici et ailleurs* under the auspices of the Sonimage production company. The forsaken *Jusqu'à la victoire* was resurrected not in the spirit of victory in which it was originally produced but in a moment of retreat—both Godard's seeming retreat from the project of militant cinema and the more general retreat of the Left in France and elsewhere.

Composed, partially, of footage taken in Jordan of Palestinian militants intended for *Jusqu'à la victoire, Ici et ailleurs* juxtaposes images of the PLO with consumer society in France. Though *Ici et ailleurs* offers only subtle hints as to what *Jusqu'à la victoire* might have looked like, the title suggests that the original intention of the footage of the PLO shot in early 1970 was to produce a film about the movement toward revolutionary victory. *Ici et ailleurs,* on the other hand, seems to be a film about defeat, or at least, about counterrevolution. But what was the counterrevolution that was already evident in the mid-1970s aside from the violent suppression of the Palestinian movement in Jordan? *Ici et ailleurs* intimates that the failure of the New Left movements of 1960s was not only the product of counter-revolutionary force. In addition to the violent suppression with which so many movements of the long 1960s were met, the film also speaks of a reconfiguration of quotidian life under capitalism, a counterrevolution by other means. In doing so, it develops a concept of counterrevolution in line with Paolo Virno's understanding of the term, as discussed in chapter 3, in the sense of a "revolution in reverse."[3] Enveloping the cinema of the New Left within an image of its present, *Ici et ailleurs* endeavors to capture the affective dimensions of the counterrevolution that we call the 1970s. While starting with political violence, I will argue the film arrives at a structural theory of counterrevolution that is at the same time a reflection on the fate of New Left cinema and its many revolutionary images.

Ici et ailleurs begins with the image of a monitor set in a stark mise-en-scène upon which the words "Mon, Ton, Son Image" appear, with the word "image" blinking. Employing this screen-within-a-screen technique, the film immediately places "my, your, his/her image" at a distance, as a voice-over presents an enigmatic statement that frames the entire film: "In 1970, the film was called *Victory*. In 1974, the film is called *Here and Elsewhere*." This statement is then repeated over footage of PLO members holding a machine gun, which cuts to a white, French family gathered around a television set. The images that compose the film had to be given a new name and recomposed in a new form.

Jusqu'à la victoire is embedded *here* within the film *Ici et ailleurs* as an implicit structuring principle, while at the same time existing *elsewhere* as a film that could not be finished. The opening segment of the film consists of footage shot with the PLO, as a voice-over describes, in the past conditional tense, how the film would have been structured. Over a monitor with the words "en repensant à cela" (thinking back to this), a voice-over states,

> It was in the middle or the beginning of 1970 that we go to the Middle East. Who is this "we"? In February there is I, there is you, there is she, there is he who go to the Middle East, amongst the Palestinians to make a film. And we shot things in this order and we organized it. She, you, he, I organized a film like that.

The voice-over continues with a description of how the images of the PLO would be assembled in an additive fashion:

> The people's will plus armed struggle equals the people's war, plus the political work equals the people's education, plus the people's logic equals the people's war extended, extended until victory of the Palestinian people—until victory. And this is what you, I, she, he had shot elsewhere.

Soon after, over a screen that reads "Ici," the voice-over states,

> And then we came back home, I came back, you came back. From that away and we haven't recovered yet. She, you, he finally came back here, in France. It didn't go well. It doesn't go well anywhere. Nowhere does it go well.

As the voice-over states "nowhere does it go well," the screen with the words "en repensant à cela" appears, and the letters from the word "cela," "that," begin to disappear.

The film goes on to reveal its own impossibility after "Black September" in Jordan, a military clash that resulted in the death of thousands of Palestinians, among them many of the fighters to be featured in *Jusqu'à la victoire*. The image of revolution toward victory becomes an image of death, and the film *Until Victory* becomes *Here and Elsewhere*. *Ici et ailleurs* is born from *Jusqu'à la victoire,* as the screen reads, "because all the actors are dead." Intercut with images of massacred Palestinians, the following text appears on the screen: "death is represented in this film by a flow of images, a flow of images and sounds that hides a silence, a silence that becomes deadly because it is prevented to come out alive." Both the revolution and the counterrevolution are inscribed in the image. D. N. Rodowick speaks of the structure of the film as one of an "incommensurable series"; he writes, "The series of images, and images and sounds, can neither be unified in a transcendent perspective nor reconciled into a whole that will confer a retroactive sense on the history, indeed histories, that the film presents. 1970 *and* 1974: the film holds the two times together in their incommensurability."[4] The interstice between these "incommensurable" spaces, times, and events is marked, in this sequence, by the finality of death that followed the violent suppression of a revolutionary movement.

For *Ici et ailleurs,* however, this radical finality from which nothing can be recovered is not an end but a kind of beginning, as it is, for the most part, a film that deals with the indeterminacy of life in the aftermath of struggle, dwelling in the interstice that is produced by this incommensurable set of times, spaces, and images. In doing so, it provides us with a different theory of counterrevolution, one that far exceeds military defeat. As the voice-over suggests, it was to be a film composed of the sum of revolutionary images added in a sequence that tended toward an unquantifiable, revolutionary end. *Ici et ailleurs* seems to take on a similar task, to add up images of revolution. However, the sum of these images adds up to zero, as we see in a sequence that appears toward the beginning of the film in which a hand attempts to add up revolutionary moments on a calculator: 1789 + 1968 + 1917 . . . The result always seems to come out as zero, and the voice-over states, "Since we find ourselves near zero, we didn't add, but subtract; or rather, it's the negative that's been added first." This impossible mathematics, adding up the unquantifiable toward infinity can only equal zero, a zero that is at the same time everything and nothing.

Through this impossible calculation, *Ici et ailleurs* folds the image of revolution into a chain of zeros. At this pivotal moment within the film, a hand erases the words "vive la revolution" from a chalkboard and begins to write zeros, as the voice-over asks what becomes a central question of the film: "How does capital function?" Beyond the orthodox responses to this question, the film proffers an answer that is anything but conventional:

A bit like this, perhaps:

Someone poor and a zero equals someone less poor.
Someone less poor and a zero equals someone even less poor.
Someone even less poor and a zero equals someone richer.
Someone richer and again a zero equals someone even more rich.
Someone even more rich and again a zero equals someone even richer again.
Capital functions like that.
At a given moment it adds up, and what it adds up are zeros.
But zeros which represent tens, hundreds, thousands of you(s) and me(s).
So not really zeros after all, the capitalist would say.

Ici et ailleurs's unconventional response to the question "how does capital function?" points to the need to produce new answers to fundamental questions about capitalism after the long 1960s. If *Jusqu'à la victoire* was to be composed with the addition of revolutionary elements, *Ici et ailleurs* is composed by the addition of the zero, an inverted image of revolution. The effect of adding another zero produces wealth into an infinity, but it also multiplies the human image, which begins to resemble a zero, as the infinite sea of faces from quotidian life begin to resemble the infinite proliferation of zeros. The voice-over continues,

We must see, learn to see, that when the time comes to add up all the defeats and victories, very often we have been fucked and we've been fucked because we, I, didn't want to see, you, she, he, nobody wanted to see that their dreams are represented . . . he didn't want to see that all his dreams are represented at a given moment, and given and taken back, by zeros which multiply them. Yes, but as they're zeros, they multiply and simultaneously cancel out; and we haven't had the time to see that it's at that moment, at that place, that our hopes have been reduced to zero.[5]

The purpose of the zero in *Ici et ailleurs* is to simultaneously multiply and negate revolutionary dreams. It is a kind of nodal point, a boundary at which revolution becomes counterrevolution. This boundary is, consequently, much more than the geographical distance between France and Jordan. As later in the film, over a shot of the bourgeois family watching television, the voice-over states, "It has been said that the images of the

Figure 31. Film still, hand drawing zeros to illustrate how capitalism functions, *Ici et ailleurs* (1974).

sum will have nothing to do with the sum of the images." The totality of zeros that are the image of capital can never equal the unquantifiable form of the image of/as/toward revolution; it can only attempt to nullify it—incessantly multiplying and negating revolutionary struggles and the utopian dreams that undergird them. The unorthodox answer to the question "how does capital function?" that the film tenders is one that brings into view the mechanism through which our dreams "have been reduced to zero." The early militant cinema of the Dziga Vertov group, like *Le Gai savoir* (The joy of learning, France, 1969), aspired to return to a zero point in order to rebuild sounds and images in a new, revolutionary configuration. In contrast, the zero in *Ici et ailleurs* is a place to which the revolutionary image endlessly returns, but without being able to move beyond its blank impotence. The zero transforms itself into a figure that compounds a sense of hopelessness—with each addition, it inverts revolutionary possibility.

In addressing the endless return of revolutionary dreams in a muted form, the zero, *Ici et ailleurs* tries to capture a political experience in which revolutionary aspirations are not simply extinguished but transfigured. The film's meditation on this transfiguration at the level of the image is encapsulated in a statement made toward the end of the film in which the voice-over laments, "Poor revolutionary fool, millionaire in revolutionary images." In contrast to sentiments expressed by New Left cinema practitioners discussed in the last chapter and throughout the book, *Ici et ailleurs* does not seem to share the belief that the endless production of more, better, and different revolutionary images is itself revolutionary. Instead, the proliferation and cancellation of revolutionary images, like the proliferation and cancellation of revolutionary dreams, becomes simultaneous. In other words, the value of revolutionary images in the 1970s becomes, like money, inflated, inflation being defined as the diminution of value through the very process of multiplication.

To further unpack the meaning of *Ici et ailleurs*'s "poor revolutionary fool," let us look at inflation as a political economic problem that shaped daily life in the 1970s. The inflationary crisis that swept much of the industrialized world in that decade was both the indication of a systemic crisis within capitalism—a "signal" crisis, to use Arrighi's term—and a process that cancelled out the wage gains of the 1960s, effectively consuming the victories of the working class. Inflation, according to Antonio Negri, is the result of the "unification of socialized work," meaning that monetary inflation is the result of organized labor's gains but also a mechanism to control them.[6] In the postwar era, the management of inflation had become of a strategy to contend with demands of labor and promote full employment. The economic thinking of John Maynard Keynes was central to this strategy, his *General Theory* arguing that the goal of full employment—a method of placating organized labor—and the maintenance of rates of profit can be reached only through measured inflation.[7] Instead of contracting the monetary supply in order to foreclose the problem of monetary crisis, Keynes suggests that increasing wages, thus stimulating inflation, is beneficial for the capitalist for no other reason than it addresses the demand for wage increases and employment while stagnating, or even depressing, real wages:

This result [leveling out of wage gains] follows from the assumption that the factors of production, and in particular the workers, are disposed to resist a reduction in their money rewards, and that there is no corresponding motive to resist an increase.[8]

Keynes's observation is as simple as it is brilliant: if you attempt to reduce wages, you will encounter resistance, but if you increase wages in a way that produces inflation, thus devaluating real wages, you can suppress wage gains without precipitating organized resistance.[9] In the midst of the Great Depression, Keynes recognized that the deflationary methods of the old school were no longer viable because of the realities of organized labor and that inflation could be a useful tool in mollifying the demands of workers while preventing the rise of the proportion of their wages. In essence, *the function of inflation is to both multiply and negate.*

However, Keynes's inflationary logic, which had more or less effectively managed the demands of labor in the postwar moment, went into a kind of chaotic overdrive in the midst of global struggles of the late 1960s and early 1970s, as if the controls on the system had gone haywire and the ability to steer the inflationary mechanism back in favor of capital had been disrupted by the massive political upheaval of that period. This process was exacerbated by Richard Nixon when he ended the Bretton Woods agreement and the gold standard in 1971 to prevent the drawing down of U.S. gold reserves and currency collapse in the face of international panic regarding the value of the dollar. The "closure of the gold window," as it was called, indicated the crisis of U.S. hegemony instigated by imperial wars and domestic unrest. The resulting unwieldy price inflations, precipitating the infamous period of "stagflation," set the stage for a radical shift in political strategy and discursive practices around labor management, which moved from a concern over rates of employment to the containment of inflation.[10]

As Fredric Jameson puts it in his essay "Periodizing the '60s," the end of the 1960s (which Jameson dates around 1972–74) signifies a shift from one "infrastructural or systemic stage of capitalism to another. The 60s were in that sense an immense and inflationary issuing of superstructual credit; a universal abandonment of the referential gold standard; an extraordinary printing up of ever more devalued signifiers."[11] The experience of inflation, in this account, is not simply an economic one. Instead, inflation's capacity to simultaneously proliferate and depreciate is linked to the destabilization of meaning that Jameson and others associate with postmodern culture. This process of destabilization and depreciation helps to illuminate how it is that *Ici et ailleurs*'s "poor revolutionary fool" can be at the same time a "millionaire in revolutionary images." Inflation provides a conceptual tool to theorize the manner in which resistance is met not simply with suppression but with a more insidious counterrevolutionary apparatus. Accordingly, inflation functions to undermine resistance though dilution rather than force.

We find a cinematic precedent for *Ici et ailleurs*'s "poor revolutionary fool" in Hans Richter's essay film *Inflation: A Counterpoint of Declining People and Growing Zeros* (Germany, 1928). Richter, as discussed in chapter 1, was a central figure of European interwar avant-garde cinema who coined the term *essay film,* and *Inflation* is an early attempt, or *essai,* at exploring the possibilities of the moving image to engage with a historical crisis—the hyperinflation of Weimar Germany—in a manner that not only describes or represents it but also generates an analysis by creating a cinematic concept of inflation. *Inflation* is organized around the rapidly shifting exchange rates of the German mark, its tempo speeding up incrementally as the German currency is devalued to the point of incomprehensibility, a counterpoint of decline measured with the addition of each zero ($1 = 100 DM, $1 = 1,000 DM, $1 = 1,000,000 DM, etc.). The film subjects each image, be it of money or of faces, to a dual process of multiplication and devaluation. In a sequence that anticipates *Ici et ailleurs,* faces of individuals are fractured and propagated, multiplied and transformed into zeros. *Inflation* is a formal exploration of the measured evisceration of the German republic through the unbearable proliferation of devalued notes. An ever-expanding number of paper notes falling in front of the camera is superimposed over many of the images in the film, producing a saturated and claustrophobic atmosphere. The immeasurable quantity of the money gives way to the quality of decline, as witnessed in one of final moments of the film, in which a middle-class man is instantaneously transformed into a beggar through the use of stop-motion reminiscent of Méliès's cinematic magic. He stands with his arm outstretched within a virtual sea of money, fully permeated by it, yet at the same time impoverished. Though made in a different historical context with a different set of concerns, *Inflation*'s cinematic expression of the affective dimensions of inflation—the simultaneous multiplication and negation of value—resonates with *Ici et ailleurs*'s meditation on the zero as a function that both multiplies and negates revolutionary impulses and images. *Ici et ailleurs* develops the idea that the proliferation of images produces a simultaneous disempowerment through two formal techniques: multiple screens and video pastiches. Following innovations with the use of multiple screens in the 1960s, such as the installation work of Charles and Ray Eames and Andy Warhol's cinema, the use of multiple screens in *Ici et ailleurs* continues to refine Godard's experimentation with this technique that started in the late 1960s. As Anne Friedberg argues, the 1960s cinematic multiple breaks with renaissance perspective and anticipates a new visual interface that becomes dominant in the digital era.[12] Exploring this un-unified barrage of images through the multiple, *Ici et ailleurs* presents a shot of four television monitors with constantly changing images—varying from Henry Kissinger to football matches, maps of the Middle East to Palestinian revolutionaries. The accompanying voice-over explains:

> My daily image will be part of a vague and complicated system where the whole world enters and leaves at each moment—no simple images...
> The whole world, that's too much for one image. "Not too much," says international capitalism, which builds all its wealth on this truth.... We have become many in one and are replaced by an uninterrupted chain of images enslaving one another. Each image at its place, each of us at our place, in the chain of events in which we have lost all power.

Suggesting that the whole world can be contained in one image, the totality of global capitalism is made manifest in the simultaneous proliferation and devaluation of images. Images are no longer simple but rather form an unending chain that usurps, absorbs, and dilutes any image by placing it within the system of image production and consumption. The chain of images enslaving one another and their corresponding subjects later populate a stark mise-en-scène, in which five figures sit behind five television

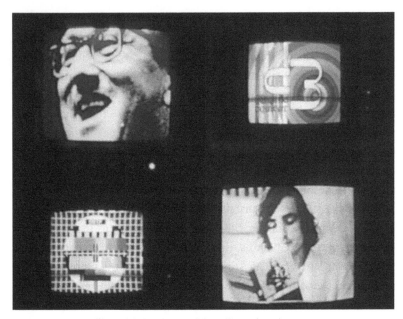

Figure 32. Film still, multiple screens, *Ici et ailleurs* (1974).

monitors all broadcasting the word "ici." Though the New Left aspired to produce and distribute images as a form of liberation, the personal screen and the uninterrupted chain of images that make up "ici" point to the deformation of power that takes place when the image is shrunken and personalized. The subject is given a place on the chain only because each individual image is diminished within the "chain of events in which we have lost all power." If modernity is characterized by what W. J. T. Mitchel, among others, have called the "pictorial turn," then postmodernity might be characterized by the inflation of the image. What inflation as a concept offers is not only a theorization of the multiplication and proliferation of images but, more importantly, the notion that each individual image and its power is devalued and subsumed within the superabundant volume of images in circulation.

Like the practitioners of the guerrilla television movement, *Ici et ailleurs* is preoccupied with the image, particularly the televisual image, as a form of information that circulates throughout society. However, unlike the guerrilla television movement, *Ici et ailleurs* does not suggest that the possibility of more, better, and different information is necessarily revolutionary, as I mentioned before. Instead, the film contends with the ways that revolutionary images get trapped within a counterrevolutionary flow and with the way that the sheer proliferation of images cancels out any revolutionary possibility. In a series of video pastiches, two images are placed within the same frame of information, allowing an image literally to invade and cover another while not displacing it entirely. For example, an image of the Popular Front from 1936 is slowly covered over with an image of Hitler. Another screen modulates between images of Israeli prime minister Golda Meir, a Palestinian fighter, and an erotic pulp cartoon. Within this video pastiche, each image enters and leaves the frame of information through a constantly scrolling limit between one still image and another whose associations are constantly changing and variable. Over a screen that scrolls between Henry Kissinger and a naked woman's behind, the voice-over states, "Any image from daily life will be a part of a vague and complicated system, where the whole world enters and leaves at each moment. Any image. Any image. Quotidian. Quotidian. The Whole World. The Whole World." Everyday life is part of this single, constantly transforming image that is yet seemingly capable of encompassing the totality of life. No longer can we separate out a revolutionary image from a reactionary one—they are engulfed in one and the same transmutable image.

Through this conundrum, *Ici et ailleurs* shows that the image *here* is the multiplication and cancellation of the image as/toward revolution. *Jusqu'à la victoire* is trapped within *Ici et ailleurs,* a film within a film that cannot emerge because there are too many images and sounds that surround it, too many counterrevolutionary forces that seek its cancellation. Its image of revolution is only allowed to appear in an inflated form that depletes its meaning, its force undermined in the very act of its appearance. *Ici et ailleurs* thus leaves us with a disheartening take on the fate of the New Left's cinematic project. Just as the beggar in Richter's *Inflation* is impoverished while surrounded by a sea of money, the revolutionary filmmaker becomes a "poor revolutionary fool, millionaire in revolutionary images." *Ici et ailleurs* concludes with a montage that cuts between footage from *Jusqu'à la victoire* of Palestinian fighters planning a battle and a French family watching television. The voice-over contends that we have lost the capacity to see and to listen in a meaningful way and implores us to see and hear differently: "learn to see here in order to understand elsewhere. Learn to understand speech in order to see what 'others' do, the 'others' who are the 'elsewhere' of our 'here.'" With this, *Ici et ailleurs* implies that there might be another way of seeing and understanding these images of revolution that lie "elsewhere," which would allow for an alternate way of relating these images to "here." Rather than simply viewing these images as caught within an endless chain from which there is no escape, they might also be able to show and tell us something important not only about a revolutionary past that is "elsewhere" but about the situation we face "here."

ON THE VISIBLE AND INVISIBLE IN
LE FOND DE L'AIR EST ROUGE

How do cinematic images know, or come to know, more than their producers might have intended? This question operates as something like the idée fixe for Chris Marker's 1977 essay film *Le Fond de l'air est rouge (A Grin without a Cat),* perhaps the most extensive cinematic reflection on the rise and fall of the global New Left social movements of the 1960s from the perspective of the defeats of the 1970s. A film with great affinity to *Ici et ailleurs,* the majority of *Le Fond* was filmed in the late 1960s and early 1970s, and its formal construction acts as a historical meditation on the events of the long 1960s in light of its counterrevolutionary present. Much like *Ici et ailleurs, Le Fond* takes footage of iconic moments from the 1960s—including many scenes shot by Marker himself—and imbues them with a tinge of despair, as the elsewhere of revolution points not only to geographical distance but also to the gulf of history that separates the late 1970s from 1968. More than a piece of mourning for revolutions that failed, however, the film is a rigorous historiographical essay, reappraising the cinema of the New Left and its audiovisual archive to reevaluate the narrative of the emergence and defeat of New Left social movements. As Marker sifts through this archive and presents its evidence anew, what comes across in his analysis of the New Left is something more sinister: the birth of new historical forces that come into being alongside, and in reaction to, radical social movements. In exploring Marker's diagnosis of these new historical forces, this section investigates the tensions between visibility and invisibility that run through *Le Fond* and what they might tell us about the legacy of New Left cinema.

Composed of almost four hours of filmed and found footage, *Le Fond* is divided into two sections, "Fragile Hands" and "Severed Hands," looking back on the rise and the rupture of the New Left, respectively. The titles of the two sections indicate the volatility of the movements of the 1960s and 1970s as well as their struggle against and ultimate detachment from central, organizing bodies—the state, the Communist Party, the Soviet Union, and so on. By framing a film about the New Left through the figure of the hand, Marker implicitly expands a traditional conception of both work and struggle. The fragility of the hands in the first section foregrounds the centrality of new figures of struggle, like students, not traditionally tied to the labor movement. The fragile hands of the New Left are those hands that enact the recomposition of leftist politics outside sanctioned domains, as exemplified in a montage during the first section of the film that consists of footage of hands performing various tasks: loading a gun, carrying protest signs, putting up posters, and making rice. These hands reference the many labors of the New Left, the multiple activities that are not reducible to any singular identity or aim. Over footage of a woman carrying a protest sign in earnest, the voice-over observes that "these fragile hands have left us the mark of their fragility."

In the next sequence, we come to see that this mark is left on the cinematic image itself, as *Le Fond* maps fragility onto the image by posing a question: "why do the images sometimes begin to tremble?" The question is presented through a series of intertitles, intercut with blurred and jittery footage of May 1968 in Paris. This sequence is followed by shots of Russian tanks entering Prague in 1968, all of which are "trembling," accompanied by the voice-over of a cameraman who thought that he was holding the camera perfectly still, "but the camera caught the mood." The trembling images draw a direct parallel between the fragile hands, the site of the many labors of revolution, and the hand that holds the camera. These fragile hands are the hands of anonymous New Left filmmakers, struggling alongside the other fragile hands of the New Left.

Figure 33. Film still, "fragile hands" of the New Left, *Le Fond de l'air est rouge* (1977).

The cameraman was certain he was holding the camera perfectly still, but something of the unconscious that is history, viscerally registered, made its way into the image by way of his fragile hand. These trembling images apprehend something that exceeds the given intentions of the New Left filmmakers who captured them. In the context of the historiographical strategy developed by Marker in *Le Fond,* these trembling images serve as a corporeal index of the adventitious meanings making their way into the New Left's audiovisual archive.

Of the numerous instances throughout the film in which unintended and unseen meaning arises from footage taken by the practitioners of New Left cinema, one of the most chilling occurs toward the end of *Le Fond.* As Marker looks back and comments on a sequence from the 1967 March on the Pentagon, he finds something of a defeat inscribed within the images he had originally held up as proof of a victory. Marker's voice-over states,

> Looking at these images in retrospect, you can identify the tricks the authorities played on us. In practice, no unarmed demonstrators could

pass through the lines of soldiers. In front of us were the buildings of the Pentagon, objectives of the direct action to which the organizers had called. Then when it was about to start, surprise, surprise, no soldiers, no bayonets. No steely looks, just a few policemen that are just pushed aside by some demonstrators who shout joyfully when they trespass a frontier no one seemed willing to defend. And everyone stops here at the stairs, after a symbolic attempt at getting inside. The police were clearly scared. I filmed it, and I showed it as a victory for the movement. But when I look back at these scenes again, and I unite with them the stories the police told us, about how it was they who lived the fire of the police stations in their 1968, I ask myself, weren't some of our victories in of the sixties made out of the same stuff?

The tone and quality of this reflection pervade *Le Fond,* as the film offers up characteristic images of the struggles of the 1960s and reads them against the grain, teasing out new interpretations of their significance from the standpoint of its present. As we will see, *Le Fond* transforms such images into "memories of the future," to borrow a phrase from Catherine Lupton; the images tremble, in a figurative sense, because it is they who know, or come to know, that which cannot be spoken at the time.[13] What and how these images know and what they might have to tell us today, however, are questions deserving of further consideration.

The original footage in this scene of protest was shot by Marker and used in *La Sixième face du Pentagone* (*The Sixth Face of the Pentagon,* 1968, France) to document the increasing militancy of the antiwar movement in the United States through the escalation of violence in the March on the Pentagon. This footage, like the majority of footage that composes *Le Fond,* was shot under the aegis of the Société pour la Lancement des Œvres Nouvelles (Society for Launching New Works), or SLON (later renamed Images, Son, Kinescope, Réalisation Audiovisuelle [ISKRA]), responsible for *Loin du Vietnam,* as discussed in chapter 1. As Catherine Lupton chronicles in her monograph on Marker, the period between 1967 and 1977 was one in which Marker largely abandoned his status as auteur, taking up numerous collective projects, including fund-raising for, editing, and distributing film projects allied with New Left social movements. The primary importance of Vietnam, Latin America, the Soviet Bloc, and France as sites of struggle that were central to Marker's travels and political involvement is largely reflected in the geopolitical focus of *Le Fond*. Unlike the scenes taken from the March on the Pentagon, however, much of the footage that makes up the film did not appear in previous collective productions. It was, rather, composed of outtakes and rushes that remained sitting in cans at the ISKRA office. As Lupton recounts,

> the idea of *Le Fond* as a film composed of rejected, unused materials, offcuts and outtakes would become central to Marker's conception of its historical purpose. Introducing the published script, Marker wrote that he had become curious about all the material that had been left out of militant films in order to obtain an ideologically "correct" image, and now wondered if these abandoned fragments might not yield up the essential matter of history better than the completed films.[14]

The history that *Le Fond* lays bare is something that the original films did not, and perhaps could not, show. Like *Ici et ailleurs,* Marker's film is as much a meditation on the practices and aspirations of the New Left film movements to which he devoted a decade of his life as it is a reflection on the New Left's defeat. *Le Fond* almost obsessively ruminates on the role of the cinematic image in the revolutions of the long 1960s through an encounter with the massive audiovisual archive that they left in their wake.

In a conversation with Rob White on *Le Fond,* Mark Sinker offers a reading of Marker's evaluation of the New Left, characterizing the film as "a dense and complex work of mourning: mourning for projects that failed, mourning for possibilities that turned in on themselves, mourning for a togetherness that somehow, as it encountered obstacles, increasingly became a horrible, contorted, endless, spiteful internal quarrel."[15] Rob White replies, "But there is another idea of mourning too: Jacques Derrida's account of *demi-deuil*—'half-mourning,' unfinished or unfinishable mourning—elaborated in such books as *Specters of Marx,*" indicating that the film leaves us with the feeling that we must "carry on mourning the New Left."[16] By recourse to discourses around "mourning" that have figured so prominently in historical framings of the legacy of the New Left, this conversation is emblematic of the ways Marker's film is thought to expose the inner logic of the internally divided and melancholic Left unable to exorcise its defeats and losses.[17] Despite its all-encompassing explanatory power, the discourse of melancholia offers a reading of the film that is perhaps too self-evident. I would argue that it is not simply that Marker is working to mourn, or expel the attachment to the dead (the New Left) from the living (the realities of counterrevolution), nor is he is trying to maintain some sort of fidelity to its legacy, as the reference to Derrida's notion of "half-mourning" would suggest. Framing *Le Fond* through the almost habitual recourse to the work of mourning and the figure of the melancholic, I believe, misses (or renders invisible) the most important work of the film: the task of reframing visible evidence of the New Left—its own audiovisual archive—in such a way that something new becomes visible.

In his essay on Foucault, "Strata or Historical Formations: The Visible and the Articulable," Gilles Deleuze introduces the notion of the "audiovisual archive" while mapping out the concepts of the visible and the articulable.[18] Although his understanding of the "audiovisual archive" is clearly more comprehensive than the parameters of the cinematic archive I have been working with, Deleuze's explication of the concepts of the visible and the articulable provides a framework for reading of *Le Fond* outside of discourses of mourning and melancholia. In discussing the material parameters of Foucauldian historiography, Deleuze writes, "Each historical formation sees and reveals all it can within the conditions laid down for visibility, just as it says everything it can within the conditions relating to statements. Nothing is ever secret, even though nothing is ever immediately visible or directly sayable."[19] In other words, the conditions of knowing and perception are given, a priori, within any historical conjuncture, as the thoroughly materialist precondition of their enunciation. What we can see is determined by the conditions of visibility, not the presence or form of the visible: "visibilities are not forms of objects, nor even forms that would show up under light, but rather forms of luminosity which are created by the light itself and allow a thing or object to exist only as a flash, a sparkle, or a shimmer."[20] What we can see at any historical moment is given by the preconditions of visibility, described by Deleuze as illumination or its lack.

In his reengagement with the audiovisual archive of the New Left,

Marker assembles the cinematic material in such a way as to cast a ray of light onto a kernel already in the image—something present but unseen, precisely because its conditions of visibility, the conjuncture which made it legible, had yet fully to take shape. From the perspective of the late 1970s, what Marker makes visible is not simply a chronicle of the events that led to the demise of the New Left; rather, the film assembles the outtakes of the New Left's audiovisual archive and presents these images as "memories of the future," images of revolution that foretold something of its aftermath. As Catherine Lupton writes, "the strapline for the film could be 'You never know what you're filming,' words Marker himself (in the French version) says over a grainy shot of Lieutenant Mendoza, Chile's champion show jumper at the Helsinki Olympics of 1952, who twenty years later would become General Mendoza, a member of Pinochet's *junta*."[21] "You never know what you're filming" is a statement that speaks to the fact that the meaning of the documentary image is never given outside of the conditions of possibility laid down for what is visible and knowable within a particular era; its meaning endures in the sense that it opens itself up to multiple temporalities (as we saw in chapter 3).

Put differently, the historiographical strategy that animates Marker's reexamination of the audiovisual archive starting in 1967 from the perspective of the late 1970s could be said to align with Marx's famous argument in the beginning of the *Grundrisse* that "human anatomy is the key to the anatomy of the ape."[22] That is, in the words of George Henderson, "the future is the key to the past, rather than the other way around. It is only the unfolding of events that make clear what the past was as a force in the world."[23] What *Le Fond* shows, then, is not simply a process of mourning for something lost but rather the reframing of the 1960s by way of a reevaluation of its own statements and visibilities from the standpoint of the world for which it was a kind of midwife. As Marker reflects upon the images that he himself shot at the Pentagon, he notices a becoming-visible of a defeat that at first appeared to be a victory. As he wrote in his director's statement, *Le Fond* grapples with the ways that "the figures of an intricate game are developing, a game whose de-coding will give historians of the future—if they are still around—a very hard time. A weird game. Its rules change as the match evolves."[24] The state steps aside and the protesters are allowed to cross an imaginary threshold not simply because they had won, but because at the same time new lines are being drawn elsewhere and the rules of engagement, the players, and the objectives are shifting.

The film is structured in such a way as to create a diagram of this constantly modulating terrain of revolution and counterrevolution at work within the visible evidence of the New Left, casting light onto the presence of things in and around the images. One of the most poignant examples of Marker's strategy occurs near the beginning of the film as it chronicles the events of 1967 and the birth of the New Left in France. Explaining scenes from the labor unrest and antiwar protests of 1967, the voice-over describes a new form of protest in which protesters and the police face off, creating an empty space between them. This space becomes filled with a novel form of conflict not between the police and the protesters but between the Maoists and the French Communist Party. With chaotic scenes of infighting and arrests, a female voice-over states, "And this is where the New Left was born. But maybe what did not get much attention in the year of 1967 was the arrival of the New Right." Her words "*nouvelle droit*" linger over the images of protests so characteristic of our memory of the 1960s and create a sound bridge to the following shot, which is of Valéry Giscard d'Estaing, France's future president, skiing down a mountain slope, passing under a banner that reads "ARRIVEE." This shot, also from 1967, could not be more disjointed with the sequence that precedes it. Rather than the violent and intense encounters within a new political terrain that ushered in the New Left, the New Right arrives in the most banal and sterile spectacle imaginable, a prescient glimpse of the counterrevolution to come. The shot of the ski race is followed by footage of Giscard playing football and, later, squeezing an accordion while joking with the audience at a political rally. The film does not linger on these images or the legacy of Giscard other than by alluding to the formation of France's new conservative party, the Independent Republicans, which was spearheaded by Giscard in 1966. What is remarkable about this sequence, however, is that Marker casts a ray of light on what is imperceptible to, or at least did not garner the studied consideration of, those New Left revolutionaries at the time. Before the film can flesh out the details of this "revolution within the revolution" taking form in 1967—new labor struggles, Cuba, student movements—it must pause to show us the counterimage to the New Left that comes to constitute its

Figure 34. Film still, Valéry Giscard d'Estaing as representative of the New Right, *Le Fond de l'air est rouge* (1977).

aftermath, another and more silent revolution taking shape that infuses the remainder of the film with its imprint. In the chaos of 1967 in France, the New Right's emergence was hidden in plain sight. We could say that elements of the New Right existed in 1967 as potential but only became legible in retrospect because they had been sutured together in a new, counterrevolutionary constellation that was rapidly ascending in 1977. But what is this banal spectacle of counterrevolution, embedded within the watershed year of 1967, that arrives on the scene in sheep's clothing?

In 1979, two years after the release of *Le Fond,* Michel Foucault starts to systematically address this new formation that was coming into being alongside the revolutions of the 1960s. In a series of lectures at the Collège de France titled "The Birth of Biopolitics," Foucault famously charts the rise of neoliberal thought in the mid-twentieth century. On the precipice of Thatcher's and Regan's revolutions, when this new form of governance is starting to become legible on a global scale, Foucault accounts for Giscard's appearance on the French political scene in the late 1960s as emblematic of the shift in France from one paradigm of governance to another. Giscard, who served as France's finance minister from 1969 to 1974 before being elected to president, is in Foucault's account the Trojan horse that ushered in the transformation of French society based on neoliberal, market-centered principles.[25] For Foucault, Giscard's new breed of politics signals not simply the rise of the Republican Party in France but, more importantly, the arrival of a German brand of neoliberalism that posed a real alternative to the Gaullist-Keynesian French state. Through a close reading of Giscard's writings during his time as finance minister, Foucault demonstrates how it is that Giscard reframes the discourse around the role of the government within French society, separating economic and social objectives so as to serve market principles and produce an entrepreneurial society.[26] What Marker sees in retrospect two years earlier Foucault then diagnoses as a new regime of government. Just as the rise of the New Right compels Marker to reconsider the narrative of the rise of the New Left, the appearance of the New Right forces Foucault to reevaluate his own ideas about governance and subjectivity, arguing that in neoliberalism, the principles of disciplinary societies are undermined by powerful discursive formations that begin to take shape on a global level.

Le Fond's brief digression on Giscard's arrival on the scene of 1967 is illustrative of its intuitive ability to place into the scene those images deemed irrelevant at the time, images that capture, in profound and untold ways, the changing rules of the game. The immensity of the archive that Marker contends with in *Le Fond,* and its weight at a moment of defeat and counterrevolution, recalls *Ici et ailleurs*'s comment "poor revolutionary fool, millionaire in revolutionary images." Like *Ici et ailleurs,* it is a film that adds up images of revolution only to arrive at zero. However, if in *Ici et ailleurs* the image of revolution is embedded within the image of counterrevolution, then the reverse is true in *Le Fond.* In Marker's reflection on the cinema of the New Left, the image of counterrevolution becomes visible within the image of revolution—the two exist simultaneously in an intricate relay. *Le Fond* thus explores the contrapuntal development of the New Left and the New Right within the 1970s, portending the collapse of the image of revolution into a crystallized defeat that we call the 1980s. As emblematic reflections on both the failures of the 1960s and the endurance of their images—politically, cinematically, and otherwise—

both *Ici et ailleurs* and *Le Fond* are exemplary, though in different ways, of the fate of New Left cinema in the 1970s.

Le Fond is a film made in a moment of retreat, both of the Left in general and Marker's particular retreat from the anti-auteur goals and objectives of New Left cinema to which he had so fully ascribed. In reading the visible and the invisible in the case of Marker's film, what materializes is neither a simple narrative of defeat nor a practice of mourning. Instead, the film is a discerning commentary on the cinema of the New Left and its practitioners who took to the streets in an effort to build the movement with an ardent, and perhaps naive, belief in the power of the cinematic image to intervene in and transform the world. It is with the utmost affection that Marker dedicates *Le Fond* to these filmmakers in the final credits. His implicit assessment of these many fragile hands and trembling images speaks not simply to the truth of the events that unfolded but also to the complicated and shifting terrain of visibility and invisibility, insight and blindness, that shaped New Left social movements. In tracking the rise of the New Left's counterimage, the New Right, and the inchoate counterrevolution to come, *Le Fond* provides an important argument about the inextricability of revolution and counterrevolution in this era.

However, it also leaves us with the sense that the meaning of the New Left's cinematic archive is still open to interpretation. It is true: we continue to inhabit the aftermath of the New Right's victory, the regime of governance that Foucault's assessment of neoliberalism so aptly describes. Yet, perhaps as the decades unfold and new historical conjunctures come into being, something new will become visible in the audiovisual archive of the New Left. If, as Fernando Solanas argues, a militant film cannot be completed until its social objectives have been achieved, perhaps the unfinished film of New Left cinema is, in a sense, still in production. What *Le Fond*'s historiographic strategy ultimately shows us is that the potential for counterrevolution was present within New Left social movements, but not as a preordained future. Instead of reading Marker's film as an exercise in mourning that turns this counterrevolutionary potential into a determinism, we must ultimately understand that the narrative of defeat does not exhaust the meaning of the New Left cinema.

In fact, is not the presupposition that the defeat of these revolution-

Figure 35. Film still, wolf staring at camera before its death, *Le Fond de l'air est rouge* (1977).

ary movements was a forgone conclusion a necessary condition for the belief that, in Margaret Thatcher's words, "there is no alternative" to the neoliberal agenda (a statement that encapsulates what Mark Fisher calls "capitalist realism")?[27] Though the last quarter of *Le Fond* chronicles internal fissures, losses, and defeats, culminating in Salvador Allende's murder in Chile, Marker chooses to end the film with a more enigmatic figure: a wolf. In a somber allegory for the defeat of the New Left, the film concludes with footage of a helicopter shooting down wolves to control the population. However, Marker's voice-over, added in 1993, complicates these images, as he leaves us with the "comforting thought that, fifteen years later, there are still some wolves left." As a wolf stares back at us, frozen at the moment before its slaughter, Marker's hopeful statement wrests it from its imminent fate. Capitalism may have won the battle, if not the war, as the voice-over tells us toward the end of the film. Nevertheless, the face of this wolf spurs us to reencounter it and perhaps to see its vitality and potential in addition to its extermination and finitude.

Epilogue

A FUTURE HISTORY?

This book ends where our present begins, in 1979, a year that marked a new era in which inchoate counterrevolutionary forces coalesced into a coherent apparatus, a moment when neoliberal governing technologies— already tested in places like Chile—returned to the centers of capitalist command. Looking back on this moment, we can sketch out, in the spirit of Marker, some intertwining scenes from in and around 1979 that compose "memories of the future," standing out as harbingers of things to come, glimpses of our present and the New Right that came to dominate it. The spectacle, as Debord originally conceived it, did not remain unchanged by the assaults launched against it. Instead, at the end of the 1970s, we arrive at a spectacle that had been profoundly transformed by global New Left struggles—a spectacle (or spectacles) of counterrevolution.

As the 1970s drew to a close, three interrelated phenomena— financialization, the rise of a new populism, and the expansion of authoritarian "law and order"—took shape, particularly in the United States, as counterformations to the social movements of the previous decade. Each of them was formed through and contributed to the counterrevolutionary spectacle that arose in reaction to the political possibilities opened up by the New Left. In August 1979, Paul Volker was appointed chair of the U.S. Federal Reserve, initiating a monetarist policy that would come to be known as the Volker Shock. Rather than simply solving the problem of inflation, Volker's turn to monetarism wove the late-1970s backlash against labor into the very fabric of U.S. economic policy, thus ensuring that precarity would become a permanent economic and social condition. As Volker brashly announced, "the standard of living of the average American has to decline."[1] Volker's implementation of neoliberal monetarist policies, in addition to causing massive unemployment and a devastating blow to the labor movement in the United States, served as one of the central forces in the financialization of the U.S. economy in the 1980s.[2] From the standpoint of our present, Volker's arrivée onto the scene of U.S. history in 1979 set into motion the rise of the New Right, which brought about the present state of precarity and the realization of a financialized global culture.

The month before Volker's appointment, another counterrevolutionary spectacle broke out in Chicago's Comiskey Park under the name of the "Disco Demolition Night." Steve Dahl, a local DJ and anti-disco crusader, dressed in military fatigues, rode onto the field and detonated a crate filled with fifty thousand disco records, sparking a riot of seven thousand people who stormed the field. Disco had opened up spaces for a burgeoning, openly gay community whose music brought together African American, Latinx, and white participants throughout the 1970s. Part of the homophobic backlash against this formation, the "disco sucks" vanguard Steve Dahl created an Anti-Disco Army, which had recruited more than ten thousand card-carrying members who had staged a series of violent direct actions against disco performers and enthusiasts.[3] The relentlessly individuated subject that Foucault and others argue is endemic to the neoliberal project needed as its counterpart collective affects that lubricated its transmission into social and political space. According to Lauren Berlant, "affective responses may be said to exemplify a shared historical time."[4] In the face of the dismantling of organized labor, affects that come forward at the dawn of the neoliberal era, I argue, are embodied in the misdirected rage expressed at the Disco Demolition Night. Appropriating the hyperbolic rhetoric of the most radical elements of New Left social movements that had shaken American society a decade earlier, the "disco sucks" campaign and the riot that ensued produced a counterrevolutionary farce of the political protests and rebellions that had swept across the country a decade earlier. In this case, rather than in the streets of U.S. cities, in factories, or on college campuses, the spectacle played out in the commodified, sacrosanct space of the all-American game. The riot in Comiskey Park had ties to a growing brand of white, blue-collar populism that the Right had been working to channel since the implementation of Nixon's Southern Strategy. It was, in many ways, the realization of the populism displayed in New York's "Hard Hat Riot" of 1970—in which a group of mostly white, male construction workers attacked antiwar protesters—in the arena of popular culture. In the disco sucks movement, we can identify the counterrevolutionary populism, rooted in a long tradition of white supremacy, that consolidated in the Trump presidency. Both the Volker Shock and the disco sucks movement erupted into the political vacuum left by the defeat of a viable leftist project, capitulating to the collective sense that, in Margaret Thatcher's words, "there is no alternative."

Volker's shock and the escalation of right populism took place against the backdrop of a more systematic counterrevolution identified by Stuart Hall et al. in their 1978 study of moral panics around crime, *Policing the Crisis: Mugging, the State, and Law and Order*. In it, they consider another, interrelated aspect of the spectacle of counterrevolution that had been gaining traction throughout the 1970s: the rise of "law and order" as a discourse that worked to control dissent through racialization and criminalization of sections of the population deemed a threat. For the authors, the multifaceted New Left was presented to the public as "a hydra-headed conspiracy against a whole way of life."[5] To combat this threat, the notion of "civil order," a new authoritarianism, became paramount to the state and capitalism's reassertion of power against the movements of the long 1960s. In the United States, criminalization and the rise of the carceral state were already identified as counterrevolutionary tools for controlling minority populations by Third World Newsreel's *Teach Our Children* (1972), which takes the 1971 Attica prison revolt and its violent suppression as a starting point for a cinematic manifesto that draws parallels between life inside and outside of the prison for poor, segregated black and Puerto Rican communities. As one interviewee avers, the only difference is that outside the prison, you cannot see the bars. Through the language of self-defense and decolonization, *Teach Our Children* advances an argument that foresees the rise of mass incarceration in the following decades. Like many of the films I discuss in this book, it anticipates the counterrevolution against the movements of the 1960s while developing nascent strategies of resistance to it. For the authors of *Policing the Crisis,* 1968 represents "an incomplete and unfinished revolution. Its seismic impact reverberated outwards from its principle terrain in social and political life; its eddies are not yet fully spent."[6] But how do we relate to this "unfinished" quality of a revolutionary moment, as we inhabit the myriad, often devastating effects of counterrevolution?

Chris Marker's *Sans Soleil* (*Sunless,* France, 1983), I believe, proffers something of an answer to this question. Often depicted as a meditation on abstract concepts like time and memory, *Sans Soleil* reveals itself, at moments, to circle around a specific memory, which is simultaneously an impossible and stubbornly persistent memory—that of the recent past. In the film, a fictional character, a stand-in for Marker, narrates his travels in a series of letters, and the majority of the film is an account of his return to Japan. At a pivotal moment, the narrator is taken to a protest against the Narita airport taking place in the early 1980s:

> I went back to Narita for the birthday of one of the victims of the struggle. The demo was unreal. I had the impression of acting in Brigadoon, of waking up ten years later in the midst of the same players, the same blue lobsters of police, the same helmeted adolescents, the same banners and the same slogan: "Down with the airport." Only one thing had been added: the airport precisely. But with its single runway and barbed wire that chokes it, it looks more besieged than victorious.

The narrator's uncanny experience at the airport is an apt analogy for the temporal rupture between here and elsewhere experienced by the participants of the movements of the 1960s in their aftermath. What separates here from elsewhere is not simply the passage of time but the addition of a new element: "the airport precisely." How does one endure such an unpleasant experience—holding, in the same moment, the images of resistance and the appearance of everything that is antithetical to them? The solution, the narrator suggests, exists in a form of science fiction, and the film introduces a character who has invented a machine, an image synthesizer, that can process and manipulate images to transform memory:

My pal Hayao Yamaeko has found a solution: if the images of the present don't change, then change the images of the past. He showed me the clashes of the sixties treated in his synthesizer: pictures that are less deceptive he says—with the conviction of a fanatic—than those you would see on television. At least they proclaim themselves to be what they are: images, not the portable and compact form of an already-inaccessible reality. Hayao calls his machine's world the "Zone," an homage to Tarkovsky.

The narration is accompanied by distorted images of 1960s protests, reduced to radiating blocks of color, from which only the outlines of figures can be discerned. The "Zone," a dangerous and verdant place where desires are fulfilled in Andrei Tarkovsky's *Stalker* (USSR, 1979), is an invention that places these images of past struggles at a distance; they are mediated images, not portals. But the Zone also opens a space where these images can be made anew, transformed, unfixed from the stagnation of the present. We cannot use these images to create a coherent, complete memory of the past that might easily be integrated into the present. Instead, what unfurls is a sense of possibility, of remembering again, remembering differently. Outside of the Zone, *Sans Soleil* paints the past as that which is inseparable from the present, a mark that persists. The narrator notes, "I met the peasants there who had come to know themselves through the struggle. Concretely it had failed. At the same time, all they had won in their understanding of the world could only have been won through struggle." The besieged airport and the peasants whose sense of self and the world had been "won through the struggle" are testaments to the fact that something happened that changed, fundamentally, the course of history—despite all the outward indications of "failure." It is within the relay between these material traces of the past and the Zone, an inaccessible place where the past's images are mediated and made again, that an incomplete and "unfinished" sense of the history resides. Starting from this "unfinished" sensibility, I would argue, allows us to begin to break with the sense that "there is no alternative" to the present and its empty repetition. Moreover, this unfinished sensibility creates a clearing from which to renew a belief in the future.

New Left cinema operates in this relay, as both an ongoing practice and as a set of images of the past that inhabit something like *Sans Soleil*'s "Zone." As a practice that opened up domains of cinematic inquiry, New Left cinema did not simply recede into the dustbin of history with the dawn of the neoliberal era but was part of an ethos whose influence endured in the midst of counterrevolution. This is most obvious in the numerous cinematic collectives that developed from the late 1970s forward, including the Mariposa Film Group, Sankofa Film and Video Collective, Black Audio Film Collective, Groupo Chaski, Paper Tiger Television, and many, many others. Beyond collectives that modeled themselves, either consciously or unwittingly, on earlier New Left iterations, I contend that New Left cinema endures in untold gestures that produce and disseminate images that seek to generate different ways of knowing the world, a participatory impulse that insists that anyone with a camera has the capacity to make cinematic interventions. On the other hand, New Left cinema also endures outside of linear history, in a zone where the images of the past are untethered and can resurface as new conditions of visibility coalesce. Recall Fernando Solanas's statement that a film about liberation "cannot be anything but an unfinished film, a film open to the present and the future of this act of liberation."[7] As I have argued here, New Left cinema is "unfinished" in both the sense that it is an ongoing project and in the sense that its meaning is "unfinished," an aperture through which we can remember anew, remember differently.

Since the 2008 financial meltdown, numerous scholars have indicated that another seismic historical shift is afoot, what some have called a "crisis of neoliberalism."[8] Whether or not we are facing neoliberalism's crisis or its further entrenchment remains to be seen. What is clear, however, is that in the present, we need alternatives to the genre of capitalist realism or the narration of the present that evacuates all alternatives, a "slow cancellation of the future."[9] While tracing the emergence of the counterrevolution that is our present, I have also worked to propose an alternative genre through the New Left and its cinema: an "essayistic politics of the common." In doing so, I have endeavored to affirm various *essais* to produce new, collective forms of sense making that diverge from the present and chart a different path, through the past, toward the future. Reflecting on the labor movement of the 1960s and 1970s in Italy, Paolo Virno writes that it "constitutes (to use Hannah Arendt's beautiful expression) a 'future at our backs,' the *remembrance* of the potential class struggles that may take place in *the next phase,* a future history."[10] Even if we cannot easily integrate images of the past into the present, might images of resistance that endure, against all odds, be woven into "a future history"?

Acknowledgments

It seems odd to me to be presenting a story of collective research and collaborative politics in the form of a single-authored manuscript. Though I claim ultimate responsibility for its contents, the book is the product of the ongoing support and insight that I have received from many friends, mentors, colleagues, and comrades along the way. Starting with my political education as an undergraduate at UC Santa Cruz, and then as a graduate student at the University of Minnesota, I learned an immense amount from more than a decade of struggles within, against, and beyond the neoliberal university. These struggles, and the remarkable people I met in the course of them, formed the backdrop against which this project was first conceived. In its earliest stages, this project also was guided by the invaluable mentorship of Cesare Casarino and John Mowitt, each of whom modeled committed, interdisciplinary scholarship.

My time at Duke University as an American Council of Learned Societies New Faculty Fellow was critical to shaping this book into its current form. Michael Hardt, my mentor at Duke, helped me to look at the project with fresh eyes and reconsider its fundamental questions. Conversations I had with Ben Trott, Jasper Bernes, Elise Thorburn, Kathi Weeks, and N. Katherine Hayles were enormously productive. At Macalester College, this project has benefited from the encouragement of terrific colleagues, particularly Leola Johnson, Karin Aguilar–San Juan, and Zeynep Gürsel. John Kim has been a steadfast supporter and has aided the conceptualization of this book at several crucial moments. I am grateful to my research assistants, Zosha Winegar-Schultz and Arianna Feldman, who worked diligently to help me bring the book to completion. I must also extend my gratitude to Macalester College for awarding me a Wallace Scholarly Activities Grant that allowed me to finish archival research in Italy.

Many thanks to my editors at the University of Minnesota Press, Danielle Kasprzak and Anne Carter, for their help and patience throughout the publishing process, and to Jason Read and an anonymous reviewer for their careful reading and thoughtful comments on the manuscript at various stages. Others have helped me with the arduous task of tracking down films and providing indispensible context for them, especially Annamaria Licciardello, Sabu Kohso, and Abé Mark Nornes. A number of friends and mentors have assisted in bringing this book to fruition by reading drafts, talking through problems, and taking my thought in new directions. Among them are Erin Trapp, Courtney Helgoe, Paige Sweet, Miranda Trimmier, Andrea Gyenge, George Henderson, Jason E. Smith, Andrew Knighton, Ben Stork, Sam Gould, Paula Rabinowitz, Ronald Greene, Charmaine Chua, and Sarah Hamblin. Please forgive me if I am forgetting anyone. And I would be remiss if I failed to mention Christopher Connery, who planted the seed for this book long ago in his course on the 1960s I took as an undergrad.

The intellectual friendship and exceptional editorial skills of Sara Nelson have made this book far better than it would have been otherwise. My sister Evy provided laughter that sustained me through difficult moments in the writing process, and the love and support of my parents, Diane and Tom, have been a constant without which I could never have written a page. And finally, Bruce Braun has shared with me all of the stages of this book, being the most patient and generous partner, friend, interlocutor, and editor I could have asked for. It is to him that I owe my greatest thanks. And, of course, thanks to Gus.

Notes

INTRODUCTION

1 Guy Debord, *Society of the Spectacle*, trans. Donald Nicholson-Smith (New York: Zone Books, 1995).

2 Guy Debord, "On *The Society of the Spectacle*," in *Complete Cinematic Works, Scripts, Stills, Documents*, trans. and ed. Ken Knabb (Oakland, Calif.: AK Press, 2003), 221.

3 Debord, *Society of the Spectacle*, 12.

4 Some examples include Phillip N. Howard and Muzammil M. Hussain, *Democracy's Fourth Wave? Digital Media and the Arab Spring* (Oxford: Oxford University Press, 2013); Manuel Castells, *Networks of Outrage and Hope: Social Movements in the Internet Age* (Cambridge: Polity Press, 2012); Peter Snowdon, "The Revolution *Will* Be Uploaded: Vernacular Video and the Arab Spring," *Culture Unbound* 6 (2014): 401–29; Ben Lezner, "The Emergence of Occupy Wall Street and Digital Video Practices: Tim Pool, Live Streaming, and Experimentations in Citizen Journalism," *Studies in Documentary Film* 8, no. 3 (2014): 251–66; and Kjerstin Thorson, Kevin Driscoll, Brian Ekdale, Stephanie Edgerly, Liana Gamber Thompson, Andrew Schrock, Lana Swartz, Emily K. Vraga, and Chris Wells, "Youtube, Twitter and the Occupy Movement: Connecting Content and Circulation Practices," *Information, Communication, and Society* 16 (2013): 421–51.

5 In *Marxism and Literature* (Oxford: Oxford University Press, 1977), Raymond Williams describes emergent cultural formations as "the formation of a new class, the coming to consciousness of a new class, and, within this, in actual process, the (often uneven) emergence of elements of a new cultural formation" (124).

6 See Michael Denning, *Culture in the Age of Three Worlds* (London: Verso, 2004), 8; Van Gosse, *Rethinking the New Left: An Interpretative History* (New York: Palgrave Macmillan, 2005); Gosse, *Where the Boys Are: Cuba, Cold War, and the Making of the New Left* (London: Verso, 1993); Kristen Ross, *May '68 and Its Afterlives* (Chicago: University of Chicago Press), 40–64.

7 Gosse, *Rethinking the New Left*, 35–36.

8 Denning, *Culture in the Age of Three Worlds*, 43.

9 George Katsiaficas, *The Imagination of the New Left: A Global Analysis* (Boston: South End Press, 1987), 23.

10 Katsiaficas, 25.

11 Gosse, *Rethinking the New Left*, 20–23.

12 Andrew Cornell, *Unruly Equality: U.S. Anarchism in the Twentieth Century* (Oakland: University of California Press, 2016), 240–79.

13 Ross, *May '68 and Its Afterlives*, 20.

14 Samuel Steinberg, *Photopoetics at Tlatelolco: Afterimages of Mexico, 1968* (Austin: University of Texas Press, 2016).

15 Jean-Luc Godard and Fernando Solanas, "Godard on Solanas/Solanas on Godard," in *Reviewing Histories: Selections from New Latin American Cinema*, ed. Coco Fusco (New York: Hallwalls, 1987), 83.

16 Jacques Rancière, *Disensus: On Politics and Aesthetics*, ed. and trans. Steven Corcoran (London: Bloomsbury, 2010), 139. In its attempts to create new forms of collective enunciation, the practices of New Left cinema are aligned with Rancière's understanding of the "aesthetics of politics" in that the "'aesthetics of politics' consists above all in the framing of a *we*, a subject of collective demonstration whose emergence is the element that disrupts the distribution of social parts" (141–42). For Rancière, the "aesthetics of politics" differs significantly from the "politics of aesthetics," which "frames new forms of individuality and new haecceities" (142).

17 For examples of these practices in the case of alternative media, such as print and radio, see John McMillian, *Smoking Typewriters: The Sixties Underground Press and the Rise of Alternative Media in America* (Oxford: Oxford University Press, 2011), and McMillian, *Radical Media: Rebellious Communication and Social Movements*, ed. John D. H. Downing et al. (Thousand Oaks, Calif.: Sage, 2001).

18 Jane Gaines, "Political Mimesis," in *Collecting Visible Evidence*, ed. Jane M. Gaines and Michael Renov, 84–102 (Minneapolis: University of Minnesota Press, 1999).

19 Readers familiar with Chris Robé's *Breaking the Spell*, which was published as this book was going to press, will note an overlapping set of concerns and documentary traditions addressed in each study. For readers interested in the legacies of 1960s and 1970s cinema movements, Robé's book offers an excellent history of activist video in the United States that spans the last half-century and is unique in its ethnographic approach. Though I differ with his characterization of what I refer to as New Left cinema as

defined within a specifically "anarchist" tradition, I share his interest in the problems of decentralization and prefigurative politics as they are manifest in these cinematic movements. Robé, *Breaking the Spell: A History of Anarchist Filmmakers, Videotape Guerrillas, and Digital Ninjas* (Oakland, Calif.: PM Press, 2017).

20 Among the many books looking at narrative cinema and politics from this period, see James Tweedie, *The Age of New Waves: Art Cinema and the Staging of Globalization* (Oxford: Oxford University Press, 2013); Peter Cowie, *Revolution! The Explosion of World Cinema in the 60s* (London: Faber and Faber, 2006); and *L.A. Rebellion: Creating a New Black Cinema,* ed. Allyson Field, Jan-Christopher Horak, and Jacquline Najuma Stewart (Berkeley: University of California Press, 2015).

21 Starting with Todd Gitlin's *The Whole World Is Watching: Mass Media in the Making and Unmaking of the New Left* (Berkeley: University of California Press, 1980), scholars have focused on the topic of how popular media representations make or break social movements. Devorah Heiter's *Black Power TV* (Durham, N.C.: Duke University Press, 2013) offers an excellent discussion of the ways that social movements gained a voice in mainstream television, and in *New Hollywood Cinema* (New York: Columbia University Press, 2002), Geoff King provides a comprehensive history of the ways New Left social movements transformed Hollywood, opening space for new voices and concerns in the midst of the crises of Hollywood in the 1960s and 1970s.

22 See, e.g., Roderick A. Ferguson, *The Reorder of Things: The University and Its Pedagogies of Minority Difference* (Minneapolis: University of Minnesota Press, 2012).

23 Michael Denning, *Culture in the Age of Three Worlds* (London: Verso, 2004), 19.

24 See, e.g., the discussion of film theory that arose from May 1968 in France in Sylvia Harvey, *May '68 and Film Culture* (London: British Film Institute, 1978), and D. N. Rodowick's discussion of the evolution of film theory in relationship to the political ruptures of the 1960s and the backlash against them in *Elegy for Theory* (Cambridge, Mass.: Harvard University Press, 2014), 211, 264.

25 Eve Kosofsky Sedgwick, *Touching Feeling: Affect, Pedagogy, Performativity* (Durham, N.C.: Duke University Press, 2003), 149.

26 Raoul Vaneigem, *The Revolution of Everyday Life,* trans. Donald Nicholson-Smith (London: Rebel Press, 2001), 21.

27 Denning, *Culture in the Age of Three Worlds,* 4–6.

28 Denning, 9.

29 Ayn Rand, *The New Left: The Anti-Industrial Revolution* (New York: Signet, 1971).

30 See Franco "Bifo" Berardi's discussion of alienation and the early Marx in thinkers like Herbert Marcuse in *The Soul at Work: From Alienation to Autonomy*, trans. Francesca Cadel and Giuseppina Mecchia (Los Angeles, Calif.: Semiotext(e), 2009), 27–73.

31 Vaneigem, *Revolution of Everyday Life*, 236.

32 See, e.g., Giorgio Agamben, "Marginal Notes on *Commentaries on the Society of the Spectacle*," in *Means without End: Notes on Politics*, trans. Vincenzo Binetti and Cesare Casarino (Minneapolis: University of Minnesota Press, 2000); Jonathan Beller, *The Cinematic Mode of Production: Attention Economy and the Society of the Spectacle* (Hanover, N.H.: Dartmouth University Press, 2006); and Paolo Virno, *A Grammar of the Multitude: For an Analysis of Contemporary Forms of Life*, trans. Isabella Bertoletti, James Cascaito, and Andrea Casson (Los Angeles, Calif.: Semiotext(e), 2004).

33 Debord, "On *The Society of the Spectacle*," 221.

34 Debord, *Society of the Spectacle*, 24.

35 Debord, 12.

36 Steven Shaviro, *The Cinematic Body* (Minneapolis: University of Minnesota Press, 1993), 14.

37 Claire Bishop, *Artificial Hells: Participatory Art and the Politics of Spectatorship* (London: Verso, 2012).

38 Gilles Deleuze, *Difference and Repetition*, trans. Paul Patton (New York: Columbia University Press, 1994), 128.

39 Deleuze.

40 Gilles Deleuze, *Cinema 2: The Time-Image*, trans. Hugh Tomlinson and Robert Galeta (Minneapolis: University of Minnesota Press, 1989), 131.

41 D. N. Rodowick, "The World, Time," in *Afterimages of Gilles Deleuze's Film Philosophy*, ed. D. N. Rodowick (Minneapolis: University of Minnesota Press, 2010), 111.

42 Rodowick, 108. For Rodowick, the reason that the time-image has this capacity is because "time is defined not as space, but rather as force, the Open, or the virtual—the eternally recurring potentiality for new creation in each passing present" (108). For Rodowick, the time-image is expressive of Deleuze's ethics, which presents us with the choice to affirm this becoming—through time—to restore our belief in the world, "choosing to believe in the ever-renewable possibility of beginning again—eternal recurrence" (112).

43 Gilles Deleuze, *The Logic of Sense*, trans. Mark Lester with Charles Stivale (New York: Columbia University Press), 265.

44 According to Deleuze, "the diagram stems from the outside but the outside does not merge with the diagram, and continues, instead, to 'draw' new ones. In this way the outside is always an opening on to a future: nothing ends, since nothing has begun, but everything is transformed. In this sense force displays potentiality with respect to the diagram containing it, or possesses a third power which presents itself as the possibility of 'resistance.' In fact, alongside (rather than opposite) particular forces present particular features of resistance, such as 'points, knots, or focuses' which act in turn on the strata, but in such a way as to make change possible. Moreover, the final word on power is that *resistance comes first,* to the extent that power relations operate completely within the diagram with the outside from which the diagrams emerge. This means that the social field offers more resistance than strategies, and the thought of the outside is a thought of resistance." Gilles Deleuze, *Foucault,* trans. Dean Hand (Minneapolis: University of Minnesota Press, 1988), 89–90.

45 Cesare Casarino, "Grammars of Conatus; or On the Primacy of Resistance in Spinoza, Foucault, and Deleuze," in *Spinoza's Authority,* ed. A. Kiarina Kordela and Dimitris Vardoulakis (London: Bloomsbury, 2017), 1:57–85. Casarino read's Deleuze's concept of resistance through Spinoza's concept of *conatus,* or a mode's striving to persevere in its being. In the concept of *conatus,* however, Casarino accentuates not a utilitarian conception of self-preservation but rather the affirmation of a life worth living, a life in common.

46 Casarino, 80.

47 Jason E. Smith, "Guy Debord, Filmmaker," *Grey Room* 52 (2013): 8.

48 In the cinematic version of *Society of the Spectacle,* Debord reorders the book's contents in such a way as to place material from chapter 8, "Ne tion and Consumption in the Cultural Sphere," before the selections chapter 3, "The Commodity as Spectacle."

49 Situationist International, "The Decline and Fall of the Comm Spectacle," in *Situationalist International Anthology,* ed. and tra Knabb, 153–59 (Berkeley, Calif.: Bureau of Public Secrets, 1981

50 For more on riots as a form of resistance, see Joshua Clover, *R Riot: The New Era of Social Uprisings* (London: Verso, 2016).

51 In *Cinema 2,* the time-image, and particularly the "crystal-im which exposes multiple temporalities. Deleuze, *Cinema 2,*

52 Paolo Virno, "Do You Remember Counterrevolution?," in *R in Italy: A Potential Politics,* ed. Paolo Virno and Michael apolis: University of Minnesota Press, 2006), 243.

53 Guy Debord, script for *Society of the Spectacle,* in Knabb

54 Similarly, the film version of *Society of the Spectacle* includes several images of the earth from space, including the famous "Earthrise" image. While these images of the whole earth "can be seen as a crowning moment in the history of spectacular accumulation," as Alberto Toscano and Jeff Kinkle write, they also portend the consciousness of a growing planetary environmental crisis that we have come to call the Anthropocene. Toscano and Kinkle, *Cartographies of the Absolute* (Winchester, U.K.: Zero Books, 2015), 32.

55 Giovanni Arrighi, *The Long Twentieth Century: Money, Power, and the Origins of Our Times* (London: Verso, 1994), 9.

56 Arrighi, 220.

57 I have explored the possibilities of understanding the image beyond the commodity form in the face of the financialization of culture elsewhere. See Morgan Adamson, "Closure of the 'Gold Window': From 'Camera-Eye' to 'Brain-Screen,'" *Film-Philosophy* 17 (2013): 245–64.

58 Steven Shaviro, *Post-Cinematic Affect* (Winchester, U.K.: Zero Books, 2010), 2.

59 Kristen Ross, *Communal Luxury: The Political Imaginary of the Paris Commune* (London: Verso, 2015).

W LEFT'S ESSAY FILM

un and Ros Gray, "The Militant Image: A Cine-Geography," , no. 1 (2011): 1–12.

tradition of filmmakers and scholars, from the dialectical Eisenstein to the film theories of Gilles Deleuze, who re how images can be vehicles for thought, different as, written language.

Essay Film: From Montaigne, after Marker (New ess, 2011), 6.

ay as Form," in *Notes to Literature*, ed. er Nicholson (New York: Columbia

Subjective Cinema and the Essay

ive nature of documentary re on documentary cinema but by Brian Winston, who argues for the fallacy of any notion of scientific objectivity in documentary film-making. Winston, "Doumentary Film as Scientific Inscription," in *Theorizing Documentary*, ed. Michael Renov (New York: Routledge, 1993), 37–57.

9   Adorno, "Essay as Form," 20.

10   Corrigan, *Essay Film*, 55.

11   Corrigan, 64, claims that the early 1940s were the "watershed years" of the development of the genre in which Hans Richter coins the term *essay film* and in which a more organized culture of film criticism and spectatorship evolves from the 1920s practice of cine-clubs in France.

12   Corrigan.

13   Hans Richter, "The Film Essay: A New Form of Documentary Film," in *Schreiben Dilder Sprechen: Text zum essayistischen Film*, ed. Christa Blümlinger and Constatin Wuldd (Vienna: Sonderzahl, 1992), 197. Online translation by Richard Langston, http://www.unc.edu/courses/2007spring/germ/060/001/readings.html.

14   Corrigan, *Essay Film*, 56.

15   John Mowitt, "The Essay as Instance of Social Character of Experience," *Prose Studies* 12, no. 3 (1989): 274–84.

16   The discourse on both "the common" and "the commons" has been most notably articulated by Michael Hardt and Antonio Negri, *Commonwealth* (Cambridge, Mass.: Harvard University Press, 2009); Jason Read, "The Production of Subjectivity: From Transindividuality to the Commons," *New Formations* 70 (2010): 113–31; Massimo De Angelis, "Social Revolution and the Commons," *South Atlantic Quarterly* 113, no. 2 (2014): 299–311; and George Caffentzis and Silvia Federici, "Commons against and beyond Capitalism," *Community Development Journal* 24 (2014): 92–105.

17   Mowitt, "Essay as Instance of Social Character of Experience," 282.

18   Mowitt, 283.

19   Guy Debord, "On the Passage of a Few Persons through a Rather Brief Unity of Time," in Knabb, *Guy Debord,* 23.

20   Corrigan contends that public circulation of experience is an essential part of the essay film. Corrigan, *Essay Film,* 182.

21   Sooyoung Yoon, "Cinema against the Permanent Curfew of Geometry: Guy Debord's *Sur le passage de quelques personnes à Travers une assez courte unité de temps* (1959)," *Grey Room* 52 (2013): 38–61.

22   Yoon, 52.

23   Thomas Y. Levin, "Dismantling the Spectacle: The Cinema of Guy Debord," in *Guy Debord and the Situationist International: Texts and Documents,* ed. Tom McDonough (Cambridge, Mass.: MIT Press, 2004), 258–59.

24 Ross, *May '68 and Its Afterlives*, 3.

25 Ross, 4.

26 Ross, 5.

27 Ross, 78–79.

28 For a comprehensive history of militant cinema production in France in the years leading up to and following 1968, including groups not discussed here, such as ARC, Cinélutte, and Cinéthique, see Paul Douglas Grant, *Cinéma Militant: Political Filmmaking and May 1968* (New York: Columbia University Press, 2016).

29 Thomas Waugh, "Far from Vietnam: A 'Left Bank' Collective Film," *Jump Cut: A Review of Contemporary Media* 53 (2011), http://www.ejumpcut.org/.

30 Christopher Leigh Connery, "The World Sixties," in *The Worlding Project: Doing Cultural Studies in the Era of Globalization,* ed. Rob Wilson and Christopher Leigh Connery (Berkeley, Calif.: North Atlantic Books, 2007), 89n10.

31 Connery, 89.

32 For a thorough account of Godard's activities in the Dziga Vertov group, see William Winston-Dixon, *The Films of Jean-Luc Godard* (Albany: State University of New York Press, 1997).

33 Deleuze, *Difference and Repetition,* 139.

34 Deleuze.

35 Trevor Stark, "'Cinema in the Hands of the People': Chris Marker, the Medvedkin Group, and the Potential of Militant Film," *October* 139 (Winter 2012): 117–50.

36 Grant, *Cinéma Militant,* 136.

37 Grant, 126–27.

38 Alberto Toscano, "Destructive Creation, or the Communism of the Senses," in *Make Everything New: A Project on Communism,* ed. Grant Watson, Gerrie van Noord, and Gavin Everall (Dublin: Bookworks/Project Arts Centre), 127. Quoted in Eshun and Grey, "The Militant Image," 7n27.

39 Much of the recent literature around films produced by these groups centers on fixing their cinematic utterances to the development of the work of each individual auteur by tracing the differences in the lineages of their auteur predecessors (Medvedkin, Vertov, etc.) or describing infighting and accusations of plagiarism, for example, Debord's claim that Godard stole his ideas or Marker's accusation that Godard was too far removed from the working class. (For more details on the nature of these accusations, see Stark, "Cinema in the Hands of the People," and Smith, "Guy Debord, Filmmaker.") When addressing collectively or anonymously

authored projects, there seems to be a compulsion to identify the hallmarks of an individual auteur's particular stylistic choices and an insistence that we uncover the truth of *who* is actually behind any particular argument, mode of production, or stylistic genius. While inquiries into differences among particular auteurs in this period of collective experimentation may yield certain insights regarding political differences among prominent filmmakers and provide hypotheses about origins of particular cinematic techniques, the consistent narration of these collective projects within the oeuvre and artistic development of particular auteurs serves to distract from understanding the emergence of these cinematic practices from broader critiques of hierarchy and specialization mentioned earlier. This critical fixation on the author, despite the attempts to collectively move beyond it, is paradoxical, given the ways that individual authorship was under attack across the Left in France and beyond during this period. For example, Sam Steinberg describes a similar process with *El grito* (The scream, Mexico, 1968), a film collectively produced about the student movements in Mexico City during 1968 to which Leobardo López Arretche's name was later attached. See Sam Steinberg, *Photopoetics at Tlatelolco: Afterimages of Mexico, 1968* (Austin: University of Texas Press, 2016), 1.

40 Michel Foucault, "What Is an Author?," in *Language, Counter-memory, Practice: Selected Essays and Interviews by Michel Foucault,* ed. Donald F. Bouchard (Ithaca, N.Y.: Cornell University Press, 1977), 130. As Foucault insists, "Perhaps the time has come to study not only the expressive value and formal transformations of discourse, but its mode of existence: the modifications and variations, within any culture, of the modes of circulation, valorization, attribution and appropriation. Partially at the expense of themes and concepts that an author places in his work, the 'author-function' could also reveal the manner in which discourse is articulated on the basis of social relationships" (137). Perhaps now a cliché for the set of discourses emerging in and around the events of May 1968 that came to be known as poststructuralism, Foucault's words nevertheless offer an important rejoinder to framings of the essay film as a mode of "expressive subjectivity" and the constant reinscription of the author-function into collective and anonymous forms of cinema that might expand the theoretical and historical framings of contemporary film studies.

41 Sylvia Harvey, *May '68 and Film Culture* (London: British Film Institute, 1980), 30.

42 Harvey, 30.

43 Harvey, 17.

44 Harvey, 16.

45 In *May '68 and Film Culture,* Harvey gives a selection of the proposals put forward by the EGC, such as "reverse the mode of production so that '"the spectators become producers," and admission to all films would be free' (Proposal 4); make a 'radical break' with the existing system, and ... spoke of the need to bring about the 'destruction of the old structures of French cinema' (Proposal 16); expand the distribution of films to extend far more into quotidian life by showing films in 'factories and firms, schools and universities, youth clubs and cultural centers, ships, trains, aeroplanes and other means of transport, and mobile production units created in suburban and country areas' (Proposal 19); operate on principles of autonomy and self-management ... based on the total absence of profit-making as a goal (Proposal 22)" (22–26). For a list of all the EGC, see *Cahiers du cinéma* 202 (1968), later translated by Diana Matias in *Screen* 13, no. 4 (Winter 1972).

46 Harvey, *May '68 and Film Culture,* 26.

47 Though uncredited, the tracts were later attributed to Jean-Denis Bonan, Gérard Fromanger, Philippe Garrel, Jean-Luc Godard, Jean-Pierre Gorin, Jacques Loiseleux, Chris Marker, Jackie Raynal, and Alain Resnais.

48 Winston-Dixon, *Films of Jean-Luc Godard,* 103. For an excellent discussion of Chris Marker's involvement with *Cinétracts* and his later experimentation with the form, see Sarah Hamblin, "Chris Marker's Overnight: *Cinétracts* Then and Now," *The Cine-Files* 12 (2017), http://www.thecine-files.com/sarah-hamblin.

49 Ross, *May '68 and Its Afterlives,* 23.

50 Nora Alter, "Translating the Essay into Film and Installation," *Journal of Visual Culture* 6, no. 44 (2007): 44–57.

51 Connery, "World Sixties," 84.

52 For an anthology of seminal essays of New Latin American cinema, such as Glauber Rocha's "Aesthetic of Hunger" and Fernando Birri's "Cinema and Underdevelopment," see Michael Martin, ed., *New Latin American Cinema, Theory, Practices, and Transcontinental Articulations,* vol. 1 (Detroit, Mich.: Wayne State University Press, 1997). Also see Julio García Espinosa, "For an Imperfect Cinema," trans. Julianne Burton, *Jump Cut: A Review of Contemporary Media* 20 (1979, 2005), https://www.ejumpcut.org/archive/onlinessays/JC20folder/ImperfectCinema.html.

53 Fernando Solanas and Octavio Getino, "Towards a Third Cinema," in *Film and Theory: An Anthology,* ed. Robert Stam and Toby Miller (Malden, Mass.: Blackwell, 2000), 268.

54 Fernando Solanas and Octavio Getino, "Towards a Third Cinema," in

Movies and Methods: An Anthology, ed. Bill Nichols (Berkeley: University of California Press), 45.

55 Though the basic tenets and examples of the cinema of the New Left, as they are articulated in this book, relate closely to Solanas and Getino's concept of third cinema, I choose not to use this term to describe the totality of New Left cinema precisely because of the ways in which the *term* third cinema has been translated into differing contexts and debated in the past several decades. While Solanas and Getino identify documentary as the primary vehicle for the project of third cinema, since its publication, many films identified as narrative film, such as *Cinema Novo,* have come to be identified with the third cinema movement, despite the rejection of such movements by Solanas and Getino as being too identified with "author" cinema. Second, as mentioned earlier, third cinema has gained the valence of being a cinema strictly coming out of a Third World context, which, as mentioned, does not conform to Solanas and Getino's definition. In their special issue introduction, Eshun and Gray make a similar argument in "The Militant Image" and refute the reconfiguration of the third cinema in the Anglo-American academy, pointing to the ways that Solanas and Getino themselves later refined the concept in a later essay titled "Militant Cinema: An Internal Category of Third Cinema," in which they argue that militant cinema, defined as documentaries directly intervening in politics that are produced and distributed outside of official domains of production and distribution, is the most radical manifestation of third cinema. Eshun and Gray, "The Militant Image," 1–12.

56 For a comprehensive account of the translation of the text and its reconfiguration for an American audience, see Jonathan Buchbaum, "One, Two . . . Third Cinemas," *Third Text* 25 (2011): 13–28.

57 Fernando Solanas and Jean-Luc Godard, "Solanas por Godard, Godard por Solanas," *Cine del Tercer Mundo* 1, no. 1 (October 1969): 48–63.

58 Godard's turn toward the essay film and the transformation in his practice as a filmmaker was formed by the force of the events of the late 1960s and is evident in his discussions of May 1968: "The 'May Events' have brought us fantastic liberation. 'May' has imposed its truth, it has forced us to talk and articulate the problems in a different light. Before 'May' here in France all the intellectuals had an alibi which permitted them to live comfortably, that is, to have a car, an apartment. . . . But 'May' has created a very simple problem, that of changing our lifestyles [*mode de vie*], breaking with the system" (85). In fact, when asked by Solanas, "How do you ideologically define this type of 'author film?'" Godard responds with a list of auteurs, including "Godard before 'May'" (86).

Looking at vast writings on the trajectory of Godard's career, it is difficult to find criticism of his work, even his work that is collectively authored, that paints it as anything but the product of an auteur. For the most part, even criticism of his most radical films maintains this presupposition. In the late 1960s, particularly with the films produced by the Dziga Vertov group, "Godard" must come to stand not only for an auteur but also as the shorthand for a collective reevaluation and reconstitution of cinema that emerged in and around the events of May. Moreover, he must stand for a redrawing of the geography of New Left cinema that centers Third World struggles and moves beyond unilateral understandings of European auteurs influencing Third World filmmakers. Jean-Luc Godard and Fernando Solanas, "Godard on Solanas/Solanas on Godard," *Reviewing Histories: Selections from New Latin American Cinema,* ed. Coco Fusco (New York: Hallwalls, 1987), 85, 86.

59   In speaking the ways that the production of his films have moved outside of traditional channels of production and distribution, Godard again conjures the image of the Vietnamese struggle, denouncing his earlier "imperialist" work: "I refer to the use the Vietnamese give to the bicycle in combat or resistance. Here a champion cyclist could not make use of a bicycle as a Vietnamese does." Vietnam is the reference point to which all of these conversations return. Godard and Solanas, 88.

60   Godard and Solanas, 83.

61   Godard and Solanas.

62   In their essay "Militant Cinema: An Internal Category of Third Cinema," Solanas and Getino cite Grupo Cineliberation as one among many militant cinema groups forming in Latin America, including the Third World Cinematique in Uruguay, Popular Columbian Cinema, and the Realizadores de Mayo in Argentina. Fernando Solanas and Octavio Getino, "Militant Cinema: An Internal Category of Third Cinema," *Third Text* 25 (2011): 52–53.

63   Mike Wayne, *Political Film: The Dialectics of Third Cinema* (London: Pluto Press, 2001), 129.

64   Octavio Getino, "The Cinema as a Political Fact," *Third Text* 25, no. 1 (2011): 45. Octavio Getino later elaborated on a theory of the cinematic essay in *Cine, cutlura y descolonización,* a book of essays on militant cinema and culture by Solanas and Getino published in 1973. In his essay "Cinema as a Political Fact," Getino argues that there is "no single model for militant cinema;" rather, militant cinema is defined first by its by its relationship to strategic or tactical objectives. Nevertheless, he identifies several subgenres of militant cinema, of which the essay film is listed first

and seems to serve as a principal category. Other genres of militant cinema discussed by Getino include informational, pamphlet, documentary, and inconclusive cinema, and Getino acknowledges that these categories are fluid (45–47). Getino further divides the essay film into subcategories of strategic or tactical essay films, and he identifies a number of examples from Latin American political cinema. "Within a *strategic essay cinema* we can identify for example *La hora de los hornos* (Argentina), *Tercer Mundo, Tercera Guerra Mundial* (Cuba). And in a *tactical essay film*, to give a rough example, *Ya es tiempo de violencia, Argentina: Mayo 1969* (Argentina), *Venceremos* (Chile); *Revolución* (Bolivia)" (author's emphasis), 47.

65 Robert Stam argues that in the 1960s, there developed "two avant-gardes" and that one (located in the auteur) tradition promoted passive spectatorship and cinephilia, while the other, exemplified by *Hour of the Furnaces,* challenged the passivity and thus transformed cinephilia: "cinephilia, at times a surrogate for political action in the United States and Europe, became in Argentina a life-endangering form of praxis, placing the spectator in a booby-trapped space of political commitment." Robert Stam, "The *Hour of the Furnaces* and the Two Avant-Gardes," in *Documenting the Documentary: Close Readings of Documentary Film and Video,* ed. Barry Grant and Jeannette Sloniowski (Detroit, Mich.: Wayne State University Press, 1998), 257.

66 Theotonio Dos Santos, "The Structure of Dependence," in *Contemporary Latin American Social and Political Thought: An Anthology,* ed. Iván Márquez (Lanham, Md.: Rowman and Littlefield, 2008), 238.

67 See V. I. Lenin, *Imperialism: The Highest Stage of Capitalism* (Sydney: Resistance Books, 1999); Rosa Luxemburg, *The Accumulation of Capital,* trans. Agnes Schwarzschild (London: Routledge and Kegan Paul, 1951); and Kwame Nkruma, *Neo-Colonialism: The Last Stage of Imperialism* (New York: International, 1965).

68 Lauren Berlant, *Cruel Optimism* (Durham, N.C.: Duke University Press, 2011).

69 As Michael Denning argues, the Latin American dependancy theorists consistently overlooked the importance of culture, understanding it to be little more than "perfume." Denning, *Culture in the Age of Three Worlds* (London: Verso, 2004), 9.

70 Solanas and Getino, "Towards a Third Cinema," in *Film and Theory,* 268.

71 Guy Debord, "Perspectives for Conscious Alterations in Everyday Life," in *Situationist International Anthology,* ed. and trans. Ken Knabb (Berkeley, Calif.: Bureau of Public Secrets, 1989), 70.

72 For a full account of the 2001 sovereign debt crisis and the legacy of

dependence, see David Rock, "Racking Argentina," *New Left Review* 17 (2002): 55–86.

73 For example, Maurizio Lazzarato identifies debt as a social relation central to the production and reproduction of inequality in neoliberal capitalism. Like most theorists and historians of the topic, he signals the mid-1970s as the onset of the neoliberal era and thus debt's predominance as a technology of subjugation. Lazzarato describes the rise in consumer debt in the United States and Europe and the rise of neoliberal entrepreneurial subjectivity at the root of the 2008 subprime crisis, along with the sovereign debt crisis in Europe that persists in the present. However, his Eurocentric analysis does not account for the ways that debt was intrinsic to colonial and imperial projects preceding the neoliberal era. Lazzarato, *The Making of the Indebted Man: An Essay on the Neoliberal Condition,* trans. Joshua David Jordan (Los Angeles: Semiotext(e), 2011).

74 Randy Martin, *The Financialization of Daily Life* (Philadelphia: Temple University Press, 2002).

75 Solanas and Getino, "Towards a Third Cinema," in *Film and Theory,* 282.

76 Solanas and Getino.

77 Claire Bishop, *Artificial Hells: Participatory Art and the Politics of Spectatorship* (London: Verso, 2012), 104.

78 Bishop, 79.

79 Bishop, 105.

80 Bishop, 123–24.

81 Bishop, 127.

82 Jacques Rancière, *The Emancipated Spectator,* trans. Gregory Elliott (London: Verso, 2011), 17.

83 Bishop, *Artificial Hells,* 27.

84 Jasper Bernes, *The Work of Art in the Age of Deindustrialization* (Stanford, Calif.: Stanford University Press, 2017), 16.

85 Toscano, "Destructive Creation," 125.

86 Bernes, *Work of Art,* 16.

2. TOWARD A NEW MODE OF STUDY

1 Stefano Harney and Fred Moten, *The Undercommons: Fugitive Planning and Black Study* (New York: Minor Compositions, 2013), 67–68.

2 Katsiaficas, *Imagination of the New Left,* 37.

3 Nick Mitchell, "Alternate Trajectories," paper presented at the annual meeting of the American Studies Association, Toronto, Ontario, October 8–11, 2015.

4   For a discussion of the relation between unemployment of capital, see Fredric Jameson, *Representing Capital: A Reading of Volume One* (London: Verso, 2011), 149.

5   Roderick A. Ferguson, *The Reorder of Things: The University and Its Pedagogies of Minority Difference* (Minneapolis: University of Minnesota Press, 2012), 34.

6   Ferguson, 50.

7   Translation and discussion of Mario Tronti's famous quotation from Gigi Roggero, "Five Theses on the Common," *Rethinking Marxism* 22, no. 3 (2010): 358.

8   Harney and Moten, *Undercommons*, 110.

9   Harney and Moten, 68.

10 Harney and Moten, 108.

11 I use the idea "new mode of study" in a similar register as Eli Meyerhoff and Fern Thompsett, who contrast alternative modes of study to the idea of "education" and argue for the importance of this alternative study in a politics of decolonization in their essay "Decolonizing Study: Free Universities in More-Than-Humanist Accompliceships with Indigenous Movements," *Journal of Environmental Education* 48, no. 4 (2017): 234–47.

12 Julio García Espinosa, "For an Imperfect Cinema," 1979, trans. Julianne Burton, *Jump Cut: A Review of Contemporary Media* 20 (2005), https://www.ejumpcut.org/archive/onlinessays/JC20folder/ImperfectCinema.html.

13 Espinosa.

14 Espinosa.

15 Espinosa.

16 Ross, *Communal Luxury*, 59.

17 Kristin Ross and Manu Goswami, "The Meaning of the Paris Commune," *Jacobin*, May 4, 2015, https://www.jacobinmag.com/2015/05/kristin-ross-communal-luxury-paris-commune.

18 Ross, *Communal Luxury*, 48.

19 Jonathan Kahana, *Intelligence Work: The Politics of American Documentary* (New York: Columbia University Press, 2008), 177.

20 Kahana, 177.

21 Michael Renov, "Newsreel: Old and New—towards an Historical Profile," *Film Quarterly* 41, no. 1 (1987): 24.

22 Robert Kramer, Norm Fruchter, Marilyn Buck, and Karen Ross, "Newsreel," *Film Quarterly* 22, no. 2 (1968–69): 46.

23 Renov, "Newsreel," 24.

24 Bill Nichols sees the Workers Film and Photo League (1928–35) as the

only historical precedent to the Newsreel's collective production methods in the United States. Nichols, "Newsreel: Film and Revolution," *Cinéaste* 5, no. 4 (1973): 7.

25 Cynthia A. Young, *Soul Power: Culture, Radicalism, and the Making of the U.S. Third World Left* (Durham, N.C.: Duke University Press, 2006), 104.

26 Young, 119.

27 Young, 119.

28 Joanne Grant, *Confrontation on Campus: The Columbia Pattern of Protest* (New York: Signet Books, 1969), 5.

29 Columbia Strike Coordinating Committee, "Columbia Liberated," in *The Sixties Papers: Documents of a Rebellious Decade,* ed. Judith Clavir Albert and Stewart Edward Albert (Westport, Conn.: Praeger Press, 1984), 233.

30 Columbia Strike Coordinating Committee, 234.

31 Columbia Strike Coordinating Committee, 234.

32 Gosse, *Rethinking the New Left,* 115.

33 Stefan M. Bradley, *Harlem vs. Columbia University: Black Student Power in the Late 1960s* (Chicago: University of Illinois Press, 2009), 29–30.

34 Bradley, 40–53.

35 H. Rap Brown, "Die Nigger Die!," in Albert and Albert, *Sixties Papers,* 157.

36 Young, *Soul Power,* 157.

37 Bradley, *Harlem vs. Columbia University,* 61.

38 Bradley, 62.

39 For more on the history of Newsreel and its Third World turn, see Young, *Soul Power*; Bill Nichols, *Newsreel: Documentary Filmmaking on the American Left* (New York: Arno Press, 1980); Renov, "Newsreel"; and Michael Renov, *The Subject of Documentary* (Minneapolis: University of Minnesota Press, 2004).

40 Nichols, *Newsreel,* 52.

41 For an excellent account of the history of black militancy on college campuses in the United States, see Martha Biondi, *The Black Revolution on Campus* (Berkeley: University of California Press, 2012).

42 Young, *Soul Power,* 111.

43 Roz Payne, "Early History of Newsreel," *Newsreel Films: Roz Payne's Archives,* http://www.newsreel.us/life.htm.

44 Espinosa, "For an Imperfect Cinema."

45 Judith Butler and Athena Athanasiou, *Dispossession: The Performative in the Political* (Cambridge: Polity Press, 2013), 2.

46 Butler and Athanasiou, 4.

47 Abé Mark Nornes, *Forest of Pressure: Ogawa Shinsuke and Postwar Japanese*

Documentary (Minneapolis: University of Minnesota Press, 2007), 38.

48 Nornes, 45.

49 Nornes, 45.

50 Nornes, 41.

51 As mentioned in chapter 1, both the Newsreel collective and "Japanese student movements" (266) are mentioned in Solanas and Getino's essay "Towards a Third Cinema," 278–79.

52 Nornes, *Forest of Pressure,* 89.

53 Nornes, 41.

54 Nornes, 154.

55 Nornes, 47.

56 Nornes, 53.

57 David Apter, "A 60s Movement in the 80s: Interview with David Apter," in *The Sixties, without Apology,* ed. Sohnya Sayres (Minneapolis: University of Minnesota Press, 1984), 80.

58 According to David E. Apter and Nagayo Sawa, "the proposed Narita airport became a 'military' airport, a symbol of U.S. imperialism and Japanese subservience to American military needs. In turn the farmers saw their own resistance as part of a common 'front' with 'progressive forces' in Vietnam and elsewhere, and as part of a peasant struggle of classic proportions, especially after some of them had visited China during the Cultural Revolution." Apter and Sawa, *Against the State: Politics and Social Protest in Japan* (Cambridge, Mass.: Harvard University Press, 1986), 6.

59 Apter and Sawa, 81.

60 Apter, "A 60s Movement in the 80s," 79.

61 David Harvey, *The New Imperialism* (Oxford: Oxford University Press, 2013), 137.

62 Apter and Sawa, *Against the State,* 89.

63 Adam Bingham, "Filmmaking as a Way of Life: Tsuchimoto, Ogawa, and Revolutions in Documentary Cinema," *Asian Cinema* 20, no. 1 (2009): 168.

64 Nornes, *Forest of Pressure,* 140–41. Also see Barbara Hammer's documentary on Ogawa Pro, *Devotion* (United States, 2000).

65 In *Cinema of Actuality,* Yuriko Furuhata argues that Ogawa Pro's style was far more literal, and thus more susceptible to commodification, than later films of the period, such as the "landscape" cinema of Masao Adachi represented in *A.K.A. Serial Killer* (1969), and, in its confrontational relation to its viewer, leaves no space for contemplation. This criticism may be true, but I would argue that it makes the documentary style of Ogawa

Pro no less sophisticated or demanding of its viewer. Furuhata, *Cinema of Actuality: Japanese Avant-Garde Filmmaking and the Season of Image Politics* (Durham, N.C.: Duke University Press), 123–25.

66 Nornes, *Forest of Pressure,* 100.

67 Nornes, 100.

68 Nornes, 99.

69 Nornes, 103.

70 Columbia Strike Coordinating Committee, "Columbia Liberated," 240.

71 Ross, *Communal Luxury,* 29.

72 Ross, 5.

73 Columbia Strike Coordinating Committee, "Columbia Liberated," 246.

74 Harney and Moten, *Undercommons,* 110.

75 Clover, *Riot, Strike, Riot,* 189.

76 Ross, *Communal Luxury,* 50.

77 Ross, 48.

78 Joanne Grant, *Confrontation on Campus,* 138–39.

79 Ferguson, *Reorder of Things,* 75.

80 See Morgan Adamson, "The Financialization of Student Life: Five Propositions on Student Debt," *Polygraph* 21 (2009): 107–20.

81 Clover, *Riot, Strike, Riot,* 190.

82 Roggero, "Five Theses on the Common," 358.

83 "Communiqué from an Absent Future," *We Want Everything: Critical Theory and Content from the Nascent California Student Occupation Movement* (blog), September 24, 2009, http://wewanteverything.wordpress.com/.

84 "Communiqué from an Absent Future." I also want to acknowledge here how these calls to occupy have been subsequently criticized by indigenous scholars in the settler colonial contexts of the United States and Canada as ignoring the original violence of settler occupation and imagining settler futures. Such critiques could also be leveled against the Columbia protests discussed in this chapter. A more thorough analysis of the political potentials of occupation as a tactic today would have to take these critiques into account. For a good summary of these critiques by indigenous scholars, see Adam J. Barker, "Already Occupied: Indigenous Peoples, Settler Colonialism and the Occupy Movements in North America," *Social Movement Studies* 11, no. 3–4 (2012): 327–34.

85 Annie McClanahan, *Dead Pledges: Debt, Crisis, and Twenty-First-Century Culture* (Stanford, Calif.: Stanford University Press, 2017), 196–97.

3. *FINALLY GOT THE NEWS* AT THE END OF
THE SHORT AMERICAN CENTURY

1 Gabriela Aceves, "'*Cosa de Mujeres?*': Feminist Networks of Collaboration in 1970s Mexico," *Artelogie* 5 (2013), http://cral.in2p3.fr/artelogie/spip .php?article230.

2 Ian Baucom, *Specters of the Atlantic: Finance Capital, Slavery, and the Philosophy of History* (Durham, N.C.: Duke University Press, 2005), 21.

3 Baucom, 23.

4 Baucom, 24. Whereas Benjamin finds the allegorical form embedded in the commodity culture of the nineteenth century, Baucom identifies a "speculative discourse" emerging in conjunction with the birth of modern finance in the eighteenth century (22). This "speculative discourse," developed around the slave trade in places such as Liverpool, enabled the accumulation of capital through new forms of insurance and credit that not only persist but are intensified and expanded within the present system of finance.

5 Fredric Jameson, *Postmodernism; or, The Cultural Logic of Late Capitalism* (Durham, N.C.: Duke University Press, 1990), xx.

6 Jameson, xxi.

7 The periodization of the American Century corresponds to both the height of U.S. industrialism and the duration of the Bretton Woods agreement, formulated in the wake of World War II, which confirmed the U.S. dominance in global monetary exchange through the gold standard. While it is certainly accurate to describe this era as typified by the Fordist mode of production, I would argue that the dual nature of what I call the *Keynesian pact* allows for a more comprehensive theorization of continuity among global financial markets, state institutions, an industrial mode of production, and labor relations in the American Century. Any understanding of the transformation between industrial modernity and our present, accordingly, must account for the dual nature of this reorganization and the ways that new forms of both labor and financial control are inextricably linked. See also Antonio Negri, "Keynes and the Capitalist Theory of the State," in *Labor of Dionysus: A Critique of the State-Form,* by Michael Hardt and Antonio Negri, 23–52 (Minneapolis: University of Minnesota Press, 1994).

8 As B. J. Widick demonstrated in *Detroit: City of Race and Class Violence* (Detroit, Mich.: Wayne State University Press, 1989), Ford utilized his connections with the community to put prominent figures, such as preachers and politicians, to work as his hiring agents. Ford's paternalistic network

for selecting African American workers essentially meant that these workers were taken "not from the open market, but on the recommendation
of a favored individual or organization" (30).

9 David Lewis-Colman, *Race against Liberalism: Black Workers and the UAW
in Detroit* (Chicago: University of Illinois Press, 2008), 24.

10 See Lewis-Colman. In the early 1950s, the House Un-American Activities
Committee held hearings on the Communist Party in Michigan. Among
the UAW members subpoenaed were a large number of prominent black
union leaders and activists. Lewis-Colman remarks that the hearings "unleashed forces that the union's black militants could not survive," namely,
a wave of violence against black workers within the plants (42–43).

11 Lewis-Colman, 46.

12 James Boggs, *The American Revolution: Pages from a Negro Worker's Notebook*
(New York: Monthly Review Press, 1963), 21.

13 Lewis-Colman, *Race against Liberalism,* 93.

14 Lewis-Colman, 98.

15 Dan Georgakas and Marvin Surkin, *Detroit: I Do Mind Dying—a Study
in Urban Revolution* (New York: South End Press, 1999), 20.

16 Georgakas and Surkin, 22.

17 Georgakas and Surkin, 22.

18 Baucom, *Specters of the Atlantic,* 320.

19 Baucom, 313.

20 Baucom, 314.

21 For Cedric J. Robinson, capitalism as a system evolved from, and was
inextricably tied to, forms of racism that were intrinsic to feudal society in
Europe. Racial violence in the form of slavery, colonialism, and imperialism are therefore constitutive of capitalism as a system. Robinson, *Black
Marxism* (Chapel Hill: University of North Carolina Press, 1983), 9–29.

22 Georgakas and Surkin, *Detroit,* 115.

23 See Clover, *Riot, Strike, Riot.* Joshua Clover likens the coexistence of urban
rebellion and the strikes in Detroit to the transformation between one era
of social struggle defined by the strike to our present era, which he defines
as *riot prime,* in which riots, struggles that take place within the sphere
of circulation, are paramount to resistance to capital. The wildcat strikes
of Detroit and elsewhere during this period are indicative, for Clover, of
the move toward struggles over reproduction, which he defines as "the
confrontational struggle for social reproduction outside the sphere of
production" (115).

24 The Detroit riots of summer 1967 came as a shock to the populace of
Detroit and to the country. In his comprehensive historical account of

the riots, *Violence in the Model City: The Cavanagh Administration, Race Relations, and the Detroit Riot of 1967* (East Lansing: Michigan State University Press, 2007), Sidney Fine characterizes the riots as an obliteration of Detroit's image as the exemplary American case of the successful governance of industrial urbanism and racial reconciliation. In the wake of the liberal urban renewal policies pursued under the administration of mayor Jerome Cavanaugh, Detroit was heralded as "a racial model," the "All American City," and was lauded by the popular press and academic circles alike (34). Fine argues that Detroit was a city where blacks enjoyed "above average income" and greater racial equality as compared to the black population nationally (37). Like many liberal accounts of the riots, Fine attributes the racial violence expressed in the riots to the increased militancy in the black community. He argues that the growing visibility of groups, such as the Revolutionary Action Movement and UHURU, that organized around both Marxist and separatist principles posed a "threat" to the liberal black leadership in Detroit typified in the NAACP by pushing a more radical agenda and set of tactics (27). Much like black militants within the factories, liberals scapegoated these organizations as catalysts for the violence of the riots that shattered the illusion of racial stability and compromise that the city was thought to embody.

25 Lewis-Colman, *Race against Liberalism*, 101.

26 H. Rap Brown, "Die Nigger Die!," in Albert and Albert, *The Sixties Papers*, 155.

27 Georgakas and Surkin, *Detroit*, 88.

28 Ross, *May '68 and Its Afterlives*, 80.

29 Ross, 81.

30 Ross, 81.

31 Jordan T. Camp, *Incarcerating the Crisis: Freedom Struggles and the Rise of the Neoliberal State* (Oakland: University of California Press, 2016), 67.

32 Jameson, *Postmodernism*, 415.

33 Jameson, 414.

34 Jameson, 414–15.

35 Fred Moten, *In the Break: Aesthetics of the Black Radical Tradition* (Minneapolis: University of Minnesota Press, 2003), 211.

36 For Moten, the interruption of sound into the image generates a form of aural totality. This interruption "reconfigures the aesthetic as a mode of inhabiting and improvising the space [of the film] that ironically represents a corollary mode of inhabiting and improvising social/global space" (221). In other words, sound within the film is a material force that introduces

a sensuality that Moten associates with the role of music in what he calls the "black radical tradition." In his reading, the politics of sound are also associated with the "politics of how you sound" and interrupt the image, introducing the space that blackness occupies within labor itself (223). Moten works against Jameson's narrative of failure and defeat by arguing that, within the politics of sound in the film, a "revolutionary tone carries forth," and "the rhythm of the iron industry is broken as the beat goes on by the tone of DRUM" (230). Implicit within the "sound of a lecture" is the sound Moten associates with the "material/maternal motif of back radicalism," which he uses to frame his critique of Jameson (230). Through his analysis of the film's use of sound, Moten puts forward an alternate form of totality that answers the narrative of defeat that Jameson gives the film (230).

37 Georgakas and Surkin, *Detroit,* 114.

38 From Georgakas and Surkin: "Those who were most dubious about the film were the people most concerned about the dangers of national exposure, of coalitions with whites, and of the use of mass media. They expressed their uneasiness in many ways. During the early stages of the shooting, they did not stop nationalistically oriented workers from running off camera crews, and they often failed to inform the filmmakers about key public events. Many of the League units under their personal supervision never appeared in the film" (114).

39 Georgakas and Surkin, 119.

40 Robé, *Breaking the Spell,* 61.

41 Georgakas and Surkin, *Detroit,* 119.

42 Georgakas and Surkin document that Newsreel members who stayed behind and who were credited for the film were Stewart Bird, René Lichtman, and Peter Gessner (119).

43 Georgakas and Surkin, 113.

44 See Nichols, *Newsreel: Documentary Filmmaking on the American Left* (New York: Arno Press: 1980). (Publication of his 1977 dissertation that chronicles the Newsreel movement.)

45 Despite this argument, the film cannot be seen as comprehensive or without its own internal hierarchies. For example, the film has been criticized by later League members, for example, A. Muhammad Ahmad argues in "1968–1971: The League of Revolutionary Black Workers," http://libcom .org/library/league-revolutionary-black-workers, that the film's focus on the League's "leaders" overemphasizes their historical importance to the movement.

46 Boggs, *American Revolution,* 26–27.

47 Boggs, 25, 22.

48 Peter Linebaugh and Bruno Ramirez, "Crisis in the Auto Sector," *Zerowork: Political Materials* 1 (1975): 61–85.

49 Linebaugh and Ramirez, 64, 76.

50 Linebaugh and Ramirez, 74.

51 Linebaugh and Ramirez, 76.

52 Jonathan Kahana, *Intelligence Work: The Politics of American Documentary* (New York: Columbia University Press, 2008), 171.

53 Linebaugh and Ramirez, "Crisis in the Auto Sector," 64.

54 Linebaugh and Ramirez, 81.

55 In many ways, my critique of Jameson's account of the League within his theoretical and historical account of postmodernity is similar to the numerous autonomists' critiques of the Regulation School. For example, see Ferruccio Gambino, "A Critique of the Fordism of the Regulation School," *Common Sense*, no. 19 (June 1996): 139–60. There is some debate about whether labor struggles actually caused the crisis of the Fordist mode of production, as other scholars, following Robert Brenner, argue that intercapitalist competition was to blame. Nevertheless, as Jasper Bernes notes, "what these struggles did do, however, is make it more difficult for capitalists to solve the crisis through conventional methods, motivating instead a full-scale reconstruction of work and workplace relations, and the social relations of capitalism overall, undertaken during the long period of low growth and stagnation that lasted from the 1970s to the present (with a short period of affluence in the late 1990s), sometimes referred to as "the long downturn." Bernes, *The Work of Art in the Age of Deindustrialization* (Stanford, Calif.: Stanford University Press, 2017), 17. For my purposes, what is essential to underscore in this debate is the centrality of labor struggles, especially those that challenged racial hierarchies, in transforming capitalist relations.

56 For Marx, the system of modern finance develops in, through, and around the "conquest, enslavement, robbery, murder, in short, force," of primitive accumulation. In tandem with the growth of modern banking, joint-stock corporations, and national debt is the "power of relation," the *force* of the mechanisms of primitive accumulation from which capital emerges "dripping from head to toe, from every pore, with blood and dirt." Karl Marx, *Capital, Volume 1: A Critique of Political Economy*, trans. Ben Fowkes (New York: Vintage, 1977), 874.

57 As Gilles Deleuze and Félix Guattari argue in *Anti-Oedipus*, "primitive accumulation is not produced just once at the dawn of capitalism, but is continually reproducing itself." Recast in a nonteleological language by

David Harvey as "accumulation by dispossession," the historical mechanisms of primitive accumulation are repeated and intensified in the neoliberal era. Deleuze and Guattari, *Anti-Oedipus: Capitalism and Schizophre-
nia,* trans. Robert Hurly, Mark Seem, and Helen R. Lane (Minneapolis:
University of Minnesota Press, 1983), 231. Also see David Harvey, *The
New Imperialism* (Oxford: Oxford University Press, 2013), 137.

58 Jason Read, "Primitive Accumulation: The Aleatory Foundation of Capitalism," *Rethinking Marxism* 14, no. 2 (2002): 35.

59 Marx, *Capital, Volume 1,* 916.

60 Greta Krippner, *Capitalizing on Crisis: The Political Origins of the Rise of
Finance* (Cambridge, Mass.: Harvard University Press, 2011), 3.

61 Paolo Virno, "Do You Remember Counterrevolution?," in *Radical Thought
in Italy: A Potential Politics,* ed. Paolo Virno and Michael Hardt (Minneapolis: University of Minnesota Press, 2006), 240.

62 See Carlo Vercellone, "The Crisis of the Law of Value: The Becoming
Rent of Profit," in *Crisis in the Global Economy: Financial Markets, Social
Struggles, and New Political Scenarios,* ed. Andrea Fumagalli and Sandro
Mezzandra, 85–118 (Los Angeles, Calif.: Semiotext(e), 2010).

63 David Harvey, "A Financial Katrina," address, City University of New
York Graduate Center, October 29, 2008.

64 Gary A. Dymski, "Racial Exclusion and the Political Economy of the
Subprime Crisis," *Historical Materialism* 17 (2009): 149–79.

65 Dymski, 162.

66 The wild speculations of the 1980s that resulted in the savings-and-loan
crisis gave way to a system of mortgage securitization in which loan making
was separated from risk bearing, thus producing the conditions in which
the subprime mortgage market could flourish in the 1990s. Dymski, 160.

67 Dymski, 162.

4. ITALIAN FEMINIST COLLECTIVES AND
THE "UNEXPECTED SUBJECT"

1 Deleuze, *Cinema 2,* 218.

2 Deleuze, 219.

3 Deleuze, 223.

4 Carla Lonzi, "Let's Spit on Hegel," in *Italian Feminist Thought: A Reader,*
ed. Paola Bono and Sandra Kemp (Oxford: Basil Blackwell, 1991), 59.

5 Rivolta Fimminile, "Manifesto," in Bono and Kemp, 40.

6 Fimminile.

7 Kathi Weeks, *The Problem with Work: Feminism, Marxism, Antiwork Politics,*

and Postwork Imaginaries (Durham, N.C.: Duke University Press, 2011), 93–94.

8 Georgy Katsiaficas, *The Subversion of Politics: European Autonomous Social Movements and the Decolonization of Everyday Life* (Oakland, Calif.: AK Press, 1997), 18.

9 Potere Operaio vento-emiliano, "La lotta dei vietcong ci insegna che la rivoluzione è possibile," *Potere Operaio* 1 (1967). Quoted in Steve Wright, *Storming Heaven: Class Composition and Struggle in Italian Autonomous Marxism* (London: Pluto Press, 2002), 132.

10 Wright, *Storming Heaven,* 134.

11 Wright.

12 Georgakas and Surkin, *Detroit,* 120.

13 For further examples of this debate and the ways that African American feminists distinguished their struggle from white second-wave feminist discourses, especially on the point of labor and the legacies of slavery, see, among others, Frances Beale, "Double Jeopardy: To Be Black and Female," in Albert and Albert, *The Sixties Papers,* 500–508, and Angela Y. Davis, *Women, Race, and Class* (New York: Vintage Books, 1981).

14 Chris Robé makes a similar point with regard to the production of the film in his essay "Detroit Rising: The League of Revolutionary Black Workers, Newsreel, and the Making of *Finally Got the News,*" *Film History* 28, no. 4 (2016): 125–58. In this essay, Robé argues that unacknowledged labor of black women in the League's organizing activities is reflected in the film's dismissive attitude toward so-called unproductive labor (148–49).

15 A seminal example in 1970 being Louis Althusser, *On the Reproduction of Capitalism: Ideology and Ideological State Apparatuses,* trans. G. M. Goshgarian (London: Verso, 2014).

16 Mario Tronti, *Operai e capitale* (Turin: Einaudi, 1971), 56. Quoted in Wright, *Storming Heaven,* 38.

17 Silvia Federici, *Revolution at Point Zero: Housework, Reproduction, and Feminist Struggle* (Brooklyn, N.Y.: Common Notions, 2012), 7.

18 Katsiaficas, *Subversion of Politics,* 22.

19 Giuliana Bruno and Maria Nadotti, "On the Margins of Feminist Discourse: The Experience of the '150 Hours Courses,'" in *Off Screen: Women and Film in Italy,* ed. Giuliana Bruno and Maria Nadotti (London: Routledge, 1988), 98.

20 Katsiaficas, *Subversion of Politics,* 26.

21 Lonzi, "Let's Spit on Hegel," 41.

22 Lonzi, 43.

23 Leopoldina Fortunati, *The Arcane of Reproduction: Housework, Prostitution,*

Labor, and Capital, trans. Hilary Creek (Brooklyn, N.Y.: Autonomedia, 1995), 11.

24 Collettivo Femminista di Cinema-Roma, "Per un cinema clitorideo vaginale," trans. Arianna Feldman and Morgan Adamson, http://www .nelvento.net/archivio/68/femm/aggettivo.htm.

25 Implicitly taking up Demau's antiauthoritarianism, Lonzi advocated for new alliances between feminists and other countercultural groups— students, hippies, and so on—that she saw as attempting to reconfigure sexual relations and social life beyond the nuclear family. Lonzi, "Let's Spit on Hegel," 51.

26 Demau, "Manifesto," in Bono and Kemp, *Italian Feminist Thought,* 34.

27 Federici, *Revolution at Point Zero,* 5–6.

28 Michel Foucault, preface to Deleuze and Guattari, *Anti-Oedipus,* xiv.

29 Hannah Arendt, *Between the Past and the Future* (New York: Penguin Books, 2006), 117.

30 Arendt, 119.

31 Arendt, 110.

32 Arendt, 136.

33 Annamaria Licciardello, "Io sono mia: experienze di cinema militante femminista negli anni settanta," *Zapruder* 39 (2016): 86–87. Licciardello notes that, though produced by and attributed to the collective, the film was the thesis project of Rony Daopoulo, who was studying at the time at the Centro sperimentale di cinematografia.

34 Licciardello, 88.

35 Collettivo Femminista di Cinema-Roma, "Per un cinema clitorideo vaginale."

36 Collettivo Femminista di Cinema-Roma.

37 Licciardello, "Io sono mia," 88.

38 Collettivo Femminista di Cinema-Roma, "Per un cinema clitorideo vaginale."

39 Collettivo Femminista di Cinema-Roma.

40 Collettivo Femminista di Cinema-Roma.

41 The manifesto sets forward a nonhierarchical code of documentary ethics based on its feminist approach to epistemological questions: "Women and children are not the object of our work, but active subjects of a joint research." Advocating, like many movements discussed in this book, that its films be shown in alternative contexts, such as schools, factories, and neighborhoods, the collective posits a cinema that is thoroughly integrated into and functions as a pretext for political organization and dialogue: "creativity becomes revolutionary when it does not remain limited to the

operation of the 'artistic,' but becomes creation of life itself." Collettivo
Femminista di Cinema-Roma.

42 Claire Johnson, "Women's Cinema as Counter-Cinema," in *Working
Together: Notes on British Film Collectives in the 1970s*, ed. Petra Bauer and
Dan Kidner (London: Focal Point Gallery, 2013), 97.

43 Johnson.

44 For a reading of early feminist cinema in the United States, see Julia
Lesage, "The Political Aesthetics of the Feminist Documentary Film,"
Quarterly Review of Film Studies 3, no. 4 (1978): 507–23, and Paula Rabinow-
itz, "Medium Uncool: Women Shoot Back; Feminism, Film and 1968—
A Curious Documentary," *Science and Society* 65, no. 1 (2001): 72–98.

45 For further discussion of these films, see Bauer and Kidner, *Working
Together*.

46 Ros Murray, "Raised Fists: Politics, Technology, and Embodiment in 1970s
French Feminist Video Collectives," *Camera Obscura* 91, no. 31 (2016):
94.

47 Aceves, "*Cosa de Mujeres?*"

48 Linda Nochlin, "Why Have There Been No Great Women Artists?," *Art
News* 69, no. 9 (1971): 22–39.

49 Simone de Beauvoir, *The Second Sex*, trans. Constance Borde and Sheila
Malovany-Chevallier (New York: Vintage Books, 2011), 283. The collective also directly cites de Beauvoir's classic in the final credits of the
film.

50 Maya Gonzalez and Jeanne Neton, "The Logic of Gender: On the Separa-
tion of Spheres and the Process of Abjection," in *Contemporary Marxist
Theory: A Reader*, ed. Andre Pendakis, Jeff Diamanti, Imre Seeman, and
Josh Robinson (London: Bloomsbury, 2014), 154.

51 Gonzalez and Neton, 150.

52 Carol Hanisch, "The Personal Is Political," in *Notes from the Second Year:
Women's Liberation*, ed. Shulamith Firestone (New York, 1970), 76–77.

53 Victoria Herford, *Feeling Women's Liberation* (Durham, N.C.: Duke University Press, 2013), 124.

54 Herford.

55 Herford.

56 Paola Bono and Sandra Kemp, "Introduction: Coming from the South,"
in Bono and Kemp, *Italian Feminist Thought*, 9.

57 This technique of documenting political conversations of groups of people
is also found in Cesare Zavattini's *Cinegiornale libero di Roma no. 1* (Italy,
1968).

58 Rather than seeing the individual and collective as distinct or even

dialectically opposed, Jason Read argues, drawing on Gilbert Simondon, that "transindividuation is the process by which the individual and the collective are constituted." Read, *The Politics of Transindividuality* (Leiden, Netherlands: Brill, 2016), 6.

59 Étienne Balibar, "The Genre of the Party," *Viewpoint*, March 15, 2017, https://www.viewpointmag.com/2017/03/15/the-genre-of-the party/.

60 In "Io sono mia," Licciardello argues, the feminist films made by the collective feminist cinema were the most formally innovative of the militant films coming out of Italy during this period (90).

61 Katsiaficas, *Subversion of Politics*, 27.

62 Katsiaficas, 30.

63 Mario Mieli, *Towards a Gay Communism: Elements of a Homosexual Critique*, trans. David Fernback with Evan Calder Williams (London: Pluto Press, 2017).

64 Mieli.

65 Katsiaficas, *Subversion of Politics*, 27.

66 Collettivo Editoriale Femminista, *Siamo Tante, Siamo Donna, Siamo Stufe!*, ed. Chiara Gamba, Franca Geri, Adriana Monti, and Grazia Zerman (Padua, Italy: Nuovi Editori, 1975), 10. Translation by Arianna Feldman and Morgan Adamson.

67 Federici, *Revolution at Point Zero*, 6.

68 Mariarosa Dalla Costa and Selma James, "The Power of Women and the Subversion of the Community," in James, *Sex, Race, and Class,* 56.

69 Federici, *Revolution at Point Zero*, 8.

70 Federici, 15.

71 Federici, 18.

72 Weeks, *Problem with Work*, 129.

73 Silvia Federici and Nicole Kox, "Counterplanning from the Kitchen," in Federici, *Revolution at Point Zero*, 30.

74 Federici and Kox, 38.

75 Also decentering narratives of feminist legacies and influence, Federici later argues that the origins of the feminist movement, particularly the critique of domestic labor, lie in these struggles of women receiving Aid for Dependent Children and not in the publication of Betty Friedan's *The Feminine Mystique*. Federici, *Revolution at Point Zero*, 43.

76 Collettivo Editoriale Femminista, *Siamo Tante, Siamo Donna, Siamo Stufe!*, 18.

77 In Milan in particular, the 150 Hours Courses became a locus of feminist activity, where courses based in the techniques of *autocoscienza* allowed students, many of them housewives, to explore themes of sexuality,

domestic labor, and identity through creative writing, performance, and the visual arts. Adriana Monti, a member of Gruppo Femminista Milanese per il Salario al Lavoro Domestico who worked on *Siamo stufe*, went on to make *Scuola senza fine* (School without end, 1983), an essay film about the 150 Hours Courses that documents the experience of "housewives [who] are called to get out of their home and take some time to think about themselves: they never regret it," as a woman asserts in an opening interview of the film. "Script of the film *Scola senza fine,*" in Bruno and Nadotti, *Off Screen*, 83.

78 For a description of these paracinematic experiments, see Paul Douglas Grant, *Cinéma Militant: Political Filmmaking and May 1968* (New York: Columbia University Press, 2016), 130.

79 Collettivo Editoriale Femminista, *Siamo Tante, Siamo Donna, Siamo Stufe!*, 11.

80 Foucault, *"Society Must Be Defended,"* 243.

81 Collettivo Editoriale Femminista, *Siamo Tante, Siamo Donna, Siamo Stufe!*, 29.

82 Collettivo Editoriale Femminista, 32.

83 Collettivo Editoriale Femminista, 31.

84 Miranda Joseph, *Debt to Society: Accounting for Life under Capitalism* (Minneapolis: University of Minnesota Press, 2014), 90.

85 Collettivo Editoriale Femminista, *Siamo Tante, Siamo Donna, Siamo Stufe!*, 32.

86 Mariarosa Dalla Costa, "A General Strike," in *All Work and No Pay: Women, Housework, and the Wages Due*, ed. Wendy Edmond and Suzie Flemming, 125–27 (Bristol, U.K.: Falling Wall Press, 1975).

87 Weeks, *Problem with Work*, 131.

88 Weeks.

89 Federici, *Revolution at Point Zero*, 39.

90 Federici, 45.

91 Michael Hardt and Antonio Negri, *Empire* (Cambridge, Mass.: Harvard University Press, 2000), 274.

92 Federici, *Revolution at Point Zero*, 50.

93 Morini, "The Feminization of Labour in Cognitive Capitalism," *Feminist Review* 87 (2007): 43.

94 Nancy Fraser, "The Contradictions of Capital and Care," *New Left Review* 100 (2016): 103.

95 Fraser, 100.

96 In capitalist centers, the organization of social reproduction within capitalism in its industrial and financial centers imposes ideals like the "family

wage," in the case of Fordism, or the "two-earner family," in the case of post-Fordism, that are impossible for most workers to achieve. Fraser, 104.

97   Fraser, 114.
98   Gonzalez and Neton, "Logic of Gender," 166.
99   Gonzalez and Neton, 172.
100 Weeks, *Problem with Work*, 147.
101 Weeks, 149.
102 Madaline Lane-McKinley, "Nine Notes on 'Gender Strike,'" *Blind Field: A Journal of Cultural Inquiry*, April 28, 2017, https://blindfieldjournal.com/2017/04/28/nine-notes-on-gender-strike/.
103 Lane-McKinley.

5. CYBERNETIC GUERRILLA WARFARE

1   David Joselit, *Feedback: Television against Democracy* (Cambridge, Mass.: MIT Press, 2007), 9.
2   Joselit, 15–17, 26.
3   G. Roy Levin, *Documentary Explorations: 15 Interviews with Film-makers* (Garden City, N.Y.: Doubleday, 1971), 387.
4   I adopt this phrase from a famous line in Spinoza's *Ethics*, in which he argues, "For no one has so far determined what a body can do." Spinoza, *Ethics*, ed. and trans. G. H. R. Parkinson (Oxford: Oxford University Press, 2000), 167.
5   Fred Turner, *From Counterculture to Cyberculture: Stewart Brand, the Whole Earth Network, and the Rise of Digital Utopianism* (Chicago: University of Chicago Press, 2006).
6   Videobase made three video essays on struggles within the social factory in Rome in the early 1970s: *Carcere in Italia* (Prison in Italy, Italy, 1973), *Policlinico in lotta* (General hospital in struggle, Italy, 1973), and *Quartieri popolari di Roma* (Working-class neighborhoods of Rome, Italy, 1973).
7   B. London, "Electronic Explorations," *Art in America* 80, no. 5 (1992): 120–31.
8   Roberto Faenza, ed., *Senza Chiedere Permesso: Come rivoluzionare l'informazine, con un manuale sulla televisione alternativa e gli audiovisivi in Italia, Nordamerica e America latina* (Milan: Giangicomo Feltrinelli, 1973).
9   Andrew Ingall, "Videofreex: The Art of Guerrilla Television," in *Videofreex: The Art of Guerrilla Television*, ed. Andrew Ingall (New Platz, N.Y.: Samuel Dorsky Museum of Art, 2015), 61.
10 See, among others, Melinda Barlow, "Feminism 101: The New York

Women's Video Festival, 1972–1980," *Camera Obscura* 18, no. 3 (2003): 2–39; Ros Murray, "Raised Fists: Politics, Technology, and Embodiment in 1970s French Feminist Video Collectives," *Camera Obscura* 31, no. 1 (2016): 93–121; and Malin Hedlin Hayden, *Video Art Historicized: Traditions and Negotiations* (New York: Routledge, 2015).

11 Ingall, "Videofreex," 61.

12 Kenneth Marsh, "Alternatives for Alternative Media: People's Video Theatre Handbook," *Radical Software* 1, no. 2 (1970): 18.

13 Robé, in *Breaking the Spell*, faults video practitioners, who were mostly white and middle class, for having visions of social change that were "delusional" and who "wrongly assumed their entitled outlook would infect others" (109). Though I disagree with this overall assessment, it is important to note that the early GTV movements were riddled with the same issues around race, class, and gender that afflicted the New Left in the United States generally.

14 Ryan, along with Ira Schneider, Michael Shamberg, Louise Jaffe, Marco Vassie, and Frank Gillet, founded the Raindance Corporation. Shamberg, *Guerrilla Television*, 11.

15 Shamberg.

16 In *From Counterculture to Cyberculture*, Turner borrows the phrase "network entrepreneur" from Ronald Bert to describe the Stewart Brand and the Whole Earth network (5).

17 Beryl Korot and Ira Schneider, eds., "A Note from the General Editors of *Radical Software*, volume II," *Radical Software* 2, no. 1 (1972): 1. Quoted in Paul Ryan, "Genealogy of Video," *Leonardo* 21, no. 1 (1988): 41.

18 Eldridge Cleaver, "Letter from March 16, 1971," *Radical Software* 1, no. 4 (1971): 30.

19 Cleaver.

20 David Joselit, *Feedback: Television against Democracy* (Cambridge, Mass.: MIT Press, 2007), 88.

21 Kathleen Neal Cleaver, "Back to Africa: The Evolution of the International Section of the Black Panther Party (1969–1972)," in *The Black Panther Party (Reconsidered)*, ed. Charles E. Jones (Baltimore: Black Classic Press, 1998), 240–41.

22 Marker's involvement in the project is confirmed by the Centre Pompidou's exhibition catalog, which lists Marker as the editor: "L'évènement Congo Oye (We Have Come Back)," *Centre Pompidou*, https://www.centrepompidou.fr/cpv/resource/cTgMKA/rR57dkq.

23 Shamberg, *Guerrilla Television*, 34.

24 Shamberg.

25 Shamberg.

26 However, as Paul Ryan argues in his attempt to complicate the received institutional memory of early video, this history is often eclipsed as early video is contained by its classification as "art." Almost twenty years after the founding of *Radical Software*, Paul Ryan wrote a short genealogy of the early video movement in which he emphasized what he called a "fault line" in early video and its legacy: "the genealogy of video is a history of the struggle between the drive to use video as a tool for social change and the drive to use video as a medium of art... Activity in the video field tended toward one or the other of these diverging poles. Choices could be made according to an agenda of social change, and choices could be made that individuated oneself as an artist." Ryan demonstrates how the latter trajectory, video art, won out over social change, especially because of the existing philanthropic funding model of the art world in New York in the early 1970s. Ryan makes clear that granting institutions favored the model of the artist that, like the author, was responsible for attributing value to individual genius rather than collective projects (42–44).

Given the institutionalization of video under the rubric of art in the late 1980s, Ryan wonders who would be responsible for distilling the history of video and maintaining its cultural memory (44). These questions are crucial to Ryan's genealogical method in the essay, which, in his words, is "concerned with rediscovering struggles without shrinking away from the rude memory of conflict. It is an effort to establish knowledge, based on local memories, that is of tactical use to the reader. Whereas history is generally written as if a struggle had been resolved, a genealogy assumes that the present resolution is subject to change" (40). The tone of Ryan's genealogy is not necessarily one of lament or nostalgia but a direct confrontation with the institutional forces that would neutralize the history of early video by circumscribing it within the realm of "art": "video itself mutated from a countercultural gesture to an art genre. When video was principally a countercultural gesture, it held promise of social change unmediated by the art world. Now, whatever promise of social change video holds is mediated by the art world. That is a significant difference" (40). In situating the early GTV movement within a book on the cinema of the New Left, I signal the ways that this history—of video as a tool for social change—has been co-opted and marginalized within the narrative that has sought to contain it within the domain of "art."

In tracing the countercultural gestures of the GTV movement, I am particularly interested in how writings and practices of it give us insights into the transformation of the moving image by the New Left and countercultural movements that cannot be fully grasped when confined to the domain of the art historical, as Ryan's genealogy rightly asserts. As countercultural gestures, or in the parlance of this study, *essais,* in the reconstitution of social life through networks of the moving image, the GTV movement was an intervention into the field of "perceptual imperialism" that uniquely integrated cybernetic systems theories; new understandings of economic, political, and social organization; and new technologies of the moving image to produce a prefigurative politics of the common, albeit an ambivalent one.

27 Ryan, "Genealogy of Video," 40.

28 Stephanie Tripp, "From TVTV to YouTube: A Genealogy of Participatory Practices in Video," *Journal of Film and Video* 64, no. 1–2 (2012): 5.

29 Ryan, "Cybernetic Guerrilla Warfare."

30 Andrew Pickering, *The Cybernetic Brain: Sketches of Another Future* (Chicago: Chicago University Press, 2010), 3.

31 Some examples include Turner, *From Counterculture to Cyberculture*; Eden Medina, *Cybernetic Revolutionaries: Technology and Politics in Allende's Chile* (Cambridge, Mass.: MIT Press, 2011); N. Katherine Hayles, *How We Became Posthuman: Virtual Bodies in Cybernetics, Literature, and Informatics* (Chicago: University of Chicago Press, 1999); Christopher Hight, *Architectural Principles in the Age of Cybernetics* (London: Routledge, 2008); and Jasper Bernes, *The Work of Art in the Age of Deindustrialization* (Stanford, Calif.: Stanford University Press, 2017).

32 Pickering, *Cybernetic Brain*, 383. For examples of texts that focus on the politics of cybernetic control, see, for example, "The Cybernetic Hypothesis," *Tiqqun* 2 (2001), and Nick Dyer-Witheford, *Cyber-Proletariat: Global Labour in the Digital Vortex* (Chicago: University of Chicago Press, 2015).

33 Carolyn Kane, "The Tragedy of Radical Subjectivity: From *Radical Software* to Proprietary Subjects," *Leonardo* 47, no. 5 (2014): 482.

34 Marshall McLuhan, Quentin Fiore, and Jerome Agel, *War and Peace in the Global Village* (New York: McGraw-Hill, 1968), 134.

35 Ryan, "Cybernetic Guerrilla Warfare," 1.

36 For an interesting debate on the legacy of Bateson in early video, see William Kaizen, "Steps to an Ecology of Communication: Radical Software, Dan Graham, and the Legacy of Gregory Bateson," *Art Journal* 67, no. 3 (2008): 86–107, and also Paul Ryan's response to the article, "*Radical Software* and the Legacy of Gregory Bateson: Letter to the Editor," *Art Journal* 68, no. 1 (2009): 111–12.

37 Ryan, "Cybernetic Guerrilla Warfare," 1.

38 Ryan.

39 Ryan.

40 Ryan.

41 In the "Process Notes" of *Guerrilla Television,* Michael Shamber claims, "The term 'guerrilla' in conjunction with media was first used, as far as I know, by Paul Ryan several years ago when he coined the phrase 'cybernetic guerrilla warfare.' It was then picked up in a lame article on alternate television by a *New York Magazine* entitled 'The Alternate Media Guerrillas,' and subsequently was used straight 'Guerrilla Television' on an equally distorting *Newsweek* article." Michael Shamberg and the Raindance Corporation, *Guerrilla Television* (New York: Holt, Rinehart, and Winston, 1971), n.p.

42 Shamberg, *Guerrilla Television,* 58.

43 In *Between the Black Box and the White Cube: Expanded Cinema and Postwar Art* (Chicago: University of Chicago Press, 2014), Andrew V. Uroskie takes a dismissive attitude toward Youngblood's, and by extension *Radical Software*'s, definition of expanded cinema. Contrasting Youngblood's countercultural tendencies with art historical critics like Rosalind Krauss, Uroskie argues that "expanded cinema" should not be understood as "'consciousness raising' about sociopolitical issues" but rather as a way of using the cinema to "rejuvenate" avant-garde art practices by disrupting the modernist obsession with medium specificity (10). Focusing particularly on the use of cinema in the context of gallery installation and performance, Uroskie generates a fascinating account of the migration of the moving image from the "black box" and into art practice in the 1960s, arguing for the "homelessness" of the moving image in the process of this migration (233). While the legacy of expanded cinema he traces within the context of artistic practice certainty sets important precedent for the video movements of the late 1960s and early 1970s, confining expanded cinema to the domain of art practice, bracketing or ultimately excluding the "sociopolitical issues" that informed many of the attempts to unsettle circuits of the moving image and the flow of information within society, runs the risk of neutralizing the aims of "cybernetic guerrilla warfare" by circumscribing them within the domain of art that Ryan warns against. It also has the effect of minimizing the significance of the translation of cybernetic theories into countercultural and New Left movements, of which Youngblood's text is a prime example, in addition to the broader political economic transformations that these movements were registering and into which they were intervening.

44 Gene Youngblood, *Expanded Cinema* (New York: P. Dutton, 1970), 55.

45 Editorial statement, *Radical Software* 1, no. 1 (1970): n.p.

46 The book *Guerrilla Television,* like *Radical Software,* is at once a DIY manual, a compilation of resources and projects, and a platform for disseminating the movement's ideas about cybernetics, information, and the media. Shamberg claims that he got the title for the book from Ryan's manifesto (n.p.).

47 Shamberg, *Guerrilla Television,* 1.

48 See Neil Postman, "Media Ecology: A Growing Perspective," *Media Ecology Review* 3 (1973): 10–11.

49 Levin, *Documentary Explorations,* 402.

50 Ryan, "Genealogy of Video," 43.

51 For example, in Shamberg's take on the information economy in *Guerrilla Television,* "our first step towards an information economy doesn't mean doing away with money. What it does mean is instead of money directing information, as is now the case, information potential will direct the investment of capital" (36).

52 Paul Ryan, "Toward an Information Economy," *Radical Software* 1, no. 3 (1971): 14.

53 Norbert Wiener, *Cybernetics; or, Control and Communication in Man and Machine* (New York: John Wiley, 1348), 17–18.

54 Wiener, 18.

55 Shamberg, *Guerrilla Television,* 11.

56 Shamberg.

57 Shamberg, 93.

58 Rosalind Krauss, "Video: The Aesthetics of Narcissism," *October* 1 (1976): 50–64.

59 Kane, "Tragedy of Radical Subjectivity," 483.

60 Joselit makes a similar point, arguing that critiques of video art neglect are the broader formal questions that colored the GTV movement's understanding of communication systems: "Unlike histories of video art, which dwell on the recursive nature of the closed-circuit medium as a form of narcissism, or histories of media activism, which tend to be content-driven, Shamberg's account [in *Guerrilla Television*] treats form *as* content: the imbalance of the commercial closed circuit must be operated upon to open its pathways." Joselit, *Feedback,* 98.

61 Shamberg, *Guerrilla Television,* 12.

62 Summarizing Wiener in *From Counterculture to Cyberculture,* Turner writes, "Society could be seen as a system seeking self-regulation through the processing of messages. In Wiener's analogy, for instance, public information systems such as the media served as servomechanisms. The TV screen became to the society as a whole what the radar screen was to the

World War II gunner—a system through which to measure and adjust the system's performance. Wiener believed that the media served to 'correct' the actions of public leaders by offering them accurate information about the performance of society as a whole" (22).

63 People's Video Theater, advertisement, reprinted in Shamberg, *Guerrilla Television*, 18.

64 "Fobile Muck Truck," *Radical Software* 1, no. 3 (1971): 4.

65 Turner, *From Counterculture to Cyberculture*, 5.

66 Turner, 8.

67 Turner.

68 Turner, 35.

69 Turner, 8.

70 Adam Curtis, *All Watched Over by Machines of Loving Grace* (United Kingdom, 2011).

71 Robé, *Breaking the Spell*, 108.

72 Turner, *From Counterculture to Cyberculture*, 97.

73 Shamberg, *Guerrilla Television*, 83.

74 Shamberg, 3.

75 Shamberg.

76 Shamberg.

77 For example, a review of the reissue of Daniel Bell's *The Coming of the Post-industrial Society: A Venture in Social Forecasting* (New York: Basic Books, 1973) in *The Economist* claims that Bell was the first to make such predictions in 1973: "Post-Industrial Society: He Said it First," *Economist*, November 11, 1999, http://www.economist.com/node/258185.

78 The questions of technological innovation and postindustrialism were also being popularized at the time by text such as Alvin Toffler's *Future Shock* (New York: Random House, 1970) and William Kuhns's *The Post-industrial Prophets: Interpretations of Technology* (New York: Weybright and Talley, 1971).

79 Shamberg, *Guerrilla Television*, 92.

80 "Fobile Muck Truck," 4.

81 Shamberg, *Guerrilla Television*, 29.

82 Shamberg.

83 Shamberg, 96.

84 Shamberg, 81.

85 Take, for example, Paolo Virno's statements on exodus in "Virtuosity and Revolution: The Political Theory of Exodus": "The key to political action (or rather the only possibility of extracting it from its present state of paralysis) consists in developing the publicness of the Intellect outside

of Work, and in opposition to it. . . . On the one hand, general intellect can only affirm itself as an autonomous public sphere. . . . On the other hand, the subversion of capitalist relations of production henceforth develops only with the institution of a non-State public sphere, a political community that has as its hinge general intellect." Paolo Virno, "Virtuosity and Revolution: The Political Theory of Exodus," in *Radical Thought in Italy: A Potential Politics,* ed. Paolo Virno and Michael Hardt (Minneapolis: University of Minnesota Press, 2006), 196.

86 Michael Hardt and Antonio Negri, *Commonwealth* (Cambridge, Mass.: Harvard University Press, 2009), 152.

87 Robé, *Breaking the Spell,* 113.

88 Ingall, "Videofreex," 39.

89 Tripp, "From TVTV to YouTube," 10.

90 For good histories of how the GTV movement influenced later "alternative media" movements, see Robé, *Breaking the Spell,* and Tripp, "From TVTV to YouTube."

91 Shamberg, *Guerrilla Television,* 45.

92 Shamberg.

93 Nick Dyer-Witheford, *Cyber-Marx: Cycles and Circuits of Struggle in High-Technology Capitalism* (Chicago: University of Illinois Press, 1999), 20–21.

94 Dyer-Witheford, 37.

95 Dyer-Witheford, 29.

96 Francis Fukuyama, *The End of History and the Last Man* (New York: Macmillan, 1992), 98. Quoted in Dyer-Witheford, *Cyber-Marx,* 32.

6. INFLATION OF THE IMAGE; OR, THE IMAGE OF REVOLUTION IN THE 1970S

1 For more on the relationship between *The Red Army/PFLP* and *Ici et ailleurs,* especially with regard to the relationship between film and television, see Furuhata, *Cinema of Actuality,* 149–82.

2 Colin MacCabe, *Godard: Portrait of the Artist at Seventy* (New York: Farrar, Straus, and Giroux, 2003), 230.

3 Virno, "Do You Remember Counterrevolution?," 241.

4 D. N. Rodowick, *Reading the Figural; or, Philosophy after the New Media* (Durham, N.C.: Duke University Press, 2001), 197.

5 This translation is from Colin MacCabe, *Godard: Images, Sounds, Politics* (London: Macmillan, 1980), n.p.

6 Writing from the perspective of the neoliberal counterrevolution of the late 1980s, Antonio Negri reflects on the problem of inflation in *The Politics of*

Subversion: A Manifesto for the Twenty-First Century, trans. James Newell (Cambridge: Polity, 2005): "if the unification of socialized work generates inflation—and this seems inevitable in view of increased productivity brought about by the socialization of work—then the basic objectives will be to stop inflation. This is an act of hypocrisy that violence which hides a precise aim: that of stifling the socialized worker's force, power and desire for unification, all which lie at the root of inflation" (96).

7 In *The General Theory of Employment, Interest, and Money* (New York: Harcourt, 1964), John Maynard Keynes talks about what he calls "real," or "absolute," inflation, or inflation that expands the monetary supply as a whole but does not disrupt overall returns on capital investment (303).

8 Keynes, 303.

9 In the discussion that follows in the "Theory of Prices" section of *The General Theory of Employment, Interest, and Money,* Keynes attempts to disabuse his fellow economists of the desire to manipulate the cost of labor through deflation, as he works to prove that the monetary standard and its deflationary pressures are relics of a time "when individual groups of employers were strong enough to prevent the wage-unit from rising faster than the efficiency of production" (308).

10 As Jefferson Cowie notes in his history of the U.S. 1970s, *Stayin' Alive: The 1970s and the Last Days of the Working Class* (New York: New Press, 2010), "the early seventies therefore marks the time in which unemployment, long the bugaboo of capitalism, was being eclipsed in the minds of mainstream economists, policy makers, and politicians by fears of its new enemy—inflation" (225).

11 Fredric Jameson, "Periodizing the 60s," *Social Text* 9/10 (1984): 208.

12 In her discussion of "the multiple" in *The Virtual Window: From Alberti to Microsoft* (Cambridge, Mass.: MIT Press, 2006), Anne Friedberg charts the emergence of a new visual logic apparent in the Eames project that completely breaks with Alberti's window and prefigures the multiple and overlapping screens that come to be with the electronic and computational image. Though the use of the multiple in the cinematic image had been used sporadically throughout history, the Eames exhibitions, along with the use of "expanded cinema" with multiple screens in the work of Andy Warhol and later Jean-Luc Godard, mark a turning point in the emergence of the visual logic of the multiple, according to Friedberg (191–239).

13 Catherine Lupton, *Chris Marker: Memories of the Future* (London: Reaktion Books, 2005).

14 Lupton, 140.

15 Mark Sinker and Rob White, "Polcats: Debating Chris Marker's *A Grin*

without a Cat," *Film Quarterly,* http://www.filmquarterly.org/2012/10 /polcats-debating-chris-markers-a-grin-without-a-cat/.

16 Sinker and White.

17 It is precisely against this kind disabling melancholia that Wendy Brown argues we must fight to build social movements in the present in her essay "Resisting Left Melancholia," *boundary 2* 26, no. 3 (1999): 19–27.

18 Deleuze, *Foucault,* 50.

19 Deleuze, 59.

20 Deleuze, 52.

21 Lupton, *Chris Marker,* 142.

22 Karl Marx, *Grundrisse,* trans. Martin Nicolaus (New York: Penguin Books, 1973), 105.

23 George Henderson, *Value in Marx: The Persistence of Value in a More-Than-Capitalist World* (Minneapolis: University of Minnesota Press, 2013), 127.

24 Chris Marker, liner notes to *A Grin without a Cat,* 1977 (New York: Icarus Films, 2001), DVD.

25 Michel Foucault, *The Birth of Biopolitics: Lectures at the Collège de France 1978–1979,* trans. Graham Burchelle (New York: Palgrave Macmillan, 2008). Neoliberalism, for Foucault, is defined by new principles of the governance of society that break from liberalism as such: "Government must not form a counterpoint of a screen, as it were, between society and economic processes. It has to intervene on society as such, in its fabric and depth. Basically, it has to intervene on society so that competitive mechanisms can play a regulatory role at every moment and every point in society and by intervening in this way its objective will become possible, that is to say, a general regulation of society by the market" (145).

26 Foucault, 207. Foucault examines how it is that Giscard detaches economic and social objectives, such as the Keynesian push for full employment, by forwarding the neoliberal ideology that "the economy is basically a game, that develops as a game between partners, that the whole of society must be permeated by this economic game, and that the essential role of the state is to define the economic rules of the game and make sure they are in fact applied" (207). The application of government, then, is limited to the effectuation of the principles of neoliberal intervention, "consequently letting society develop as an enterprise society" (207).

27 Mark Fisher, *Capitalist Realism: Is There No Alternative?* (Winchester, U.K.: Zero Books, 2009).

EPILOGUE

1 Paul Volker, quoted in the *New York Times,* October 19, 1979. Quoted in Cowie, *Stayin' Alive,* 301. According to David Harvey, we can pinpoint the rise of neoliberalism as a global force to the moment when Volker institutionalized monetarism in the Federal Reserve. Harvey, *A Brief History of Neoliberalism* (Oxford: Oxford University Press, 2005), 1.

2 See Greta R. Krippner, *Capitalizing on Crisis: The Political Origins of the Rise of Finance* (Cambridge, Mass.: Harvard University Press, 2011).

3 Gillian Frank, "Discophobia: Antigay Prejudice and the 1979 Backlash against Disco," *Journal of the History of Sexuality* 16, no. 2 (2007): 276–306.

4 Lauren Berlant, *Cruel Optimism* (Durham, N.C.: Duke University Press, 2011), 15.

5 Stuart Hall, Chas Critcher, Tony Jefferson et al., *Policing the Crisis: Mugging, the State, and Law and Order* (London: Macmillan, 1978), 253.

6 Hall et al., *Policing the Crisis,* 240.

7 Godard and Solanas, "Godard on Solanas/Solanas on Godard," 83.

8 Gérard Duménil and Dominique Lévy, *The Crisis of Neoliberalism* (Cambridge, Mass.: Harvard University Press, 2011).

9 Fisher, *Capitalist Realism*; Blind Field Collective, "Against the 'Slow Cancellation of the Future': RIP Mark Fisher," *Blinfield Journal,* http://blindfieldjournal.com/.

10 Virno, "Do You Remember Counterrevolution?," 243, author's emphasis.

Index

Morgan Adamson is assistant professor of media and cultural studies at Macalester College.